The Economics of Biodiversity Conservation

Dedicated
to
the memory of

David W. Pearce

Who built institutions, careers and environmental economics,
who was a source of inspiration for many people and studies, and
who continues to live amongst us through his works and ideas.

The Economics of Biodiversity Conservation

Valuation in Tropical Forest Ecosystems

K. N. Ninan
with
*S. Jyothis, P. Babu
and V. Ramakrishnappa*

Foreword
by
Charles Perrings

London • Sterling, VA

First published by Earthscan in the UK and USA in 2007

ISBN: 1-84407-364-5   hardback
         978-1-84407-364-1   hardback

Typesetting by Composition and Design Services
Printed and bound in the UK by Cromwell Press, Trowbridge
Cover design by Philip Peake

For a full list of publications please contact:

Earthscan
8–12 Camden High Street
London, NW1 0JH, UK
Tel: +44 (0)20 7387 8558
Fax: +44 (0)20 7387 8998
Email: earthinfo@earthscan.co.uk
Web: www.earthscan.co.uk

22883 Quicksilver Drive, Sterling, VA 20166-2012, USA

Earthscan is an imprint of James and James (Science Publishers) Ltd and publishes in association
with the International Institute for Environment and Development

A catalogue record for this book is available from the British Library

Library of Congress Cataloging-in-Publication Data has been applied for

The paper used for the text pages of this book is FSC certified. FSC (the Forest Stewardship Council)
is an international network to promote responsible management of the world's forests.

Printed on totally chlorine-free paper

Contents

List of Figures, Tables and Box

Figures

Tables

Box

Foreword

Tropical forests are home to much of the world's biodiversity. They are also home to many of the world's people. This study of the economics of biodiversity conservation in tropical forests seeks to uncover the implications of these two facts for the treatment of biodiversity in one of India's two biodiversity hotspots, the Western Ghats. The study is to be welcomed for two reasons.

The first is that it offers a serious attempt to understand the local consequences of decisions to use biodiversity in different ways. Until the publication of the Millennium Ecosystem Assessment, many of the arguments for biodiversity conservation in the tropics were driven by estimates of the value people from the North placed on the existence of species in the South. While the study does review the findings of the valuation studies that supported such arguments, the empirical research it reports is fully consistent with the Millennium Ecosystem Assessment's emphasis on biodiversity as the source of ecosystem services. Using three case studies, it investigates both the positive and negative local consequences of biodiversity conservation. Since we need to understand this if we are to understand what drives local conservation, this kind of study is extremely valuable. It does not, of course, say anything about the value of conservation in the Western Ghats to people elsewhere in the world, but it does establish the local incentive/disincentive to conserve biodiversity. It is all too easy to forget that many of the costs of biodiversity conservation – in terms of the abundance of pests and predators – are borne locally. The conclusion that biodiversity conservation pays even where the local opportunity costs of conservation are high is encouraging. However, it also means that the explanation for the continuing decline in dense forest cover (as a proxy for conservation) must lie elsewhere.

A second reason to welcome this study follows from this. It is, indirectly, that it is a study of biodiversity conservation in India undertaken by Indian researchers. While the conservation of the global gene pool is clearly a global public good, conservation of many ecosystem services is a local public good. Identifying the local public good and making the case for conservation on local grounds is ultimately a far more effective route to conservation than relying on the beneficence of the international community. Dr Ninan and his colleagues should be commended for documenting the local advantages to local conservation. This is the sort of evidence that is needed to stimulate local conservation as a local public good.

Charles Perrings
Tempe
July 2006

Preface

Biodiversity conservation is part of the larger objective of promoting sustainable development. Biodiversity loss not only affects current economic growth, but also the capacity of the economy to sustain future economic growth. Biodiversity loss has both human and non-human impacts as well as intergenerational and intra-generational impacts. In view of its importance, biodiversity conservation has been receiving considerable attention in research and policy circles and from inter-national donor agencies in recent years, especially after the Rio Summit of the United Nations Conference on Environment and Development (UNCED) held in 1992. While policies for biodiversity conservation need to be addressed at dif-ferent scales – global, regional and local levels, understanding the local values of biodiversity conservation, and the incentives and disincentives for biodiversity conservation, especially those operating at the local level, is critical to devising ap-propriate strategies for biodiversity conservation. Policies for biodiversity conser-vation depend upon the perceived costs and benefits of biodiversity conservation vis-à-vis alternate use options of the concerned resource. Tropical forests, which are the most important ecosystem from the viewpoint of global biodiversity, have alternate land use options such as utilizing and sustaining agriculture, raising plantation crops, animal husbandry, tourism and recreation, and other activities. Although biodiversity conservation has received considerable attention in research and policy circles in India recently, rigorous empirical work on the subject is lack-ing. This study focuses on the tropical forests of the Western Ghat region in South India, which is one of the 25 biodiversity hotspots identified in the world, and tries to assess the comparative economics of biodiversity conservation vis-à-vis the benefits forgone or realizable from alternate land use options of tropical forests. Apart from estimating the opportunity costs of biodiversity conservation and the external costs of wildlife conservation, the study also tries to assess the extent of dependence on forests for various products and services by different socio-eco-nomic groups and regions, as well as to analyse the incentives and disincentives for biodiversity conservation. The study also attempts to analyse the perceptions and attitudes of the local communities towards biodiversity conservation in general and wildlife protection in particular, taking elephants, a keystone and threatened species in Asia and our study region as a case study. An attempt is also made to assess the Willingness to Pay (WTP) or Willingness to Accept (WTA) compensation for biodiversity conservation and wildlife protection.

To analyse the above, the study carries out an in-depth survey of 305 households located in three villages or cluster of villages representing different situations – a plantation dominant village in the Kodagu district of Karnataka State where growing plantation crops such as coffee constituted a land use option of tropical forests, a cluster of tribal villages/hamlets within and on the fringes of the Nagarhole National Park in Mysore district and two farming villages where there is close interaction between agriculture, livestock and forests within/near the Dandeli wildlife sanctuary in the Uttar Kannada district of Karnataka. Apart from a detailed socio-economic survey, a contingent valuation survey is also conducted. As a background to the in-depth study based on primary data, the study also analyses the land use and crop pattern changes, population and livestock pressure on forests and other natural resources in the study region between 1960–1961 and 1999–2000, as well as the status of biodiversity.

This study has been sponsored by the World Bank-aided India: Environmental Management Capacity Building Technical Assistance Project. We have received valuable support and advice from several people. At the outset, we would like to express our gratitude to Professor Jyothi Parikh, Chairperson, Environmental Economics Research Committee (EERC), Indira Gandhi Institute for Development Research (IGIDR), Mumbai and members of the EERC for sanctioning this project and for offering several useful comments and suggestions on the study at the Project Review Workshops. The comments of Professor Charles Perrings, York University; Dr Karl-Goran Maler, Director, Beijer International Institute of Ecological Economics, Stockholm; and an anonymous referee of the World Bank were useful for sharpening the focus and conduct of the study. We received valuable support and cooperation from officials of the Karnataka State Forest Department at various stages for the conduct of the study. Particularly we thank Mr S. K. Chakravarty, and his successor Mr Ram Mohan Ray, Principal Chief Conservator of Forests (Wildlife); Dr P. J. Dilip Kumar, Principal Chief Conservator of Forests (Western Ghats Project); Mr Muni Reddy, Mr C. D. Dyavaiah, and Mr Shivanna Gowda, then Chief Conservators of Forests at Madikeri, Mysore and Sirsi Circles, and other forest officials specially Dr A. S. Ravindra, Deputy Conservator of Forests (DCF); Mr Belliappa, Mr C. Byre Reddy and Mr Lakshman, Range Forest Officers at Madikeri, Kushal Nagar and Tithimathi ranges; Mr Krishna Gowda, DCF (Wildlife), Nagarhole; Mr T. Balachandra, Assistant Conservator of Forests (ACF), Nagarhole; Mr. A. T. Poovaiah, Assistant Forest Officer (AFO), Nagarhole; and Mr Avtar Singh, Deputy Forest Officer (DFO), Dandeli and Mr M. B. Prabhu of Institute of Tribal Development, Hunsur. Dr R. Raju, DCF (Wildlife), Hunsur, spared considerable time and gave us a lot of information and data on the Nagarhole National Park during a revisit to the park in 2004. We also had useful discussions with Mr Yathish Kumar, Deputy Conservator of Forests, Bandipur National Park. We received valuable help from Mr Nanda Subbaiah,

President, Small Growers Association, Maldari and Dr D. S. Mudappa for the conduct of the study. Mr S. Puttaswamaiah who was part of the project team in the initial stages gave valuable support in collecting some of the secondary data required for the study. We have benefited immensely from the comments and suggestions of Mrs T. S. Jeena, PhD, on an earlier draft. We are most thankful to the Director, Dr Gopal K. Kadekodi, and our colleagues in the Ecological Economics Unit for their support and encouragement. The study benefited immensely from the comments given by participants at seminars that I presented at Oxford Forestry Institute, University of Oxford, University of Paris, 10, Nanterre, National Graduate Institute for Policy Studies, Tokyo, Centre of Excellence at Kyoto University, Hitotsubashi University and University of Tokyo, and also at the Institute for Social and Economic Change (ISEC). A paper based on Chapter 3, entitled: 'The economics of biodiversity conservation – A study of a coffee growing region in the Western Ghats in India', was also presented at the 25th International Conference of Agricultural Economists held 16–22 August, 2003 in Durban, South Africa and the 8th Biennial Conference of the International Society of Ecological Economics held 11–14 July 2004 in Montreal, Canada. I would like to express our sincere thanks to the conference participants, and especially Professors John Gowdy, Clem Tisdell and Unai Pascual for their comments on the paper. A revised version of this paper has been published in *Ecological Economics* (vol 55, no 1, 2005). Professors Tisdell and Pascual also gave detailed and helpful comments on Chapter 5.

We would also like to thank the administrative, accounts and library staff of ISEC, Bangalore, especially Mr Jagadish. Mr R. Krishna Chandran provided necessary logistics and support at various stages of this study. Mr B. G. Kulkarni deserves special thanks for the care taken to prepare the set of maps required for the study. Special thanks are also due to Ms S. Padmavathy for her patience and care in word processing this study. Our immense thanks are also due to the coffee planters and other respondents in Maldari, tribals in Nagarhole and farmers in the two villages in Uttar Kannada for their cooperation in providing the necessary data and information required for this study.

This book was written and completed while I was a Visiting Professor in the Department of Agricultural and Resource Economics at the University of Tokyo during 2004–2005. I am most grateful to Professor Takeshi Sasaki, President of the University of Tokyo, Dr Katsumi Aida, Dean, Graduate School of Agricultural and Life Sciences and especially Professor Yoichi Izumida for inviting me to be a Visiting Professor. The congenial atmosphere, the excellent library, especially the ready access to several online journals, and other facilities at the University of Tokyo were most beneficial in writing this book.

My co-authors, Jyothis Sathyapalan, Pramod Babu and V. Ramakrishnappa provided able support for the study on which this book is based. While Jyothis helped in the designing of questionnaires, coding of data, computer processing and analysis of data, Babu and Ramakrishnappa helped in the data collection and field survey.

Professor David W. Pearce whom I had the privilege to meet on two occasions in 1992 and 2000 at the Centre for Social and Economic Research on the Global Environment (CSERGE), University College London very kindly agreed to write a foreword to this book despite his busy schedule and several commitments. In response to my email he wrote: 'I am happy to write a foreword. Please do NOT email the book as it will take too long to download (we live in a small village with a poor telephone service)...' Unfortunately just as I was getting ready to send the book to Professor Pearce I received the sad news of his sudden passing away. His death is a tremendous loss to the profession. Professor Pearce has made a lasting contribution to environmental economics and inspired several others, including myself. In fact no work in environmental economics or ecological economics is complete without a reference to his pioneering works. Although David is no more his ideas and works continue to live among us.

We are most grateful to Professor Charles Perrings who was the President of the International Society of Ecological Economics for very kindly agreeing to write a foreword to this book. I have had the privilege of knowing Professor Perrings for quite some time and he was also kind enough to invite me to give a seminar at York University when I visited the UK in 2000. He has always been supportive of our endeavours.

K. N. Ninan
Bangalore
July 2006

List of Acronyms and Abbreviations

ACF	Assistant Conservator of Forests
AFO	Assistant Forest Officer
BCR	benefit–cost ratio
BRT	Biligiri Rangana Temple
BOTD	Beneficiary Oriented Scheme for Tribal Development
CBD	Convention on Biological Diversity
CI	Conservation International
CIFOR	Centre for International Forestry Research
CITES	Convention on International Trade in Endangered Species of Wild Flora and Fauna
COP	Conference of Parties to the Convention on Biological Diversity
CPRs	common property resources
CSERGE	Centre for Social and Economic Research on the Global Environment
CVM	contingent valuation method
DCF	Deputy Conservator of Forests
DFID	Department for International Development
DFO	Deputy Forest Officer
DGO	Decentralized Government Organization
EERC	Environmental Economics Research Committee
EIRR	economic internal rate of return
FAO	Food and Agricultural Organization
FSI	Forest Survey of India
GEF	Global Environment Facility
GPV	gross present value
IEA	International Energy Agency
IGIDR	Indira Gandhi Institute for Development Research
IRR	internal rate of return
ISEC	Institute for Social and Economic Change
IUCN	The World Conservation Union (formerly the International Union for the Conservation of Nature)
KFD	Karnataka Forest Department

MCA	multi-criteria analysis
MFP	minor forest product
MoEF	Ministry of Environment and Forests, Government of India
MSL	mean sea level
Mtoe	million tonnes of oil equivalent
NBSAP	National Biodiversity Strategy and Action Plan
NGO	non-governmental organization
NOAA	National Oceanic and Atmospheric Administration
NPV	net present value
NTFB	non-timber forest benefit
NTFP	non-timber forest product
NTFR	non-timber forest resource
NWDB	National Wastelands Development Board
NWFP	non-wood forest product
ODA	Overseas Development Agency
OECD	Organisation for European Co-operation and Development
PV	present value
Rs	rupees
SCBD	Secretariat of the Convention on Biological Diversity
STM	sustainable timber management
TCM	travel cost method
TEV	total economic value
UNCED	United Nations Conference on Environment and Development
UNDP	United Nations Development Programme
UNEP	United Nations Environment Programme
WCMC	World Conservation Monitoring Centre
WRI	World Resources Institute
WSSD	World Summit on Sustainable Development
WTA	willingness to accept
WTP	willingness to pay
WWF	World Wildlife Fund

1
Introduction

Biodiversity conservation: Its significance and the issues

Biodiversity conservation is part of the larger objective of promoting sustainable development. Biodiversity loss not only affects current economic growth, but also the capacity of the economy to sustain future economic growth. Biodiversity loss has both human and non-human impacts as well as intergenerational and intra-generational impacts. For instance, while the benefits of biodiversity conservation will accrue to the present generation, the costs of biodiversity loss will be borne by future generations. Similarly, while the benefits of biodiversity conservation may accrue to the local and global community at large, the costs are most often borne by the local community who depend on forests for their livelihood (e.g. Wells, 1992). Poor people and less developed countries are affected the most by bio-diversity decline. Biological diversity provides the goods and services that make life on Earth possible and satisfy the needs of human societies. The variability it represents constitutes a global life insurance policy (UNEP, 2001). Biodiversity also plays a crucial role in maintaining the resilience of ecosystems to environmental shocks (Perrings et al, 1992; Tilmand and Downing, 1994, see Gowdy, 1997; Perrings, 2000). Hence, the need for conserving biodiversity is obvious. In view of its importance, biodiversity conservation is receiving considerable attention both in research and policy circles in recent years, especially after the Rio Summit of the United Nations Conference on Environment and Development (UNCED) held in 1992.

Biological diversity, or biodiversity for short, is an umbrella term used to describe the number, variety and variability of living organisms in an assemblage. Biodiversity may be described in terms of genes, species and ecosystems. Genetic diversity is the sum of genetic information contained in the genes of individuals of plants, animals and micro-organisms. Species diversity refers to the variety and variability of species in a given region or area. Ecosystem diversity can be defined as the variety of habitats, biotic communities and ecological processes in the biosphere as well as the diversity within the ecosystem (Pearce and Moran, 1994).

The developing countries are rich in biodiversity such as forests, wetlands, aquatic environments, etc. However, the biodiversity of the developing countries are under threat due to demographic and economic pressures, faulty incentive mechanisms and policies, and so on. Although much of the world's biodiversity is concentrated in developing countries, research on biodiversity is centred in developed countries.

While moral and ethical grounds can be advanced to justify biodiversity conservation, it is primarily economic forces that are driving down much of the world's biological diversity and resources (Pearce and Moran, 1994). A proper assessment of the benefits of biodiversity conservation ought to take into account the opportunity costs of biodiversity conservation in terms of the benefits forgone as well as the external costs of conservation, for example the wildlife damage costs and defensive expenditures to protect against wildlife attacks incurred by local communities living within or near forests. Even if the global community were to perceive biodiversity conservation favourably and support conservation activities, ultimately it is the perceptions and attitudes of the local communities who reside within or near forests/protected areas and depend on forests for their livelihood that will make a difference to biodiversity conservation. Understanding the local values of biodiversity conservation and the incentives and disincentives for biodiversity conservation, especially those operating at the local level, is, therefore, critical to devising appropriate strategies for biodiversity conservation. Policies for conserving biodiversity depend upon the perceived costs and benefits of biodiversity conservation. This necessitates a comparative assessment of the benefits of biodiversity conservation vis-à-vis the benefits forgone or realizable from the alternative land use options of forests such as utilizing them for and sustaining agriculture, animal husbandry, tourism and recreation, and other activities. Figure 1.1 presents a flow chart illustrating the alternate land use options of forests, namely, the preservation, conservation and development options. The preservation option precludes any human use of forests. This implies that forests are preserved in their original or natural state without any human interference. The conservation option, on the other hand, permits human uses of forests in a sustainable way, such as the sustainable extraction of timber and non-timber forest products. The development option implies the destruction of forests and conversion to non-forest uses, such as permanent or settled agriculture, establishing human settlements, industries, mining, hydro-electric and other development projects. The choice confronting most countries and societies is the conservation vs. development option. However, an assessment of the benefits of biodiversity conservation as opposed to alternate land use options poses problems and challenges, since many environmental goods and services are not traded or are difficult to measure. A number of valuation techniques such as the Contingent Valuation Method (CVM), the Travel Cost Method (TCM), hedonic pricing, etc., have been developed to value biodiversity. (For a detailed list of methods of valuing biodiversity and protected areas, see Dixon and Sherman, 1990; Pearce and Moran, 1994.) Similarly, re-

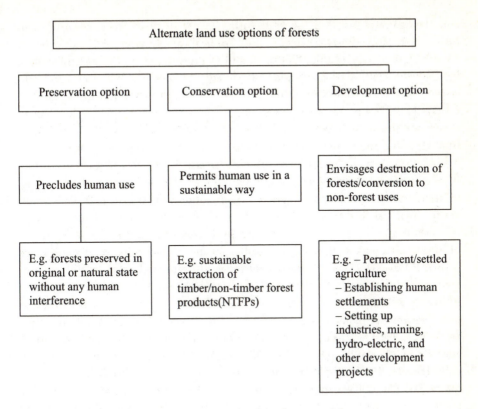

Figure 1.1 *Alternate land use options of forests*

cent policy initiatives to declare protected areas or sanctuaries to protect habitats, biodiversity and wildlife have focused attention on their social costs since most often they tend to exclude local or indigenous communities from their planning and implementation, without giving them a stake in conservation or providing sustainable livelihood options. These adverse social impacts can affect the quality of success of these policy initiatives. These initiatives also tend to ignore or under-rate the importance of traditions and customs as well as of local communities and institutions in conserving natural resources. The proposed research will probe into some of these issues as well as undertake a willingness to pay (WTP) or willing-ness to accept (WTA) study for environmental goods and services with respect to tropical forests.

Tropical forests

This study focuses on tropical forests, which are without doubt the most impor-tant ecosystem type from the viewpoint of global biodiversity. The sheer diversity of functions which they serve, the uniqueness of primary forests in evolutionary and ecological terms, and the accelerating threat to their existence justify this focus on tropical forests (Pearce, 1991). Tropical forests cover 14 per cent of the Earth's land surface (8,000,000km^2) and are exceptional in the wealth of their biodiversity. Half of all vertebrates, 60 per cent of known plant species and possibly 90 per cent of the world's total species are found in tropical forests (ODA, 1991). There are more species in total and per unit area in the tropics than in temperate and polar regions (UNEP, 2001). Besides biodiversity, cultural, spiritual, aesthetic and recreational benefits, tropical forests also provide vital environmental services such as helping to protect watersheds in terms of water retention, flood protection, helping to prevent soil erosion, nutrient and carbon cycling, influencing local and global climate functions, and so on. (Pearce, 1991; Perrings, 2000). Tropical forests provide a wide range of products and services, including several useful plant species for agriculture, medicine and industry. Examples of important crops include banana, coffee, cocoa, citrus fruits, vanilla and black pepper (ODA, 1991). Conservation of the wild relatives of these species is necessary to maintain their productivity. Cross breeding with wild varieties is essential to maintain resistance to diseases and pests. It is stated that cross breeding has saved sugarcane, banana and cocoa crops from major damage (Leonard, 1987, see Pearce, 1991). Tropical forests also house many insects that are the natural enemies of plant-damaging pests, and plant chemicals that are used as insecticides (Pearce, 1991). Estimates suggest that tropical forests are being cleared at the rate of 140,000km^2 per year or approximately 1.8 per cent of the remaining forest cover (Myers, 1989, see ODA, 1991). The rate of tropical deforestation appears to have accelerated over recent decades. For instance, Pearce (1991) notes that during the late 1970s 6,540,000 hectares (ha) of closed forests were deforested annually, but that this rose to 14,220,000ha by the late 1980s. As a proportion of the remaining forest, the rate of deforestation rose from 0.6 per cent in the late 1970s to 1.8–2.1 per cent in the late 1980s (Pearce, 1991). In the *State of the World's Forests 2005* the Food and Agriculture Organization (FAO) notes that over the period 1995–2000 about 9,400,000ha of forests were deforested annually across the world. The annual deforestation rate was the highest in Africa (5,300,000ha), followed by South America (3,700,000ha), North and Central America (600,000ha), Asia and Oceania (each 400,000ha). Europe was the only continent to register an increase in the forest cover at 900,000ha annually (FAO, 2005). Deforestation and forest degradation are currently more extensive in the tropics than in the rest of the world (World Resources Institute (WRI), 2005). Tropical deforestation has disastrous consequences on species and tropical forest ecosystem services. The Millennium Ecosystem Assessment Report (WRI, 2005) notes that current species extinction rates are up to 1000 times higher than the fossil record of less than one species per 1000 mammal species becoming extinct every millennium (WRI, 2005). The projected future extinction rate is more than ten times higher than the current rate. It is also reported that 12 per cent of bird species, 25 per cent of mammals and 32 per cent of amphibians are threatened with extinction over the next century (WRI, 2005). One estimate suggests that if current deforestation continues at the same rate, approximately one quarter of the world's plant species will be lost over the next 20 years (IUCN, 1990, see ODA, 1991). Although biodiversity conservation is being emphasized in policy circles in India, there is a dearth of rigorous empirical and theoretical work focusing on India. This study seeks to bridge this gap.

Factors causing biodiversity loss

Economic and demographic pressures, market failures, faulty incentives and policy distortions, the divergence between the private and social values of biodiversity and the failure to capture the global values of biodiversity are among several factors contributing to biodiversity loss (ODA, 1991; Perrings et al, 1992; Pearce and Moran, 1994; Swanson, 1995; Perrings, 2000). The Millennium Ecosystem Assessment Report 2005 notes that biodiversity change is influenced by direct and indirect drivers (WRI, 2005). Drivers are any natural or human induced factors that directly or indirectly cause a change in an ecosystem such as habitat change, climate change, invasive species, overexploitation and pollution. Indirect drivers are the real cause of ecosystem changes such as change in economic activity, demographic change, socio-political, cultural and religious factors, scientific and technological change, etc. (WRI, 2005). There are both fundamental and proximate causes that account for biodiversity loss. Logging, clearance of forestlands for agricultural and non-agricultural purposes and pollution are some of the proximate causes behind biodiversity loss; but the fundamental causes are rooted in economic, institutional and social factors. The pressure to develop itself poses a major threat to biodiversity. It is acknowledged that there could be trade-offs between development and biodiversity loss, and that some biodiversity will be lost even if development becomes more sustainable. Population growth along with poverty is a major source of biotic impoverishment, habitat loss, species and genetic decline in developing countries. Environmental goods such as biodiversity, the costs and benefits of which are both uncertain and concentrated in the future, are heavily discounted which accelerates biodiversity loss. Pearce and Moran (1994) and ODA (1991) identify two major types of failures contributing to biodiversity loss, namely market failure and intervention failure. Market failures arise from distortions due to 'missing markets' or the inability of existing markets to capture the 'true' value of natural resources. Market failures are of two types, local market failure and global market failure. Local market failure refers to the inability of markets to capture some of the local and national benefits of biodiversity conservation. For example, with respect to land conversion it refers to the failure of markets to account for the external costs of biodiversity loss because of land conversion. Many of the goods derived from biodiversity are public; but there are also considerable externalities present, and such limited markets that do exist are not competitive. The 'market' in biodiversity is non-existent, incomplete or distorted. As a result market prices do not reflect true social values. These market failures arise due to ill-defined property rights, externalities, uncertainty and irreversibility of certain environmental processes, market imperfections and policy distortions. Global market failure or global appropriation failure is another type of market failure. Biodiversity conservation yields external benefits to people outside the boundaries of the nation faced with the development vs. conservation choice. This, therefore, refers to the failure of the global community and outside countries – which receive these global external benefits – to give financial and other incentives for biodiversity conservation to the bio-rich countries. Hence, these latter countries have no incentive to look after their biological resources. Intervention failure arising from distortions due to governmental actions in intervening in the working of the market is another causal factor behind biodiversity loss. Financial incentives for deforestation, underpricing of water resources, are examples of intervention failure. Intervention failure can take two forms: ineffective positive intervention (such as the failure to protect demarcated natural reserves, to implement land use policies, or to enforce land use regulations and environmental legislation) and unintentional negative intervention arising from general development strategy, fiscal and monetary policy, market interventions, land tenure, etc. Thus a variety of economic, social and institutional factors account for biodiversity loss.

The economic case for valuing biodiversity

An obvious question that arises is why one needs to value biodiversity. A basic premise is that if proper economic values are assigned to biodiversity, then rational decisions are possible, especially in the case of resources such as forests, which have alternative land use options. Valuation helps society to make informed choices about the trade-offs (Loomis, 2000). Decisions on logging, management or conversion of forestlands are most frequently determined on economic criteria such as the demand for timber, for agricultural land or the need to export forest products to earn foreign exchange (Adgers et al, 1995). But market transactions provide an incomplete picture of the total economic value of forests. Those forest benefits which are not normally exchanged in markets are generally ignored in decision making. Undervaluation of these welfare-enhancing services introduces inherent distortions in efficient resource allocation. Estimating the appropriate (shadow) prices of non-marketed or partially marketed forest functions and developing appropriate mechanisms to capture the estimated economic values is required to improve the efficiency of resource allocation (Adgers et al, 1995).

The case for biodiversity conservation, however, does not rest on economic considerations alone, but is also rooted in ethical, cultural, aesthetic and social factors. There are in fact two opposing viewpoints in this regard. While one holds that moral and ethical grounds justify the case for biodiversity conservation, the other view justifies conservation of biodiversity largely on economic grounds (ODA, 1991; Pearce and Moran, 1994). The recognition that humankind is part of nature: that all species have an inherent right to exist regardless of their material value to humans, that human culture must be based on a respect for nature, and that present generations have a social responsibility to conserve nature for the welfare of future generations all provide justification for biodiversity conservation (IUCN, 1990, see, ODA, 1991; Ehrlich and Ehrlich, 1992; Flint, 1992; Gowdy, 1997). As per the first view, economics has no place in what is fundamentally an ethical issue. Advocates of the moral viewpoint as reflected in the ideas of anthropocentrism, biocentrism and ecocentrism do not favour regarding biodiversity conservation as intrinsically valuable but think of its moral value as derivative (Oksanen, 1997). As against this deep ecology advocates such as Naess argue for its intrinsic value and maintain that biodiversity conservation is a morally worthwhile end in itself (Oksanen, 1997). As per this 'the flourishing of human and non-human life on earth has intrinsic value' and that 'richness and diversity of life forms are values in themselves and contribute to the flourishing of human and non-human life on earth' (Oksanen, 1997). The economic justification for biodiversity conservation does not imply that moral and ethical considerations are not important. Existence values, for instance, represent an attempt by economists to give a reasonable proxy for moral values, and the absence of market prices does not mean the absence of economic values (ODA, 1991). Biodiversity does have positive economic values that need to be taken into account. The reality nevertheless is that choices and trade-offs have to be made in the context of scarce resources and the need for measures to conserve biodiversity. Powerful social and ethical grounds can also be mustered for programmes which are designed to improve the welfare of poor people in developing countries but which involve some reduction in biodiversity (Flint, 1992). Unless and until the social and economic implications are clearer, governments are likely to continue to give insufficient weight to biological degradation. Improving the economic case for biodiversity conservation is, therefore, an important goal (ODA, 1991).

The case for economic or monetary valuation of biodiversity rests on three grounds: it provides a way of arriving at a decision that maximizes well being; it provides a way of trading off objectives; and it is effective since it speaks in the economic language to which policy makers listen (O'Neill, 1997). However, there are others who cite the limitations of economic valuation and conventional cost–benefit analysis to justify biodiversity conservation (cf. Gowdy and McDaniel, 1995; Gowdy, 1997; Erickson, 2000). According to them, owing to the complexities, uncertainty and irreversibilities characteristic of a public good such as biodiversity, the limitations of the market and substitutability between biodiversity and monetized goods, and conflicts between economic and biological systems, relying on the precautionary principle or the safe minimum standard is the most prudent option to ensure biodiversity conservation. Establishing and maintaining a proportion of forests as protected areas is an example of observing the safe minimum standard to conserve biodiversity. Those who justify economic valuation are not denying the importance of relying on the precautionary principle or safe minimum standard to conserve biodiversity. However, establishing and maintaining protected areas is not a costless activity and requires money and for bio-rich developing countries in particular this has to compete with alternate uses. A case study presented in Chapter 4 notes that the income from Nagarhole National Park was just a fraction of the expenditure incurred by the State on the park. Unpriced and non-market benefits were not taken into account, which partly explains this discrepancy. This is where economic valuation has a major role to play in biodiversity conservation. The financial and economic benefits of conserving biodiversity are increasingly being cited by the conservation lobby as an argument for increased aid resources (ODA, 1991). For policy makers an idea of the forgone benefits accruing to the inhabitants and indigenous communities following the establishment of protected areas, would, for instance, be useful in designing rehabilitation and compensation packages for those displaced by such projects. Similarly, tropical countries like Malaysia and Indonesia, which rely on timber extraction for export earnings, would need appropriate economic incentives to forgo the development option and conserve their forest resources. An idea of the development benefits forgone would thus be useful in designing conservation policies. The economic case for valuing biodiversity is, therefore, based on strong grounds.

Total economic value of tropical forests

It would be useful to value the goods and services rendered by these forests. Following Pearce (1991, 1995) the total economic value of tropical forests could be considered as consisting of its direct and indirect use values plus the option and existence values. Direct values refer to goods and services provided by forests such as timber and non-timber products, recreation, medicines, plant genetics. Direct use values could be further subdivided into consumptive, productive and non-consumptive use values. Consumptive use values refer to the timber, non-timber, recreation, plant genetics and medicinal benefits provided by forests, whereas productive use values refer to plant breeding benefits, and non-consumptive use values to tourism benefits (ODA, 1991). Indirect use values refer to the ecological services and functions of the forests in terms of facilitating nutrient cycling, watershed protection, carbon fixing, etc. Option value is concerned with future use of both direct and indirect uses, for example the future value of drugs. Quasi-option values refer to the expected value derived from delaying the conversion of forests today. Existence value, which is a non-use value, is concerned with viewing forests as objects of inherent value that need to be conserved. Bequest value is another non-use value which refers to individuals placing a high value on the

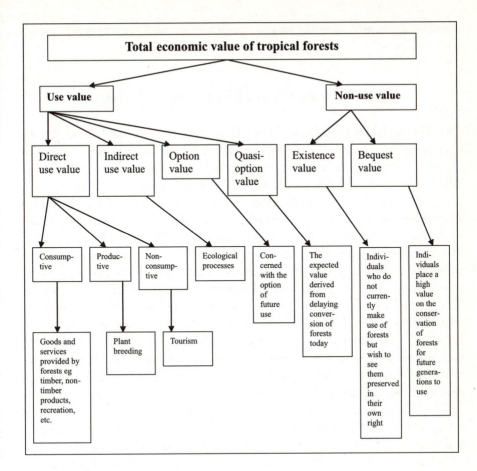

Source: Pearce (1991)

Figure 1.2 *Total economic value of tropical forests*

conservation of forests for future generations. Figure 1.2 presents a flow chart of the various components of the total economic value (TEV) of tropical forests as illustrated above.

Apart from reviewing the state of knowledge in this area, an attempt will be made to estimate the use and non-use values of tropical forests using a case study approach. A number of economic valuation procedures, such as Contingent Valuation Method (CVM), Multi-Criteria Analysis (MCA), Travel Cost Method (TCM), etc., have been evolved in developed countries. It would be useful to use some of these techniques and also evaluate their suitability from the perspective of developing countries. A probe into the opportunity costs of biodiversity conservation, the external costs of wildlife conservation, the incentives and disincentives for biodiversity conservation, the perceptions and attitudes of local communities towards biodiversity conservation and wildlife protection as well as the value preferences of the local communities for biodiversity conservation is also attempted.

The Western Ghats biodiversity hotspot

The Western Ghats region spread over six states of Southern and Western India (Kerala, Karnataka, Tamil Nadu, Maharashtra, Goa and Gujarat), is the setting for the present study. It has been identified by the United Nations as an environmentally sensitive area. The Nilgiris Biosphere is located in this region. Of the 18 (now 25) biodiversity hotspots listed in the world, two are located within the Indian subcontinent of which the Western Ghats is one, and the Eastern Himalayas (part of the Indo-Burma Biodiversity hotspot) is the other (Myers, 1990; Myers et al, 2000). Table 1.1 presents information about the 25 biodiversity hotspots in the world including the Western Ghats. As the table shows, the remaining primary vegetation in the Western Ghats (including Sri Lanka) constitutes only 6.8 per cent of the original extent of primary vegetation in this biodiversity hotspot. Out of 1073 vertebrate species found in the Western Ghats region (including Sri Lanka) 355 are endemic to this hotspot; similarly of 4780 plant species, 2180 are endemic to this hotspot. Of the 528 bird species found in the Western Ghats region (including Sri Lanka), 40 are endemic; similarly, of the 140 mammalian species, 38 are endemic; of the 259 reptile species 161 are endemic, and of the 146 amphibian species 116 are endemic (Table 1.2). The distribution of endemic vertebrates in the Western Ghats region alone (excluding Sri Lanka) are as follows: mammals – 14; birds – 19; reptiles – 97; amphibians – 94; fishes – 116; total endemic vertebrates – 340 (India, 2002). The Western Ghats also figures as one of the eight hottest biodiversity hotspots in the world in terms of five factors: the number of endemic plants, the number of endemic vertebrates, endemic plants/ area ratio, endemic vertebrates/area ratio, and remaining primary vegetation as a percentage of its original extent (Table 1.3).

The Western Ghats runs to a length of about 1600km, more or less parallel to the west coast of India starting from South Gujarat and the mouth of river Tapti in Dhule district of Maharashtra and ending at Kanyakumari, the southernmost tip of India in Tamil Nadu (Tewari, 1993). The Western Ghats cover an area of 160,000km^2 with elevations of 6000m above mean sea level (MSL). The population of this region was about 38,550,000 according to the 1981 Population Census. The region generally receives 2000–7000mm of rainfall and is rich in natural resources. Almost a third of the geographical area of the Western Ghats is under forests of diverse types – evergreen to semi-evergreen forests, moist to deciduous forests, etc. The region is rich in forest and hydel resources, and biodiversity. Most of the rivers in peninsular India such as the Godavari, Krishna, Cauvery, Kali Nadi and Periyar have their origin in the Western Ghats. The health of these water courses is intimately bound up with the health of the forest catchment areas in the Western Ghats. The water harvested from the Western Ghats provides irrigation and hydro-electric power to the eastern plains (Western Ghats Forestry Project, see Karnataka Forest Department (KFD) and Department for International Development (DFID), 1999).

The region, as stated earlier, is rich in biodiversity. It is a treasure house of several known and unknown flora and fauna, including several mammalian species on the endangered list such as the lion-tailed macaque (*Macaca silenus*), four-horned antelope (*Tetracerus quadricernis*), fishing cat (*Felis viverrina*), loris (*Loris targligradus*), Nilgri langur (*Presbytis johni*), Nilgri tahr (*Hemitragus hylocrius*), mouse deer (*Tragulus memmina*), Indian gaur (*Bos gaurus*), Brant Malabar squirrel (*Ratufa indica*) and the Malabar civert (*Viverricula megaspita*). The forests of the Western Ghats harbour some of the best wildlife areas of the Indian subcontinent with the last remnant populations of such major animals as the Royal Bengal tiger, panther, Asian elephant, gaur or Indian bison. Other groups, for example birds and amphibians, are equally rich in species. For example, Daniels recorded some 343 bird taxa (species) over five years of observation in the 7000km^2 of the North Kanara forests (KFD and DFID, 1999). A study by Madhav Gadgil (1987, see KFD and DFID, 1999) indicates that of the 13,000 species of flowering plants found in India, some 3500 are found in the Western Ghats alone. Of these, some 1500 are unique to this mountain range. These include wild relatives of many economically valuable plants such as pepper, cardamom, ginger, mango, jackfruit, varieties of millets and rice. It is also held that the Western Ghats may have been a centre for origin of many species. The specialized climatic conditions of the Western Ghats may also explain the restricted distribution or 'endemism' of many species. The climax vegetation of the wet tract is an evergreen forest dominated by trees of *Cullenia, Persea, Dipterocarpus, Diospyros, Holigarna* and *Memcylon*. The deciduous forest tract is dominated by *Terminalia, Lagerstroemia, Pterocarpus, Xylia, Tectona* and *Anogeissus* species which are some of the most valuable commercial timbers in the world (KFD and DFID, 1999). Commercial forestry and various other human interventions in the forests have unintended effects on the wildlife. Animals like the lion-tailed macaque are dependent on a narrow range of food plants, and require sizeable stretches of undisturbed forest canopy. Fragmentation of the forest impedes migratory movements, especially of large herbivores like the elephant, resulting in lower carrying capacity and an increase in man–animal conflicts (KFD and DFID, 1999). A study of the southern parts of the Western Ghats using satellite data to estimate changes in the forest cover over a 25 year period, 1973–1995, revealed a loss of 25.6 per cent of the forest cover. While dense forests decreased by 19.5 per cent, open forests decreased by 32.2 per cent. The study observed a five-fold increase in rate of forest loss between the periods 1920–1960 and 1960–1990. The southern stretch of the Western Ghats extending to about 40,000km^2 has experienced the most significant loss during 1973–1995 with an estimated loss of 2729km^2 of forest with an annual deforestation rate of 1.16 per cent. Increase in plantation and agricultural areas due to population pres-

Table 1.1 *The 25 biodiversity hotspots in the world*

Biodiversity hotspot	Original extent of primary vegetation (km²)	Remaining primary vegetation (km²) (% of original extent)	Area protected (km²) (% of hotspot)	Plant species	Endemic plants (% of global plants, 300,000)	Vertebrate species	Endemic vertebrates (% of global vertebrates, 27,298)
Tropical Andes	1,258,000	314,500 (25.0)	79,687 (25.3)	45,000	20,000 (6.7)	3389	1567 (5.7)
Mesoamerica	1,155,000	231,000 (20.0)	138,437 (59.9)	24,000	5000 (1.7)	2859	1159 (4.2)
Caribbean	263,500	29,840 (11.3)	29,840 (100.0)	12,000	7000 (2.3)	1518	779 (2.9)
Brazil's Atlantic Forest	1,227,600	91,930 (7.5)	33,084 (35.9)	20,000	8000 (2.7)	1361	567 (2.1)
Choco/Darien/Western Ecuador	260,600	63,000 (24.2)	16,471 (26.1)	9000	2250 (0.8)	1625	418 (1.5)
Brazil's Cerrado	1,783,200	356,630 (20.0)	22,000 (6.2)	10,000	4400 (1.5)	1268	117 (0.4)
Central Chile	300,000	90,000 (30.0)	9167 (10.2)	3429	1605 (0.5)	335	61 (0.2)
California Floristic Province	324,000	80,000 (24.7)	31,443 (39.3)	4426	2125 (0.7)	584	71 (0.3)
Madagascar*	594,150	59,038 (9.9)	11,548 (19.6)	12,000	9704 (3.2)	987	771 (2.8)
Eastern Arc and Coastal Forests of Tanzania/Kenya	30,000	2000 (6.7)	2000 (100.0)	4000	1500 (0.5)	1019	121 (0.4)
Western African Forests	1,265,000	126,500 (10.0)	20,324 (16.1)	9000	2250 (0.8)	1320	270 (1.0)
Cape Floristic Province	74,000	18,000 (24.3)	14,060 (78.1)	8200	5682 (1.9)	562	53 (0.2)
Succulent Karoo	112,000	30,000 (26.8)	2352 (7.8)	4849	1940 (0.6)	472	45 (0.2)
Mediterranean Basin	2,362,000	110,000 (4.7)	42,123 (38.3)	25,000	13,000 (4.3)	770	235 (0.9)
Caucasus	500,000	50,000 (10.0)	14,050 (28.1)	6300	1600 (0.5)	632	59 (0.2)
Sundaland	1,600,000	125,000 (7.8)	90,000 (72.0)	25,000	15,000 (5.0)	1800	701 (2.6)
Wallacea	347,000	52,020 (15.0)	20,415 (39.2)	10,000	1500 (0.5)	1142	529 (1.9)

Philippines	300,800	9023 (3.0)	3910 (43.3)	7620	5832 (1.9)	1093	518 (1.9)
Indo-Burma	2,060,000	100,000 (100.0)	100,000 (100.0)	13,500	7000 (2.3)	2185	528 (1.9)
South-Central China	800,000	64,000 (8.0)	16,562 (25.9)	12,000	3500 (1.2)	1141	178 (0.7)
Western Ghats/Sri Lanka	182,500	12,450 (6.8)	12,450 (100.0)	4780	2180 (0.7)	1073	355 (1.3)
SW Australia	309,850	33,336 (10.8)	33,336 (100.0)	5469	4331 (1.4)	456	100 (0.4)
New Caledonia	18,600	5200 (28.0)	526.7 (10.1)	3332	2551 (0.9)	190	84 (0.3)
New Zealand	270,500	59,400 (22.0)	52,068 (87.7)	2300	1865 (0.6)	217	136 (0.5)
Polynesia/Micronesia	46,000	10,024 (21.8)	4913 (49.0)	6557	3334 (1.1)	342	223 (0.8)
Totals	17,444,300	2,122,891 (12.2)	800,767 (37.7)	**	133,149 (44)	**	9645 (35)

Note: Documentation of plant and vertebrate species and endemism can be found in Table 1.2.
* Madagascar includes the nearby islands of Mauritius, Reunion, Seychelles and Comores.
** These totals cannot be summed owing to overlapping between hotspots.

Source: Myers et al (2000); adapted and reproduced with permission from the publisher

Table 1.2 *Vertebrate species and endemism of 25 biodiversity hotspots in the world*

Biodiversity hotspot	Bird species and endemism		Mammal species and endemism		Reptile species and endemism		Amphibian species and endemism		Total species and endemism	
	(a)	(b)	(a)	(b)	(a)	(b)	(a)	(b)	(a)	(b)
Tropical Andes	1666	677	414	68	479	218	830	604	3389	1567
Mesoamerica	1193	251	521	210	685	391	460	307	2859	1159
Caribbean	668	148	164	49	497	418	189	164	1518	779
Brazil's Atlantic Forest	620	181	261	73	200	60	280	253	1361	567
Choco/Darien/Western Ecuador	830	85	235	60	210	63	350	210	1625	418
Brazil's Cerrado	837	29	161	19	120	24	150	45	1268	117
Central Chile	198	4	56	9	55	34	26	14	335	61
California Floristic Province	341	8	145	30	61	16	37	17	584	71
Madagascar	359	199	112	84	327	301	189	187	987	771
Eastern Arc and Coastal Forests of Tanzania/Kenya	585	22	183	16	188	50	63	33	1019	121
Western African Forests	514	90	551	45	139	46	116	89	1320	270
Cape Floristic Province	288	6	127	9	109	19	38	19	562	53
Succulent Karoo	269	1	78	4	115	36	10	4	472	45
Mediterranean Basin	345	47	184	46	179	110	62	32	770	235
Caucasus	389	3	152	32	76	21	15	3	632	59
Sundaland	815	139	328	115	431	268	226	179	1800	701
Wallacea	697	249	201	123	188	122	56	35	1142	529
Philippines	556	183	201	111	252	159	84	65	1093	518
Indo-Burma	1170	140	329	73	484	201	202	114	2185	528
South-Central China	686	36	300	75	70	16	85	51	1141	178

Western Ghats/Sri Lanka	528	40	140	38	259	161	146	116	1073	355
SW Australia	181	19	54	7	191	50	30	24	456	100
New Caledonia	116	22	9	6	65	56	0	0	190	84
New Zealand	149	68	3	3	61	61	4	4	217	136
Polynesia/Micronesia	254	174	16	9	69	37	3	3	342	223
Total endemics and % of global total	*	2821	*	1314	*	2938	*	2572		9645
		28.5%		27.3%		37.5%		53.8%		35.3%

Notes: * These totals cannot be summed owing to overlapping between hotspots.
(a) Number of species (b) Number of endemic species.

Source: Myers et al (2000); adapted and reproduced with permission from the publisher

Table 1.3 *The eight hottest biodiversity hotspots in the world in terms of five factors*

Biodiversity hotspot	Endemic plants	rank	Endemic vertebrates	rank	Endemic plants/area ratio (species per 100km²)	rank	Endemic vertebrates/area ratio (species per 100km²)	rank	Remaining primary vegetation as % of original extent	rank	Times appearing in top 10 for each of five factors
Madagascar	9704	4	771	4	16.4	8	1.3	7	9.9	9	5
Philippines	5832	8	518	9	64.7	2	5.7	2	3.0	1	5
Sundaland	15,000	2	701	5	12.0	10	0.6	10=	7.8	7	5
Brazil's Atlantic Forest	8000	5	654	6	8.7	6	0.6	10=	7.5	6	4
Caribbean	7000	6=	779	3	23.5		2.6	4	11.3		4
Indo-Burma	7000	6=	528	8	7.0		0.5		4.9	3	3
Western Ghats/Sri Lanka	2180		355		17.5	7	2.9	3	6.8	5	3
Eastern Arc and Coastal Forests of Tanzania/Kenya	1500		121		75.0	1	6.1	1	6.7	4	3

Note: The above factors do not carry equal weight, so they cannot be combined into a single quantitative ranking. For comparative purposes in qualitative fashion the above table lists the eight hottest hotspots which appear at least three times in the top ten listings for each factor.

Source: Myers et al (2000); adapted and reproduced with permission from the publisher

sure were the major factors behind this rapid loss of the forest cover in these parts of the Western Ghats (Jha, Dutt and Bava, 'Current Science', see *Deccan Herald*, 9 September 2000, p9). The above discussion shows the significance and richness of the biodiversity of the Western Ghats and its appropriateness for conducting the present study. Due to demographic and economic pressures, market failures and inappropriate policies, the biodiversity of the region is under various stages of degradation and, therefore, needs to be conserved through appropriate policies.

Survey of literature and justification for the study

While there is no dearth of literature on biodiversity conservation, economic or valuation studies of biodiversity conservation are relatively fewer. However, such studies are increasing rapidly in response to concern about the alarming decline in biodiversity and its consequences, and as a result of funds becoming available from development and donor agencies for research and development projects for biodiversity conservation. The currently existing economic and valuation studies of biodiversity conservation cover a diversity of regions and countries, and ecosystems such as tropical forests, wetlands. (For a comprehensive review of economic and valuation studies, see Pearce and Moran, 1994.) For our review, we shall concentrate on those studies that focus on tropical forests, valuations of different species and habitats and studies pertaining to India in particular.

Economic values of tropical forests: regional and cross-country estimates

Information on the economic values of tropical forests for selected regions and countries is furnished in Table 1.4. Gutierrez and Pearce (1992, see Pearce and Moran, 1994) have estimated the TEV of Brazil's Amazon forest at US$91 billion (bn) of which the direct use value is US$15 bn (16.5 per cent), the indirect use value is US$46 bn (50.5 per cent) and the existence value is US$30 bn (i.e. 33 per cent). The net present value (NPV) was estimated at US$1296 bn (Pearce and Moran, 1994). Pearce et al (1993, see Pearce and Moran, 1994) and Adgers et al (1995) estimated the non-market benefits (lower bound estimates) of 51,500,000ha of Mexican forests at about US$4214.8 million. Of this, indirect use values arising from carbon and watershed protection accounted for US$3790.6 million, that is 89.9 per cent; option and existence value at US$391.9 million, 9.3 per cent, and direct use value from tourism at US$32.2 million, 0.8 per cent. A study of the Peruvian Amazon forests by Ruitenbeek (1989, see Pearce and Moran, 1994) estimated an NPV of US$6820/ha from sustainable harvesting in 1ha compared with US$3184/ha from plantations of timber and pulpwood, and US$2966/ha from cattle ranching. Another study by Ruitenbeek (1989), pertaining to the Korup National Park in Cameroon, West Africa, indicated the minimum expected genetic value of the park at an NPV of about US$7/ha, and from tourism at US$19/ha. Indirect use value from watershed protection of the park was estimated at US$54/ha or aggregating to about US$6,800,000. A CVM survey of villagers' willingness to accept (WTA) compensation to forgo the use benefits from the creation of Mantadia National Park in Madagascar will implicitly reveal their valuation of the TEV of the resource forgone. The survey revealed a per household expected mean WTA of US$108 per annum which, aggregated over the affected number of households, amounted to a necessary one time compensation of approximately US$670,000 using a 10 per cent discount rate and a 20 year horizon (Kramer et al, 1993, see Pearce and Moran 1994). Balick and Mendelson (1992, see Pearce and Moran, 1994) conducted a study of the sustainable harvesting of medicinal plants in Belin and calculated a local market value at an NPV of US$3327/ha compared to US$3184/ha from plantation forestry with rotation felling (see Pearce and Moran, 1994). Pearce and Moran (1994) have made estimates of the lost pharmaceutical value from disappearing plant species. For the US, using the 'value of life' approach, their estimates suggested an annual loss of US$180 bn, and over US$500 bn for Organisation for European Cooperation and Development (OECD) countries, assuming that substitutes would not be forthcoming in the event that the plant species did become extinct.

A study of the Mount Kenya Forest Reserve in Kenya noted that of the estimated gross benefits of US$77 million per annum from the forest reserve, while direct benefits accounted for 29 per cent of the gross benefits, indirect benefits such as watershed protection contributed as much as 71 per cent (Emerton, 1999a). However, the study has not estimated the non-use value of the forest reserve. The direct use value from forest production in Malaysia was US$2455/ha compared with only US$217/ha from intensive agriculture (see Pearce and Moran, 1994). Beukering et al (2003) estimated the accumulated TEV of the Leuser National Park in Sumatra, Indonesia under three alternative scenarios: assuming deforestation, conservation and selective utilization. The accumulated TEV was estimated at US$7–9.5 billion (at 4 per cent discount rate over 30 years) under the three scenarios. Interestingly, under the deforestation scenario, while direct use values contributed over 70 per cent of the TEV, indirect use values such as ecological services contributed around 29.6 per cent. Under the conservation scenario, however, the contribution of direct use values to TEV dropped to over 43 per cent, while that of ecological services rose sharply to account for over half of the TEV. Under the selective utilization scenario direct use values accounted for over 53 per cent of the TEV, while indirect use values contributed approximately 47 per cent. This study also has not estimated the non-use values provided by the forest ecosystem. Overall, the above studies show that even taking a lower bound value, the TEV of tropical forests are considerable.

Table 1.5 presents the local and global conservation values for selected countries, namely, Mexico, Costa Rica, Indonesia and Malaysia. The values for timber for these countries ranged from US$1000–2000/ha for Indonesia to US$4075/ha

Table 1.4 *Economic values of tropical forests (in US$)*

Tropical forests	Direct use value	Indirect use value	Non-use value	Total economic value	Author/s
South America					
Brazilian Amazon	15 bn (16.5)	46 bn (50.5)	30 bn (33.0)	91 bn (100.0)	Gutierrez and Pearce, 1992
				NPV 1296 bn (using Krutilla Fisher)	
Mexican Forests	(Categorized annual non-market benefits of 51,500,000ha of Mexican forests)				
	Tourism 32.2 mil (0.8)	Carbon and watershed protection 3790.6 mil (89.9)	Option & existence 391.9 mil (9.3)	4214.8 mil (lower bound estimate) (100.0)	Pearce et al, 1993; Adgers et al, 1995
Peruvian Amazon	Sustainable harvesting in 1 ha, (1987) NPV – $6820/ha Clear felling – $1000/ha Plantation for timber/pulp wood – $3184/ha From cattle ranching – $2966/ha (For 126,000ha park area or 426,000 with additional buffer area)		–	–	Ruitenbeek, 1989
Africa					
Korup National Park (Cameroon)	Medicines/genetic NPV $7/ha Tourism $19/ha	(i) Watershed protection: $54/ha ($6.8 mil) (ii) Imputed value of loss from flooding: $23/ha ($2.84 mil) (iii) Benefits imputed from crop productivity decline: $8/ha ($0.96 mil)			Ruitenbeek, 1989
Mantadia National Park (Madagascar)	Villagers WTA to forgo benefits for Park creation: US$108 per annum per household				

Tropical forests	Direct use value	Indirect use value	Non-use value	Total economic value	Author/s
				US$ 0.67 mil estimated for affected households (at 10% discount rate, 20 yr horizon)	Kramer et al, 1997
Mt Kenya Forest Reserve (Kenya)	(Forest Reserve Area covers 2000km²)		NA	Gross benefits 77 mil US$ per annum	Emerton, 1999a
		Watershed protection			
	(29.0)	(71.0)		(100)	
Of which					
Local domestic use	17%				
Local cultivation	6%				
Licensed use	3%				
Government	2%				
Recreation & tourism	1%				
Asia					
Malaysia	Forest production : $2455/ha Intensive agriculture : $217/ha				Swanson, 1991 see Pearce and Moran, 1994
Leuser National Park, Sumatra (Indonesia)	(Leuser ecosystem covers 25,000km²) Ecological Services			Accumulated TEV at 4% discount rate over 30 years billion US$	Beukering et al, 2003
a) Deforestation scenario	– (70.4)	– (29.6)	–	7.0 (100)	
b) Conservation scenario	– (43.2)	– (56.8)	–	9.5 (100)	
c) Selective utilization scenario	– (53.2)	– (46.8)	–	9.1 (100)	

Notes: 1 Figures in parentheses are percentages to respective TEV/Gross Benefits.
2 Mt Kenya Forest Reserve Study – local cultivation – forest shamba cultivation; licensed use – forest products; Govt – tea zone revenue, licence fees, royalties from forest products and land rentals.
3 Leuser National Park, Sumatra study – Direct benefits includes timber; NTFPs, fisheries, agriculture, hydro-power and tourism; ecological services includes water supply, flood protection, biodiversity, carbon sequestration and fire prevention.

Source: Adapted from Pearce and Moran, 1994; Emerton, 1999a; Beukering et al, 2003

Table 1.5 *Comparing local and global conservation values (US$/ha)*

Goods/ services	Mexico (Pearce et al., 1993)	Costa Rica (World Bank, 1992b) (carbon values adjusted)	Indonesia (World Bank, 1993) (carbon values adjusted)	Malaysia (World Bank, 1991)	Peninsular Malaysia (Kumari, 1994)
Timber	—	1240	1000–2000	4075	1024
Non-timber products	775	—	38–125	325–1238	96–487
Carbon storage	650–3400	3046	1827–3654	1015–2709	2449
Pharmaceutical	1–90	2	—	—	1–103
Ecotourism/recreation	8	209	—	—	13–35
Watershed protection	<1	—	—	—	—
Option value	80	—	—	—	—
Non-use value	15	—	—	—	—

Notes: All values are present values at 8% discount rate, but carbon values are at 3% discount rate. Uniform damage estimates of US$20.3 per tonne of carbon released have been used (Frankhauser and Pearce, 1994), so that original carbon damage estimates in the World Bank studies have been re-estimated (see Pearce, 1995).
References in the table are cited in Pearce (1995).

Source: Pearce (1995)

for Malaysia. For non-timber products these values were in the range US$38–1238/ha. The carbon storage values of the forests in these countries were considerable, ranging from US$650 to US$3654/ha for Mexico, Costa Rica and Indonesia, and from US$1015 to US$2709/ha for Malaysia. The pharmaceutical values of Mexico's forests were estimated at US$1–90/ha; for Peninsular Malaysia this value was estimated at US$1–103/ha. Ecotourism or recreation values varied from US$8/ha in Mexico to US$209/ha in Costa Rica. The option value of Mexico's forests was estimated at US$80ha, and non-use value at US$15/ha (Pearce, 1995).

Table 1.6 presents summary economic values of tropical forests in comparison with temperate forests. The table illustrates that the economic value of ecological services provided by tropical forests, such as climate and watershed benefits, are significantly larger than those provided by temperate forests. For instance, in respect of watershed benefits, the economic values provided by tropical forests are in the range US$15–850/ha per annum compared with US$10–50/ha per annum provided by temperate forests. Similarly the value of climate benefits provided by tropical forests are US$36–2200/ha per annum (gross present value (GPV)) compared with US$90–400/ha per annum from temperate forests. In terms of other benefits, such as genetic information and recreation, tropical forests yield significant benefits whereas such benefits, if any, from temperate forests are low or insignificant. Even in terms of direct benefits, such as fuelwood and non-timber forest products (NTFPs), tropical forests fare better than temperate forests. It is

Table 1.6 *Summary economic values of forest goods and services
(US$/ha per annum unless otherwise stated)*

Forest good or service	Tropical forests	Temperate forests
Timber		
conventional logging	200–4400 (NPV)	
sustainable	300–2660 (NPV)	–4000 to +700 (NPV)[2]
conventional logging	20–440[1]	
sustainable	30–266[1]	
Fuelwood	40	–
NTFPs	0–100	Small
Genetic information	0–3000	–
Recreation	2–470 (general) 770 (forests near towns) 1000 (unique forests)	80
Watershed benefits	15–850	–10 to +50
Climate benefits	360–2200 (GPV)[3]	90–400 (afforestation)
Biodiversity (other than genetics)	?	?
Amenity	–	Small
Non-use values		
Option values	NA	70?
Existence values	2–12 4400 (unique areas)	12–45

Notes: 1 – annuitized NPV at 10% for illustration; 2 – Pearce and Moran (1994); 3 – assumes compensation for carbon is a one off payment in the initial period and hence is treated as a present value. It is a gross value since no costs are deducted; NPV = net present value; GPV = gross present value.

Source: *The Value of Forest Ecosystems*, CBD Technical Series No.4, Secretariat of the Convention on Biological Diversity, Montreal, Canada, November 2001, p34; reproduced with permission from the publisher (SCBD)

thus obvious that the economic values of tropical forests are high and significant when compared to those of temperate forests.

Existence valuations of endangered species and prized habitats

The existence valuations for endangered species and prized habitats by individuals across a cross-section of countries is indicated in Table 1.7. These existence values for endangered species in the US range from around US$5 per person per year for striped shiner and coyote, to US$18–21 for grizzly bear, bald eagle and northern spotted owl, to as high as US$40–64 per person per year for humpback whales. For 300 forest-related animal and plant species in Sweden the existence value was around US$7 per person per year. The existence valuations for prized habitats across selected countries under review ranged from US$3 to US$8 per person per year for recreational, virgin and natural forests in Sweden, to around US$300 per person per year for lowland wetland bogs in the UK. These estimates indicate that the existence valuations for endangered species and prized habitats are quite significant. These studies, of course, all pertain to the developed countries only. There do not seem to be any similar estimates for developing countries as yet.

Table 1.7 *Existence valuations for endangered species and prized habitats*

Country	Species or habitat	Expressed value (US$ 1990 per person per year)
Species		
Norway	Brown bear, wolf and wolverine	15.0
US	Bald eagle	19.1
	Striped shiner	5.0
	Grizzly bear	18.5
	Bighorn sheep	8.6
	Whooping crane	6.5
	Wild turkey	11.4
	Salmon	7.6
	Coyote	5.1
	Blue whale	9.3
	Bottlenose dolphin	7.0
	California sea otter	8.1
	Northern elephant seal	8.1
	Humpback whales	40–64
	Northern spotted owl (linked to old growth forest habitat)	21
Sweden	300 forest-related animal and plant species	7
Habitat valuation		
US	Grand Canyon visibility	27.0
	Colorado wilderness	9.3–21.2
Australia	Nadgee Nature Reserve	28.1
	Kakadu Conservation Zone	40–93
UK	Sites of Special Scientific Interest*	40
	Lowland wetland bog	300
Norway	Conservation of rivers	59–107
	Preservation of coniferous forests	90–140
Sweden	Recreational and virgin forest areas	3–4
	All natural forests in Sweden	5–8

* Conservation designation.

Source: Based on Samples et al (1986), Boyle and Bishop (1987), Bowker and Stoll (1988), Stevens et al (1991), Brown et al (1991), Navrud (1992, 1993), and Directorate for Nature Management (1992), see Perrings (1995)

Use and non-use values of elephants

Elephants are considered as a keystone species because of their significant impact on their environment (Mendelssohn, 1999). They have a significant impact on plant composition due to their large and varied diet, their physical impact on their surroundings and their ability to move large distances (Mendelssohn, 1999). For instance, elephants are known to have a role in African savannas and forests that includes ecosystem diversification, seed dispersal, expanding grasslands and reducing tsetse fly, all of which may be of value to livestock grazing (Western, 1989, see Perrings, 2000). Such ecological functions are important in maintaining the dynamics and health of the ecosystem, and hence its capacity to sustain the various organisms dependent on it (Perrings, 2000). Elephants are, of course, also considered an agricultural pest (Tisdell and Zhu, 1998; Tisdell, 1999; Bandara and Tisdell, 2002).

Elephants are a vulnerable species in Asia and our study region in particular, and are the focus of our CVM survey. Hence we take a look at some estimates of the use and non-use values of elephants (Table 1.8). The table shows that the productive use value of elephants as reflected in the pre-ban ivory exports from Africa averaged around US$35–45 million per year. The viewing value of elephants by tourists on safari in Kenya in 1988 was estimated through a CVM survey at around US$25 million per year. This value represents non-consumptive use values, and option and existence values of elephants in Kenya. A study by Barnes (1996), which assessed the comparative economics of alternative elephant use strategies in Botswana through different levels of government investment before and after a ban on ivory trading, indicated a positive NPV with a 6 per cent discount rate (see Mendelssohn, 1999). This study suggested that a combination of wildlife viewing, safari hunting and culling would be the most viable form of elephant use, provided culling did not deter tourists (see Mendelssohn, 1999). A study by Hoare (1992, see Mendelssohn, 1999) assessed the financial and economic viability of investing in elephant fencing and found a positive internal rate of return (IRR) of 55 per cent. The most significant benefits were value of elephant used for safari hunting and savings on staff patrol costs.

Another study by Barnes (1996) tried to estimate the economic use values of elephants in Botswana under alternative elephant management strategies. The NPVs (at 6 per cent discount rate over 15 years at 1989 prices), assuming an elephant management strategy involving viewing only with no consumptive uses, was estimated at 123.5 million Pula (approximately US$59.3 million); and for viewing with safari hunting only at 168–196.1 million Pula (approximately US$80.6 million); and under the management strategy involving viewing, safari hunting and cropping (culling) at 162.3–202.3 million Pula (approximately US$77.9–97.1 million). Thus the study observed that an elephant management strategy involving a combination of viewing, safari hunting and cropping yielded the highest economic values in Botswana as compared to other alternatives. Unlike the

Table 1.8 *Economic values (use and non-use) of elephants*

Type of value	Unit/currency	Amount	Source
Africa:			
Productive use value			
Pre-Ban Ivory Export, Africa	US$ million/year	35–45	Barbier et al, 1990
Non-consumptive use value			
Viewing Value of elephants, Kenya	US$ million/year	25–30	Brown and Henry, 1993
Economic use values of elephants in Botswana	Million Pula (approximate US$ in parenthesis)[1]		Barnes, 1996
(under alternative elephant management strategies) NPVs (at 6% discount rate over 15 years) at 1989 prices – Results of 1992 analysis)			
1 Viewing only with no consumptive uses		123.5 (59.3 mil US$)	
2 Viewing with safari hunting only		168–196.1 (80.6 mil US$)	
3 Viewing, safari hunting and cropping[2]		162.3–202.3 (77.9–97.1 mil US$)	
Asia			
Option and existence values of Asian elephants to Thai residents, Khao Yai National Park, Thailand	Thai Baht (approximate 1990–1991 US$ in parenthesis)		Dixon and Sherman, 1990; 1991
Option and existence values		122 mil Baht (4.7 mil US$)	
Average maximum WTP		181 Baht per park user (US$7)	

Willingness to pay for conservation of wild Asian elephants, Sri Lanka

	Sri Lankan Rupees (per year over next 5 years)	Bandara and Tisdell, 2003
Urban residents of Colombo	1322	
Park users[3]	1648.6	
Park non-users	995.5	
Total present value (5% discount rate over 5 years)	6009.7	
(62% of WTP was attributable to non-use values of wild Asian elephants)		

Notes: 1 Botswana Pula = US$0.48 during the time of analysis as per the author.
2 In Botswana study (Barnes, 1996), cropping includes culling for raw ivory, fresh or dried meat, meat processing, dry salted hides, hide tanning, live sale of calves (6 months to 1 year old) under alternative assumptions regarding the degree of displacement/disturbance assumed for different elephant management options.
3 Sri Lanka study (Bandara and Tisdell, 2003) Users – those urban residents who had visited national parks or sanctuaries; Non-users – those urban residents who had never visited a national park or sanctuary.

African elephant (*Loxodonta africana*), the Asian elephant (*Elephas maximus*) is a threatened species. For instance, it is estimated that while there is an estimated population of around 600,000 African elephants, the population of wild Asian elephants is estimated at just 38,000–51,000. The Asian elephant is accorded the highest level of protection in India by virtue of its inclusion in Schedule 1 of the Indian Wildlife (Protection) Act of 1972. It is also included in Appendix 1 of the Convention on International Trade in Endangered Species (CITES) of wild flora and fauna. There appear to be only two studies so far which have tried to estimate the economic values of wild Asian elephants. Dixon and Sherman (1990, 1991) estimated the option and existence values of wild Asian elephants in Khao Yai National Park, Thailand to Thai residents at about 122 million Baht, that is approximately US$4.7 million (1990–1991 US$). The Park users' average maximum WTP was estimated at 181 Baht (or US$7) per park user. A more recent study by Bandara and Tisdell (2003), who estimated the WTP for the conservation of wild Asian elephants in Sri Lanka by the urban residents of Colombo, noted that they were willing to pay Sri Lankan Rs1322 per annum over the next 5 years. While users, that is those urban residents who had visited national parks or sanctuaries, were willing to pay about Rs1648.56 per annum over the next 5 years for the conservation of wild Asian elephants, non-users, those urban residents who had never visited a national park or sanctuary, this figure was about Rs995.52. The study also noted that 62 per cent of the WTP estimate was attributable to non-use values of wild Asian elephants.

Barnes (1996) also evaluated the economic worth of elephants in Botswana during the pre- and post-ivory ban periods, that is between 1989 and 1992 (Table 1.9). The total present value of elephants in Botswana in the pre-ivory ban

Table 1.9 *Economic worth of elephants in Botswana between 1989 and 1992 – total present value in million Botswana pulas at 6 per cent discount rate at 1989 prices*

Item	Pre-ivory ban	Post ivory ban	
	1989	1990	1992
Total present value (Million Pula)[1]	293.5	155.3	133.0 (NPV)
Use category	(Percentage distribution)		
1. Tourism – viewing	44.2	70.1	71.3
2. Tourism – safari hunting	16.4	26.0	26.5
3. Cropping[2]	39.4	3.9	2.2

Notes: 1 Botswana Pula = US$0.48 during the time of analysis, according to the author.
2 Cropping refers to culling for ivory, fresh or dried meat, meat processing, dry salted hides, hide tanning, live sale of calves (6 months to 1 year old).

Source: Barnes (1996)

period (1989) was estimated at around 293.5 million Pula; whereas it declined to 155.3 million Pula in the post-ivory ban period, implying that the ivory ban reduced the economic worth of elephants in Botswana. Interestingly, during the pre-ivory ban period viewing and safari hunting accounted for 60.6 per cent of the use value of elephants and cropping (culling for ivory, fresh or dried meat, meat processing, hide tanning, selling of live elephant calves) contributed the remaining 39.4 per cent, during the post-ivory ban period the share of cropping in use value dropped sharply to just around 2–4 per cent, and bulk of the use value was accounted for by viewing value (over 70 per cent), followed by safari hunting value (around 26 per cent). In the Botswana case (as perhaps in Southern Africa as a whole), Barnes' study suggests that the ivory ban led to a reduction in the economic value of elephants.

Economics of wildlife conservation vs. alternative land use options

Forests have alternative land use options, as noted earlier. For instance, in sub-Saharan Africa commercial livestock farming competes for land use with other alternatives such as wildlife use, etc. How far commercial livestock farming is viable vis-à-vis wildlife use or a combination of wildlife and livestock use, or other alternative land use options is an important issue of interest. Evidence from Botswana, for instance, suggests that rates of return for cattle ranching are conspicuously below that from game ranching, ostrich or crocodile farming, safari hunting, etc. (Table 1.10). In fact Pearce and Moran (1994) note that in the Brazilian Amazon where livestock ranching has been a major factor behind biodiversity loss, livestock ranching yields negative rates of return and gives positive incomes to ranchers only after subsidies are taken into account. A study from Nyae Nyae in Namibia noted that a combination of wildlife and livestock use yields greater net social benefits than other alternatives such as commercial livestock farming.

A detailed review of the estimates of the values of alternative uses of forested land such as cattle ranching, growing agricultural and plantation crops, as presented in Table 1.11 are quite revealing. Although these studies are strictly speaking not comparable in terms of the methodology used, alternative land uses covered and forest sites studied, yet they seem to suggest that the NPVs of the alternative uses of forest land show wide variation across countries and land uses. For cattle ranching, these NPVs ranged between US$68 and US$1622/ha, for agricultural crops US$1440–2255/ha, and for plantation crops and tree growing US$184–4281/ha. Considering this, it appears that it is primarily the non-market and unpriced benefits of tropical forests that provide the economic justification for biodiversity conservation.

Table 1.10 *Comparative rates of return of game ranching vis-à-vis alternative land use options in Botswana and Namibia*

Country and land use	Internal rate of return (%)		Comments
	Financial	Economic	
Botswana			
Group small scale game harvesting	21	28	Biltong, skins, trophies
Ostrich farming	19	14	Skin, feathers, meat
Crocodile farming	18	14	Skin, tailmeat
Tourist lodge	18	35	
Safari hunting	16	45	<3% offtake
Game ranching	6	7	Meat, hunting
Cattle ranching	5	NA	
Namibia	(Social net benefits of wildlife conservation in Nyae Nyae)		
	NPV (1000 N $)	*EIRR (%)*	
PV of livestock	14,919.6	10.1	
PV of wildlife	26,554.9	14.5	
PV of joint use	41,474.5	12.4	

Note: NPV – Net Present Value; EIRR – Economic Internal Rates of Return; The time horizon assumed for the analysis is 21 years.

Source: Botswana study – Barnes and Pearce, 1991 see Pearce and Moran (1994); Namibia study – Kakujaha-Matundu and Perrings (2000)

Game sales market and auction prices in South Africa

Game ranching and sales has been an important feature of wildlife conservation and management in South Africa. It is noteworthy that about 20 per cent of land in South Africa is managed primarily for game (Porter et al, 2003). This consists of about 14 per cent under commercial game farms and 5.4 per cent under protected areas. Wildlife in South Africa has been recognized as having economic value since the 1960s when hunters began to pay to stalk game (Scriven and Eloff, 2003). Trading in game is stated to have enabled South Africa to achieve many conservation goals, such as facilitating the reintroduction of species into areas from which they may have been removed, providing options for genetic diversification within species, and allowing opportunities to strengthen population size through achieving a balanced predator–prey ratio (Scriven and Eloff, 2003). One of the ways trading in live game takes place in South Africa is through game auctions.

Table 1.12 presents information on game sales market and auction prices in South Africa for selected species reported in the year 2001. The data demonstrate that impala, blue wilderbeest, common blesbock and springbuck rank high among the most commonly traded species in the game market. The highest average prices

Table 1.11 *Estimates of the value of alternative uses of forested land*

Land use	Net present value alternative land use US$/ha	Net present value sustainable or conservation use US$/ha	Source
'Deforestation cycle': Ecuadorian highlands (wood, crops, cattle), near Quito	2094 (5% discount rate) 1721 (10% discount rate)	Not estimated	Wunder, 2001
Timber, Sinharaja, Sri Lanka	1129 (8%, 20 yrs) 1307 (8%, 50 yrs)	147–183	Batagoda et al, 2000
Tea, Sinharaja, Sri Lanka	4281 (8%, 20 yrs)	147–183	Batagoda et al, 2000
Small farming, Mt Cameroun, Cameroun	1440–2500 (10%, 30 yrs)	1673–4398 (all values captured)	Yaron, 2001
Oil palm, Mt Cameroun, Cameroun	Negative	1673–4398 (all values captured)	
Cattle ranching, Costa Rica	1309 (Atlantic region, 10%) 1535 (South) 893 (North)	1078–1494 (STM)[1] 1348–1616 (STM) 698–1136 (STM)	Howard and Valerio, 1996
Bean crops, Costa Rica	2255 (South) 1613 (North)	1348–1616 (STM) 698–1136 (STM)	Howard and Valerio, 1996
Corn, Costa Rica	2054 (Atlantic)	1078–1494 (STM)	Howard and Valerio, 1996
Ranching, Amazonian Ecuador	68–351	1496–3500 (NTFPs)	Grimes et al, 1994
Timber, Amazonian Ecuador	224	1496–3500 (NTFPs)	Grimes et al, 1994
Ranching, Costa Rica	1622 (8%, domestic prices)	1050 (STM)	Kishor and Constantino, 1993
Clear felling, Costa Rica	576 (8%, domestic prices)	1050 (STM)	Kishor and Constantino, 1993
Plantations, Costa Rica	3944 (8%, domestic prices)	1050 (STM)	Kishor and Constantino, 1993
Cattle ranching, Veracruz, Mexico	2000–10,000 (pasture price)	>2000–10,000 if high planting of 'mamey'	Ricker et al, 1999

Land use	Net present value alternative land use US$/ha	Net present value sustainable or conservation use US$/ha	Source
Slash and burn, Peruvian Amazon	4555 with subsidies, minus 2176 without subsidies. But positive if first two years only are considered	Sustainable use more profitable if farmers paid for carbon conservation	Smith et al, 1997
Amazonian agricultural settlements		300 (range 3–400) (permanent agriculture)	Ozorio de Almeida, 1992
Tree plantations, Brazil	184 (15%), 24 (20%) – eucalyptus grandis	–	Haltia and Keipi, 1999
Tree plantations, Chile	625 (15%), 393 (20%) – eucalyptus globules	–	Haltia and Keipi, 1999

Notes: 1 STM – sustainable timber management, assuming 2% p.a. increase in stumpage values.
References mentioned in the table are cited in SCBD (2001a).

Source: SCBD (2001a), reproduced with permission from the publisher

Table 1.12 *Game sales market and auction prices in South Africa, 2001*

Species	Number sold
Impala	3932
Blue wilderbeest	1700
Common blesbok	1520
Common springbuck	1314
Nyala	1053
Kudu	1003
Common eland	891
Burchell's zebra	815
Red hartebeest	599
Gemsbuck	563
	(Highest average prices at auction, 2001) South African Rand[1]
Black rhino	520,341 (US$60,000)
White rhino	160,170 (US$18,474)
Roan	100,959 (US$11,645)
Black impala	95,868 (US$11,057)
Buffalo (disease free)	77,019 (US$8883)
Sable	62,946 (US$7260)
Tsessebe[2]	14,461 (US$1668)
Lion	14,191 (US$1637)
Giraffe	12,411 (US$1431)
Livingstone's eland	10,744 (US$1200)

Notes: 1 Scriven and Eloff's article gives the US dollar equivalent of the highest average auction prices in South African Rand only for black rhino, whereas for the remaining species prices are presented only in South African Rand. Using the US dollar equivalent given for black rhino, we have used the given exchange rate and derived the US dollar equivalent for other species.
2 Tsessebe (*Damaliscus lunatus lunatus*) is a rare antelope.

Source: Scriven and Eloff, 2003

at the game auctions in South Africa during 2001 are quite revealing. Black and white rhinos commanded a premium in the game auction, selling at US$60,000 and US$18,474 per animal respectively. It is interesting to note that the highest average auction price for lions was about South African Rand 14,191 (approximately US$1637) which is much lower than that reported for other species such as black and white rhinos, black impala, buffalo, etc. This may partly be explained by the fact that demand for lions in game auctions may be low due to the high costs and perils of maintaining lions in game farms. This does not reflect their real economic value, since lions and other big cats rank high in tourists' viewing preferences. For instance, in studies of safari tourism to East African wildlife parks, sizeable values have been attributed to lions, elephants and other major animals (Dixon and Sherman, 1990). For instance, in the Amboseli National Park in Kenya, the value of a lion (as a visitor draw) was estimated at US$27,000 per year; an elephant herd was worth US$610,000 per year (Western and Henry, 1979, see Dixon and Sherman, 1990). Another study noted that a lion's value as a hunting or sport resource was about US$8,500 (the cost of a 21 day lion hunt) or US$960–1325 as a skin (Thresher 1981, see Dixon and Sherman, 1990). South Africa's experience in game ranching and sale of live game has been unique, as noted earlier. It is also reported that South Africa is one of the few countries in the world where the number of rare and endangered species (such as white rhinos) have increased. This is partly attributed to the value and commercial utilization of wildlife resources (Scriven and Eloff, 2003). There is a view in certain quarters that South Africa's experience in wildlife conservation and management through commercial utilization is worth emulating in other countries where biodiversity and wildlife are threatened. Whether South Africa's experience can be replicated elsewhere is, of course, debatable.

Eco-tourism and conservation values for India

Studies focusing on India are few indeed, although India is listed as one of the twelve megadiversity countries in the world, and it contains two of the 18 (now 25) biodiversity hotspots in the world. The few available studies on India have tried to estimate the eco-tourism and conservation values of protected areas in India, using TCM or CVM surveys (see Table 1.13). Of these, three studies cover the Periyar and Borivli Sanctuaries falling within the Western Ghats region of Kerala and Maharashtra, and two pertain to the Keoladeo National Park, a Ramsar site, in Rajasthan. Manoharan et al (1999) in a study covering the Periyar Tiger Reserve in Kerala estimated (using TCM) the present value of eco-tourism benefits of domestic visitors to the sanctuary at around Rs161.3 per visitor. Using CVM, the study estimated the mean consumer surplus per visitor at Rs9.89 for domestic visitors and Rs140 for foreign tourists. The study indicated the present value of eco-tourism to be around Rs84.5 million. Another study (Jyothis, 2002) covering the Periyar Tiger Reserve estimated the mean WTP per household of the local community for participatory biodiversity conservation at around Rs162.7, and of urban Kerala residents at Rs128 per respondent. Hadkar et al's (1997) study of Borivli National Park in Maharashtra, using CVM, estimated the average WTP per person per year for the next five years at Rs7.5 for domestic visitors; for Mumbai city this was estimated at around Rs20 million. A study of Keoladeo National Park in Rajasthan by Murty and Menkhaus (1994), using CVM, estimated the average WTP for recreation at Rs11.5 for domestic visitors, and much higher – Rs82.9 – for foreign visitors. The average WTP for non-use values was estimated at over Rs519 for domestic visitors; for foreign visitors this estimate was lower at Rs495.6. Chopra et al (1997) also studied the Keoladeo National Park and estimated the consumer surplus per visit through TCM at Rs427–432 for

Table 1.13 *Eco-tourism and conservation values for India (in rupees)*

Study area/forest site	Tool of analysis	Variables	Domestic visitors	Foreign visitors	Villages/city	Author
Periyar Tiger Reserve, (Kerala)	TCM	PV per visitor	161.3	–	–	Manoharan et al, 1999
	CVM	Mean consumer surplus per visitor	9.9	140	–	
Periyar Tiger Reserve, (Kerala)	CVM	Mean WTP per household for participatory conservation	–	–	–	Jyothis, 2002
		Local community	–	–	162.7	
		Urban Kerala residents	–	–	128.0	
Borivli National Park (Maharashtra)	CVM	Av. WTP per person per year for next 5 years	7.5	–	20 million (Mumbai City)	Hadkar et al, 1997
Keoladeo National Park, (Rajasthan)	CVM	Av. WTP for recreation	11.5	82.9	–	Murty and Menkhaus, 1994
		Av. WTP for non-use values	519.1	495.6	–	
Keoladeo National Park, (Rajasthan)	TCM	Consumers surplus per visit – local cost estimates	427.0	432.0	–	Chopra et al, 1997
		Non-users (Scientists) WTP Average once for all payment per capita	475.0			
		Average annual payment per capita	321.0			

Notes: TCM = Travel Cost Method; CVM = Contingent Valuation Method WTP = Willingness to Pay; PV = Present Value.

domestic and foreign visitors. The non-users' (scientists) WTP for the park was also quite significant being, on an average, an annual payment of Rs321 per capita. The few studies on India also confirm that eco-tourism and conservation values are quite significant. The available studies on India are, however, mostly focused on protected areas and neglect the other alternative land use options of tropical forests, such as converting into plantations of coffee or for agriculture, etc.

As stated earlier, although biodiversity conservation is being emphasized in policy circles in India, there is a dearth of rigorous empirical and research work focusing on India. Hence the need for the present study. Such a study needs to assess the benefits of biodiversity conservation in comparison with alternative land use options of forests. The proposed study seeks to bridge this gap by making an economic assessment of the benefits of biodiversity conservation vis-à-vis the alternative land use options of forests. It also seeks to assess both the local community's dependence on forests for various goods and services and the socio-economic and institutional factors inhibiting or promoting biodiversity conservation, the local community's perceptions and attitudes towards biodiversity conservation in general and wildlife protection in particular. This latter aspect is considered through a case study of wild Asian elephants, a keystone and threatened species in Asia and the study region. Finally, the study also seeks to assess the institutional alternatives and mechanisms for conserving biodiversity without retarding growth.

Objectives

1   To estimate the use and non-use values of tropical forests, through a survey of households.
2   To assess the extent of dependence on forests for various goods and services by different socio-economic groups and regions.
3   To estimate the opportunity cost of biodiversity conservation and the external costs such as wildlife damage costs and defensive expenditures to protect against wildlife attacks borne by the local communities due to wildlife conservation.
4   To analyse the perceptions and attitudes of the local communities towards biodiversity conservation in general and wildlife protection in particular.
5   To estimate the local community's willingness to pay (WTP) or willingness to accept (WTA) compensation for biodiversity conservation and wildlife protection.

Data and approach

Data

The study is based on both secondary and primary data. In order to provide a backdrop to the in-depth study based on primary investigation, secondary data have been collected from official records and publications such as land utilization statistics of India and Karnataka, publications of the forest departments, population and livestock census, etc., as well as from village panchayat records and publications. This secondary data has provided general information on the biodiversity of the Western Ghats and of the study regions that will allow:

1 analysis of changes in land use patterns, human and livestock pressure on land and forest resources over time in the selected districts or areas;
2 analysis of the status of biodiversity and changes in the forest cover and forest types;
3 the tracking of populations of endangered species over time in the Western Ghats region.

The data for the in-depth study have been collected through a sample survey of households/respondents. Data have been collected on the following:

1 socio-economic data of sample households, covering demographic particulars, operational holdings, income, etc.;
2 cropping patterns;
3 cost and returns from crop production and other allied activities such as livestock rearing, forest-related activities;
4 the extent of dependence on forest resources (land, timber and NTFPs, etc.) and the value of forest products extracted;
5 on-farm consumption, and marketing of forest products;
6 respondents' perceptions and attitudes towards biodiversity conservation and wildlife protection;
7 respondents' WTP or WTA (compensation) for biodiversity conservation in general and wildlife protection in particular, taking wild Asian elephants as a case study, as noted earlier.

Selection of study areas

The data for the in-depth study have been collected through a sample survey of households/respondents located in three villages or sets of villages in the Western Ghats representing different situations – a plantation dominant village where growing plantation crops such as coffee constitute a land use option for forests, two farming villages where there is a close interaction between agriculture, livestock and forests, and a cluster of tribal villages/hamlets within and on the periphery of a national park. For the present study, a coffee-growing village in Kodagu district of Karnataka, two agricultural cum pastoral villages (one within and the other on the periphery of the Dandeli Wildlife Sanctuary) in Uttar Kannada district, and a cluster of tribal villages/hamlets within and on the periphery of the Nagarhole National Park in Mysore and Kodagu districts (which has witnessed considerable tribal unrest due to the establishment of the sanctuary and is also covered under the World Bank-aided India Ecodevelopment project) were selected purposively, after consultations with forest department and village officials. Location maps of the Western Ghats in South India, and in Karnataka State, and of the sample villages selected for our study in Kodagu, Mysore and Uttar Kannada districts are appended at the end of this chapter (Figures 1.3 to 1.7). The survey covers over 300 households/respondents (for sample design see below) from the selected villages to elicit information about the extent of their dependence on forests for various socio-economic activities, their production activities and income, on-farm consumption and marketing of forest products. It was also designed to elicit the local community's perceptions and attitudes towards biodiversity conservation in general and wildlife protection in particular, and their value preferences for bio-diversity conservation.

Analytical techniques used

To analyse the above objectives, cost–benefit appraisal, opportunity cost approach, contingent valuation method (discrete choice method), logit or tobit models, de-scriptive cum tabular statistics, and averages and proportions have been used. To estimate the use and non-use values of the tropical forests, the survey method and Contingent Valuation Method (CVM), have been used. In conducting the CVM survey, the guidelines suggested by the National Oceanic and Atmospheric Administration (NOAA) Panel (1993) in the US were taken into account (i.e. pre-testing of schedules, canvassing through personal interview, sufficient sample size, etc.). For the CVM study, the dichotomous method or discrete choice method, which seeks simple 'Yes' or 'No' replies to an offered bid is used. The discrete choice method is preferred over other methods (e.g. open ended methods) because of its inherent advantages: this method would make it easier for villagers to react to the question, and also households could respond while keeping some budget constraint in view, that is the upper bound on bids could be controlled (Moran, 1994). Also this method minimizes any incentive to strategically overstate or understate WTP (Loomis, 1988; Moran, 1994). Dichotomous choice methods require the use of parametric (typically logit or probit) probability models relating yes or no responses to offer amounts, the computation of an expected mean, and relating the WTP or WTA responses to relevant socio-economic and other variables.

Sampling design

A two-stage sampling design was followed for conducting the in-depth study. In the first stage sample villages were selected purposively on the basis of the crite-ria indicated earlier. In the second stage households in the sample villages were selected on a stratified random sample basis or a cluster sampling basis. After discussions with forest and village officials, and visits to prospective areas for

Figure 1.3 *Western Ghats in South India*

selection, Maldari village in Virajpet taluk of Kodagu district was selected. This village is close to a reserve forest; coffee growing is predominant and man–animal conflicts are conspicuous. The village has a mix of coffee plantations of different sized groups, including some managed by large companies. Households in this

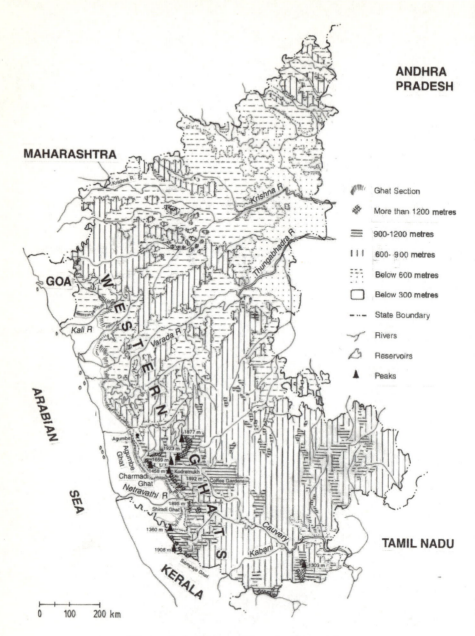

Figure 1.4 *Western Ghats in Karnataka*

village were listed and selected on a stratified random sample basis based on land holding categories and other criteria such as coffee growing, etc. In total 125 households were selected for the in-depth survey. When selecting villages in or near the Nagarhole National Park, due to the small size of the tribal villages or hamlets (some having just 10 or 15 households), we had to select a cluster of tribal

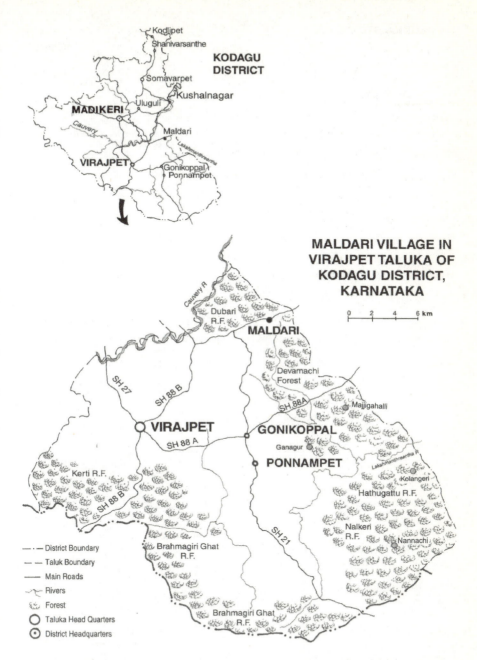

Figure 1.5 *Maldari Village in Kodagu District, Karnataka*

villages or hamlets in order to have a reasonable sample size. Due to non-cooperation in some villages (this was motivated by some NGOs that were against the
World Bank-aided India Ecodevelopment project supporting their relocation outside the national park) and non-response in some villages, a few villages had to be

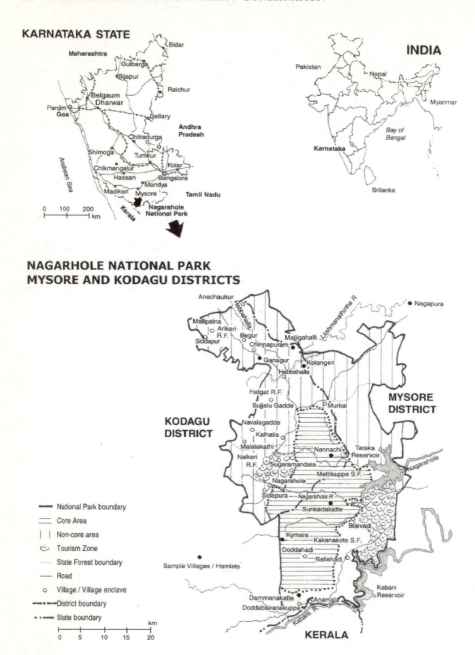

Figure 1.6 *Sample villages in or near Nagarhole National Park, Karnataka*

substituted. Finally, eight tribal villages or hamlets were selected for an in-depth survey: Nagapura, Dammanakatte, Sunkadakatte, Kaimara, Nannachi, Kolangeri, Ganagur and Majjigahalli. Of these Nagapura is a rehabilitated village located outside, on the periphery of the national park, whereas Dammanakatte is a non-

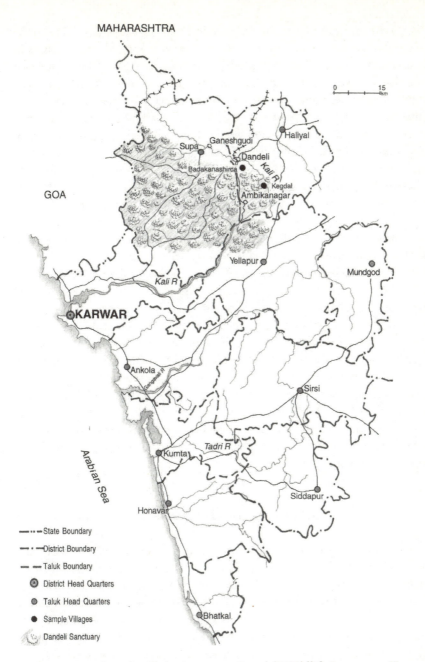

Figure 1.7 *Sample villages in or near Dandeli Wildlife Sanctuary, Karnataka*

rehabilitated village near the periphery of the national park. The remaining six tribal villages or hamlets are located within the national park. All the households within the selected cluster of villages available during the period of survey were surveyed. In total, of 250 households in this cluster of tribal villages, 100 households were covered in the survey. In the case of Uttar Kannada, again due to the small size of villages and the need to have a reasonable sample size, a cluster of two agricultural villages, Kegdal and Badaganasirada in Haliyal taluk of Uttar Kannada district, was selected for our sample survey. While Kegdal is located within the Dandeli Wildlife sanctuary or forest reserve, Badaganasirada is situated outside, on the periphery of the sanctuary. All the households in these two villages were surveyed for the in-depth study. This included 33 households from Kegdal village and 47 households from Badaganasirada village, making a total of 80 households from this region. Thus, in total our survey covered 303 households from these villages or cluster of villages located in Kodagu, Mysore and Uttar Kannada districts. Data were canvassed through a detailed, structured schedule. The schedule consisted of two parts, a socio-economic survey and a contingent valuation survey. These schedules were pre-tested in the three sets of villages and modifications were made to suit the different situations and issues covered in the three regions. For instance, whereas the WTP format was found to be appropriate in Maldari, the coffee growing village, in the tribal villages within or near the Nagarhole National Park the WTA format was found to be more suitable, as well as placing more emphasis on dependence on NTFPs. The detailed socio-economic survey canvassed information on the various parameters indicated earlier. The CVM survey tries to assess the local community's perceptions and attitudes towards biodiversity conservation in general and wildlife protection in particular, taking elephants as a case study, as stated earlier. The reference year for this study was the agricultural year 1999–2000 or as otherwise stated. The fieldwork for the survey was conducted in phases between January and June 2000. More details about the sample villages and households and methods, are spelt out wherever appropriate in subsequent chapters.

Structure of the book

The book consists of six chapters: changes in land and crop use patterns, population and livestock pressure on land and forest resources in the selected districts and regions as well as the status of biodiversity and changes in the forest cover and forest types, and the population of endangered species are presented in the next chapter. Chapters 3 to 5 analyse the economic and other related aspects of biodiversity conservation in the context of the three situations – a coffee-growing village, tribal villages within or near a national park or protected area, and agricultural-cum pastoral villages within or near a sanctuary or forest reserve. The last chapter presents a summary and conclusions, including policy recommendations.

2

Land Use and Crop Pattern Changes, Pressure on Natural Resources and the Status of Biodiversity in Selected Regions

Introduction

The decline or loss of habitats and biodiversity in several regions is being abetted by social, economic, demographic and institutional factors such as converting forests to agricultural or non-agricultural uses or for growing plantation crops, etc. Population growth along with poverty are among important factors responsible for biodiversity loss. So, also, an increase in the number of livestock, often beyond the carrying capacity of a region, has been a major factor behind degradation of forests and common property resources (CPRs) in many developing countries. Hence, in this chapter, we examine the land use and crop pattern and changes therein, population and livestock pressure on forests and other natural resources in our selected regions as well as the status of biodiversity.

Land use patterns and changes

Historically, habitat and land use changes have had the biggest impact on bio-diversity across biomes (WRI, 2005). For terrestrial ecosystems such as tropical forests, the most important driver of biodiversity loss in the past 50 years has been land cover changes (WRI, 2005). Hence, the land use pattern and changes therein between 1960–1961 and 1999–2000 for all-India, Karnataka state, and the three districts under review, Kodagu, Mysore and Uttar Kannada are analysed here. Table 2.1, which presents the relevant data, shows that the total cropped area as a proportion of the total reporting area has increased over the periods under review for India as a whole and Karnataka. While this proportion for India rose from 51.6 per cent during 1960–1961 to 1962–1963 to 62.5 per cent during 1997–1998 to 1999–2000, for Karnataka this proportion rose from 56.6 per cent to 63.2 per cent over the same time period. While the proportion of the net area sown to total reporting area rose from 44.9 per cent to 46.4 per cent between 1960–1961 and

1999–2000 for India as a whole, for Karnataka this proportion has more or less remained constant, around 55 per cent. Among the three districts the net area sown and total cropped area as a proportion of the total reporting area has increased over the time periods under review in Kodagu and Mysore districts, whereas in Uttar Kannada there is no appreciable increase. The proportion of net area sown to the total reporting area is relatively high in Mysore district, around 40–44 per cent; whereas Kodagu reports around a third of its reporting area under net area sown; for Uttar Kannada this proportion is only around a tenth of its reporting area. Interestingly the proportion of net area sown to total reporting area has more than doubled in Kodagu district between 1960–1961 and 1999–2000. While this proportion, which was around 16.8 per cent during 1960–1961 to 1962–1963, rose to over 29 per cent during 1970—1971 to 1972–1973, and still further to around 35–36 per cent during the 1980s and 1990s, in Mysore district this proportion rose from over 37 per cent during 1960–1961 to 1962–1963, to about 44 per cent during 1997–1998 to 1999–2000. An area sown more than once, as reflected in the difference between the proportion of total cropped area and net area sown, is relatively high in Mysore district, whereas both in Kodagu and Uttar Kannada it is quite low. The increase in the net area sown in these districts seems to have largely come through reducing area under other land use categories such as permanent pastures and grazing lands, land under miscellaneous tree crops and cultivable wastes. The proportion of these land use categories to the total reporting area has registered a decline in India, Karnataka and the three districts during the last four decades. The forest cover in the country and Karnataka state seems to have risen slightly over the time periods under review. For India as a whole the proportion of forest area to the total reporting area which was about 18.7 per cent during 1960–1961 to 1962–1963 rose to 21.2 per cent during the early 1970s, and thereafter it has ranged around a little over 22 per cent. For Karnataka this proportion rose from 14.4 per cent during 1960–1961 to 1962–1963 to over 16 per cent during the 1990s. Among the districts, while Uttar Kannada reports about 80 per cent of its reporting area under forests, Kodagu district has around a third of its area under forests, and Mysore district has over a quarter of its reporting area under forests. While Kodagu and Uttar Kannada report a marginal decline in their forest cover over the last four decades under review, Mysore interestingly records a marginal rise in the forest cover in the 1990s. The above, however, does not tell us anything about the state of the forests and biodiversity in these three districts which is degraded in many parts due to encroachments and other human interventions, and is under constant threat from different interest groups and factors eager to reap the potentially large economic rents available through exploitation of these forests. In fact data presented in a later section clearly show that, as per satellite imagery data, the dense forest cover in Karnataka state and these three districts, especially Kodagu and Uttar Kannada, has registered a significant decline, whereas open forest cover has increased substantially, which indicates the extent of degradation of forests in the state and districts under review.

The proportion of the reporting area under non-agricultural uses has increased steadily from 5 per cent during 1960–1961 to 1962—1963 to over 7 per cent during the 1990s for all-India, and for Karnataka this proportion rose from 4.5 per cent to 6.8 per cent during the same periods. For the three districts under review, the proportion of total reporting area put to non-agricultural uses has increased for Kodagu district from about 4.8 per cent during 1960–1961 to 1962–1963, to around 5.8 per cent during 1997–1998 to 1999—2000; for Mysore district this proportion rose from 3.5 per cent to 7.3 per cent, and for Uttar Kannada district from 1.9 per cent to 2.9 per cent respectively for the same periods. The proportion of fallow areas too has increased marginally for India as a whole, Karnataka and the three districts. The increase is relatively high for Mysore district where the proportion of fallow areas to total reporting area rose from around 5.7 per cent in the 1960s and 1970s, to around 8 per cent during the 1990s. In the other two districts this increase is only marginal although this trend over time is not smooth. In the case of barren land its proportion to the total reporting area has fallen from 11.9 per cent during 1960–1961 to 1962–1963 to over 6 per cent during the 1980s and 1990s for India as a whole; whereas for Karnataka the proportion of barren land to total reporting area has declined over the time periods under review. Among the districts, while Mysore recorded a decline in the proportion of the reporting area under this land use category over the last three and a half decade period under review, it has more or less remained constant in Kodagu and Uttar Kannada districts.

Thus, the forgoing shows significant changes in the land use pattern for all-India, Karnataka and the three districts under review. Area under cultivation has increased in all the cases, except in Uttar Kannada where the increase is marginal. The total cropped area (i.e. net area sown plus area sown more than once) which reflects the intensity of cultivation has also risen in all the situations except Uttar Kannada district. This increase in the area under cultivation has largely come through diversion of area under permanent pastures and grazing lands, land under miscellaneous tree crops and cultivable wastes. Forest areas too have been diverted to agriculture, although this is not adequately captured in the data for reasons cited earlier. The increase in cropping intensity has been facilitated by increased irrigation facilities, and particularly in the plain regions of the districts such as in Mysore district by exploiting the hydel potential of the westward flowing rivers which have their origin in the Western Ghats. This has implications for the forests and biodiversity of the Western Ghats. The forest cover has declined marginally in Kodagu and Uttar Kannada in the recent years, whereas it has registered a marginal increase in Mysore district. This, of course, as stated earlier does not reflect the true state of the forests and biodiversity in these districts which are degrading fast due to various forms of human interventions, and also facing constant threat from different interest groups eager to exploit the rich natural resources of the Western Ghats. The area put to non-agricultural uses has registered a rise in the country as a whole, Karnataka and the three districts which again may have partly come through diversion of forest area to non-forest uses.

Table 2.1 *Land use pattern and changes in India, Karnataka and Kodagu, Mysore and Uttar Kannada districts (1960–1961 to 1999–2000)*

Period	India	Karnataka	Kodagu district	Mysore district	Uttar Kannada district
	Total cropped area as % to total reporting area				
1960/1961–1962/1963	51.6	56.6	24.3	42.5	12.7
1970/1971–1972/1973	54.1	56.6	30.8	45.1	11.5
1980/1981–1982/1983	57.2	58.7	35.2	47.4	11.7
1990/1991–1992/1993	60.5	62.7	36.6	49.4	12.6
1997/1998–1999/2000	62.5	63.2	34.9	53.2	12.5
	Net area sown as % to total reporting area				
1960/1961–1962/1963	44.9	55.0	16.8	37.6	11.7
1970/1971–1972/1973	45.7	53.3	29.2	38.5	10.2
1980/1981–1982/1983	46.3	54.0	34.8	40.3	10.8
1990/1991–1992/1993	46.7	55.5	36.0	41.7	11.0
1997/1998–1999/2000	46.4	53.9	34.6	43.8	10.9
	Forest area as % to total reporting area				
1960/1961–1962/1963	18.7	14.4	33.1	26.5	81.5
1970/1971–1972/1973	21.2	15.2	33.0	26.2	81.4
1980/1981–1982/1983	22.2	15.9	32.8	26.9	81.0
1990/1991–1992/1993	22.3	16.1	32.8	27.2	81.0
1997/1998–1999/2000	22.5	16.1	32.8	27.2	79.5
	Permanent pastures and grazing lands as % to total reporting area				
1960/1961–1962/1963	4.7	9.1	12.2	3.5	1.6
1970/1971–1972/1973	4.3	8.4	8.4	3.1	1.4
1980/1981–1982/1983	3.9	6.7	4.1	2.9	1.0
1990/1991–1992/1993	3.7	5.8	2.9	2.7	0.8
1997/1998–1999/2000	3.6	5.2	2.9	2.5	1.9
	Cultivable wastes as % to total reporting area				
1960/1961–1962/1963	6.2	3.4	9.3	0.7	0.5
1970/1971—1972/1973	5.7	3.2	9.7	1.2	0.4
1980/1981–1982/1983	5.4	2.6	9.6	0.9	0.5
1990/1991–1992/1993	4.9	2.3	9.2	0.9	0.5
1997/1998–1999/2000	4.5	2.3	9.2	0.9	0.5
	Land under miscellaneous tree crops as % to total reporting area				
1960/1961–1962/1963	1.5	1.9	7.6	12.9	0.1
1970/1971–1972/1973	1.4	1.6	5.3	14.0	1.9
1980/1981–1982/1983	1.2	1.8	4.5	10.6	2.0
1990/1991–1992/1993	1.2	1.7	4.3	7.3	2.0
1997/1998–1999/2000	1.2	1.6	4.3	5.3	0.9

	Fallows as % to total reporting area				
1960/1961–1962/1963	7.3	6.9	1.5	5.7	1.3
1970/1971–1972/1973	7.2	8.8	1.8	5.7	1.2
1980/1981–1982/1983	8.0	8.9	1.0	6.7	1.3
1990/1991–1992/1993	7.9	8.2	1.5	8.0	1.2
1997/1998–1999/2000	7.9	9.9	2.9	7.6	1.6
	Area under non-agricultural uses as % to total reporting area				
1960/1961–1962/1963	5.0	4.5	4.8	3.5	1.9
1970/1971–1972/1973	5.5	5.0	5.0	5.1	1.8
1980/1981–1982/1983	6.5	5.7	5.7	5.7	1.5
1990/1991–1992/1993	7.0	6.3	5.8	6.9	1.6
1997/1998–1999/2000	7.5	6.8	2.9	7.3	2.9
	Barren land as % to total reporting area				
1960/1961–1962/1963	11.9	4.9	7.7	7.3	1.4
1970/1971–1972/1973	9.0	4.5	7.8	6.2	1.9
1980/1981–1982/1983	6.6	4.4	7.6	6.0	2.0
1990/1991–1992/1993	6.4	4.2	7.6	5.4	2.0
1997/1998–1999/2000	6.3	4.2	7.5	5.4	1.8

Source: Indian Agricultural Statistics Volumes I and II, Directorate of Economics and Statistics, Ministry of Agriculture, Government of India; Karnataka Statistics at a Glance (various issues), Directorate of Economics and Statistics, Government of Karnataka, Bangalore

The land use pattern and changes therein between 1960–1961 and 1999–2000 in selected taluks (i.e. administrative unit below district level) of Kodagu, Mysore and Uttar Kannada districts, where the sample villages are located, is examined here. Table 2.2, which presents the relevant data, indicates that in Virajpet taluk the total cropped area as a proportion of the total reporting area has increased from 32.9 per cent during 1960–1961 to 1962–1963 to over 37 per cent during 1997–1998 to 1999–2000. The proportion of net area sown to the reporting area has increased from 24 to over 37 per cent in this taluk during the period under review. The increase seems to have come about at the cost of areas under permanent pastures and grazing lands, cultivable wastes, land under miscellaneous trees, and forests whose share in the reporting area has more or less declined over the periods under review. Around 40 per cent of the reporting area in Virajpet taluk is forested. Area under forests has declined slightly from 40.7 per cent during 1960–1961 to 1962–1963 to 40 per cent during 1997–1998 to 1999–2000. Land put to non-agricultural uses has risen from 1.2 per cent to 1.9 per cent over the time periods under review.

In H. D. Kote and Hunsur taluks of Mysore district where our sample villages of Nagarhole National Park are located, the proportion of the total cropped area to the reporting area has risen fast from 24 per cent to over 40 per cent in H. D.

Table 2.2 *Land use pattern and changes in selected taluks (1960–1961 to 1999–2000)*

Land use category as % to reporting area	1960/1961– 1962/1963	1970/1971– 1972/1973	1980/1981– 1982/1983	1990/1991– 1992/1993	1997/1998– 1999/2000
Virajpet Taluk (Kodagu district)					
Total cropped area	32.9	31.8	37.0	38.4	37.7
Net area sown	24.0	29.7	36.8	34.4	37.6
Forest	40.7	40.6	40.0	40.0	40.0
Permanent pasture/ grazing lands	10.4	7.0	1.0	0.6	0.5
Cultivable wastes	9.5	8.2	8.6	7.8	5.6
Fallows	0.8	0.2	0.4	0.3	2.3
Land under miscellaneous tree crops	7.6	6.8	6.1	6.0	6.9
Land under non-agricultural uses	1.2	1.6	1.9	1.9	1.9
Barren land	5.8	5.9	5.2	5.2	5.2
H. D. Kote Taluk (Mysore district)					
Total cropped area	24.0	24.9	32.9	32.8	40.1
Net area sown	21.6	19.4	28.4	30.4	36.3
Forest	19.5	14.7	15.4	17.0	17.0
Permanent pasture/ grazing lands	2.8	6.1	7.2	8.2	7.1
Cultivable wastes	0.2	2.3	2.1	1.7	1.7
Fallows	8.1	5.8	4.3	7.0	2.2
Land under miscellaneous tree crops	35.9	35.6	26.2	17.4	17.4
Land under non-agricultural uses	1.3	1.5	4.4	9.7	9.7
Barren land	10.6	14.6	12.0	8.6	8.6
Hunsur Taluk (Mysore district)					
Total cropped area	36.2	49.4	52.5	70.6	72.5
Net area sown	32.9	40.8	46.1	63.9	64.6
Forest	3.0	8.5	7.9	7.9	7.9
Permanent pasture/ grazing lands	4.5	3.8	3.1	1.0	1.2
Cultivable wastes	0.3	0.4	0.4	0.4	0.4
Fallows	10.0	6.5	4.7	4.8	3.8
Land under miscellaneous tree crops	29.1	20.9	18.7	2.9	2.9
Land under non-agricultural uses	8.8	8.4	8.4	8.4	8.5

Barren land	11.4	10.7	10.7	10.7	10.7

Haliyal Taluk (Uttar Kannada district)

Total cropped area	22.4	20.3	21.9	27.6	30.3
Net area sown	20.3	19.3	21.1	24.0	24.9
Forest	71.8	71.5	70.6	70.6	68.2
Permanent pasture/ grazing lands	1.3	1.0	1.5	0.4	0.4
Cultivable wastes	0.001	0.6	0.8	0.8	0.3
Fallows	1.3	3.0	2.2	0.6	0.7
Land under miscellaneous tree crops	0.5	0.9	0.8	0.6	0.3
Land under non-agricultural uses	2.1	0.7	0.4	0.5	3.5
Barren land	2.7	3.0	2.6	2.5	1.7

Source: Directorate of Economics and Statistics, Government of Karnataka, Bangalore.

Kote and from 36.2 per cent to over 72 per cent in Hunsur taluk over the time periods under review. The increase is particularly sharp in Hunsur taluk where the total cropped area has doubled. The share of net area sown to the total reporting area too has risen fast in these two taluks. This increase seems to have been at the expense of land under miscellaneous tree crops and fallows in both taluks, and also permanent pastures and grazing lands in Hunsur taluk. Interestingly, while the proportion of the area under forest to the reporting area has fallen in H. D. Kote taluk from 19.5 per cent during 1960–1961 to 1962–1963 to about 17 per cent during 1997–1998 to 1999–2000, in Hunsur taluk it rose from 3 per cent to around 8 per cent over the same time span. Land put to non-agricultural uses has risen sharply in H. D. Kote taluk whereas in Hunsur taluk it was around 8.8 per cent during 1960–1961 to 1962–1963 and has registered a marginal decline thereafter.

As in the case of the other taluks, in Haliyal taluk of Uttar Kannada district too the share of the net area sown and total cropped area to the total reporting area has increased steadily over the periods under review. This taluk has over two-thirds of its reporting area under forests, although over the last three and a half decades there has been some decline from around 71.8 per cent during 1960–1961 to 1962–1963 to over 68 per cent during 1999–2000. The proportion of area under land put to non-agricultural uses and under miscellaneous tree crops, permanent pastures and grazing lands has declined during the period under review. Thus, the forgoing shows that while the net area sown and total cropped area in the taluks where our sample villages are located has risen between 1960–1961 and 1999–2000, a number of land use categories such as permanent pastures and grazing lands, land under miscellaneous tree crops and fallows have registered a decline. The forest cover too has slightly reduced in Virajpet, Haliyal and H. D. Kote taluks, whereas in Hunsur an increase is reported.

Crop patterns and changes

The loss and shrinkage of habitats, decline in forests and vegetative cover, gaps in the elephant corridors and migration paths of wildlife have aggravated man–animal conflicts. Destruction and damage to crops of those living close to or even within reserve forests and sanctuaries by wildlife such as elephants, wild boars, etc., are a common complaint. There are certain crops like rice, sugarcane, coconut, bananas, even coffee, which are most affected by attacks from wildlife. Crop pattern and changes therein may, apart from other factors, also be influenced by the pattern and intensity of attacks from wildlife. In this section the crop pattern and changes in Kodagu, Mysore and Uttar Kannada districts, and the taluks where our sample villages are located between 1960–1961 and 1999–2000 are analysed. Table 2.3, which presents the relevant data, shows that in Kodagu district and Virajpet taluk, while the area under rice declined over the periods 1960–1961 to 1999–2000, the area under coffee has increased rapidly. In Kodagu district the area under rice, which was about 44.6 per cent of the total cropped area, declined consistently to a little over 27 per cent during 1997–1998 to 1999–2000; in Virajpet taluk it declined from 40.2 per cent to 31.2 per cent during the same points of time. The reduction in rice area, apart from other factors, may be in response to the high external costs of wildlife conservation affecting rice cultivation in the region, especially since paddy crop is highly prone to damage caused by wildlife, especially wild elephants, wild boars, etc. In fact, some of the farmers surveyed by us in Maldari, the coffee-growing village analysed in Chapter 3 stated that they had stopped cultivating paddy (rice) due to frequent attacks and damages caused by wild elephants and boars to the paddy (rice) crop almost every year, and such paddy fields were now left fallow. Area under coffee in Kodagu district which was over 30 per cent of the total cropped area during 1960–1961 to 1962–1963 rose rapidly to 52.4 per cent of the total cropped area during 1997–1998 to 1999–2000. In Virajpet taluk this increase in coffee has been faster, rising from about 21.8 per cent to over 57 per cent during the same periods under review. The share of other plantation crops like cardamom, pepper, cashew and tea to the total cropped area in Kodagu district and Virajpet taluk have increased over the time periods under review. Areas under citrus fruits and banana have declined both in this district and taluk, and especially in the case of banana may be a preventive measure undertaken by farmers, since banana crops are highly prone to wildlife attacks, in the absence of appropriate protection measures. The share of non-food crops to the total cropped area in the district and taluk has increased rapidly between 1960–1961 to 1999–2000 which is largely due to the rapid growth in coffee area, as noted earlier.

Unlike in Kodagu district, as noted earlier, in Mysore district and H. D. Kote and Hunsur taluks, food crops are predominant although their relative share in the total cropped area has been consistently falling. Within the foodgrains category, shifts in area are observed. While the share of area under low value cereals

Table 2.3 *Crop pattern and changes between 1960–1961 and 1999–2000: For sample districts and taluks (per cent to total cropped area)*

Crops/crop groups	1960/1961–1962/1963	1970/1971–1972/1973	1980/1981–1982/1983	1990/1991–1992/1993	1997/1998–1999/2000
			Kodagu district		
Rice	44.6	37.1	30.3	29.9	27.3
Coffee	30.0	34.8	44.9	49.7	52.4
Cardamom	7.1	8.7	10.8	8.8	8.8
Citrus fruits	8.9	8.1	5.8	3.3	2.3
Banana	0.7	1.0	0.5	0.1	0.1
Betelnut	0.4	0.4	0.5	0.6	0.7
Pepper	0.5	0.8	0.7	0.9	0.9
Cashew	0.3	0.3	0.8	1.1	1.2
Tea	0.2	0.2	0.2	0.3	0.3
Foodgrains	47.3	41.6	33.3	32.2	28.6
All food crops	66.3	62.6	53.2	46.8	44.9
All non-food crops	33.7	37.4	46.8	53.2	55.1
		Virajpet Taluk (Kodagu district)			
Rice	40.2	44.8	36.7	35.5	31.2
Coffee	21.8	36.7	49.7	55.3	57.1
Cardamom	0.3	0.8	1.3	1.8	1.7
Citrus fruits	10.3	13.2	8.2	4.3	3.1
Banana	0.4	1.4	0.7	0.1	0.1
Betelnut	0.1	0.1	0.1	0.1	0.1
Pepper	0.3	0.7	0.5	0.9	1.1
Cashew	0.01	0.01	0.7	0.2	0.2
Tea	0.3	0.4	0.5	0.6	0.7
Food grains	42.3	44.8	36.7	35.5	31.3
All food crops	74.8	61.5	47.8	43.0	36.8
All non-food crops	25.2	38.5	52.2	57.0	63.2
			Mysore district		
Ragi (finger millet)	23.3	21.1	19.9	17.0	14.9
Jowar (sorghum)	16.5	18.0	15.1	11.8	6.1
Rice	10.9	12.8	11.0	15.7	19.1
Groundnut	5.6	6.1	4.8	4.9	4.5
Tobacco	1.3	1.2	1.4	2.5	3.2
Chilli	1.4	1.2	1.4	0.4	0.5
Coconut	1.2	1.3	1.8	2.2	2.6
Cotton	0.6	0.7	1.4	6.7	10.4
Sugarcane	0.4	0.6	1.4	2.5	3.8

Crops/crop groups	1960/1961– 1962/1963	1970/1971– 1972/1973	1980/1981– 1982/1983	1990/1991– 1992/1993	1997/1998– 1999/2000
Banana	0.2	0.2	0.2	0.1	0.2
Mulberry	–	8.7	10.3	9.2	3.6
Foodgrains	74.8	76.9	70.4	64.1	61.4
All food crops	79.0	80.0	74.7	68.3	66.7
All non-food crops	21.0	20.0	25.3	31.7	33.3
H. D. Kote Taluk (Mysore district)					
Ragi (finger millet)	39.9	33.4	30.6	23.0	23.7
Jowar (sorghum)	1.9	12.3	12.2	8.5	0.7
Rice	9.1	14.4	10.7	11.6	11.7
Groundnut	3.5	3.1	1.7	1.1	1.7
Tobacco	2.7	3.2	2.6	1.8	1.5
Chilli	2.0	1.5	1.6	0.4	0.4
Coconut	0.04	0.1	0.2	0.5	0.6
Cotton	2.6	2.0	4.9	30.8	32.3
Sugarcane	–	0.1	0.3	1.1	0.7
Banana	0.1	0.04	0.2	0.5	0.6
Mulberry	–	–	0.3	0.5	0.6
Foodgrains	79.9	82.0	78.3	58.4	55.0
All food crops	83.0	82.9	81.7	60.4	56.2
All non-food crops	17.0	17.1	18.3	40.6	43.8
Hunsur Taluk (Mysore district)					
Ragi (finger millet)	31.9	36.5	38.5	25.6	22.5
Jowar (sorghum)	6.2	5.4	3.3	7.1	0.8
Rice	8.0	14.1	12.0	11.8	14.5
Groundnut	5.5	6.9	2.2	1.4	3.8
Tobacco	5.0	2.3	8.7	8.4	9.1
Chilli	1.5	2.1	1.7	0.1	0.5
Coconut	0.5	0.6	1.1	2.1	2.5
Cotton	0.9	2.2	2.9	9.1	8.5
Sugarcane	–	0.2	0.6	0.8	0.6
Banana	0.2	0.3	0.2	0.1	0.3
Mulberry	–	0.004	0.2	1.2	0.6
Foodgrains	64.9	77.1	52.3	71.4	61.7
All food crops	78.2	79.5	79.3	72.6	64.3
All non-food crops	21.8	20.5	20.7	27.4	35.7
Uttar Kannada district					
Rice	70.3	86.0	85.8	57.4	69.8
Cotton	–	–	–	–	4.9
Fodder	18.5	0.8	1.2	1.4	1.3

Coconut	4.0	4.7	5.0	4.7	5.1
Betelnut	3.8	7.4	7.7	7.4	8.1
Banana	1.7	2.2	1.4	1.0	1.1
Sugarcane	1.0	1.5	2.0	1.8	1.3
Cashew	0.5	1.0	1.3	1.3	1.4
Pepper	0.5	0.8	0.7	0.2	0.2
Groundnut	0.3	1.6	2.7	4.8	3.1
Cardamon	0.2	0.3	0.2	0.2	0.4
Foodgrains	76.9	89.6	90.5	81.9	84.9
All food crops	83.7	91.4	90.7	90.5	92.0
All non-food crops	16.3	8.6	9.3	19.5	18.0
Haliyal Taluk (Uttar Kannada district)					
Rice	77.7	85.8	83.3	64.9	61.5
Cotton	—	—	—	—	—
odder	13.3	1.9	0.2	0	0
Coconut	0.02	0.02	0.03	0.1	0.1
Betelnut	—	—	—	—	—
Banana	0.03	0.03	0.1	0.04	0.2
Sugarcane	0.1	0.5	2.6	2.5	3.2
Cashew	0.03	0.1	0.1	0.04	0.2
Pepper	—	—	—	—	—
Groundnut	0.02	0.2	0.8	0.9	0.9
Cardamon	—	—	—	—	—
Foodgrains	85.5	97.3	94.7	78.5	76.7
All food crops	86.1	98.4	98.5	81.6	81.5
All non-food crops	13.9	1.6	1.5	18.4	18.5

Source: Directorate of Economics and Statistics, Government of Karnataka, Bangalore

such as ragi (finger millet) and jowar (sorghum) have fallen in the district and the two taluks, the proportion of rice area to the total cropped area has risen over the periods under review, although this rising trend is not smooth. The share of area under a number of crops such as coconut, cotton, sugarcane, mulberry, tobacco to the total cropped area has improved in Mysore district and the two taluks over the time spans under review, while that of other crops such as groundnut and chilli have fallen. The proportion of area under banana has increased in H. D. Kote taluk, while it is more or less constant in Mysore district as a whole and Hunsur taluk.

In Uttar Kannada district and Haliyal taluk food crops, mainly rice, are predominant. The proportion of the total cropped area under rice in the district rose from over 70 per cent during 1960–1961 to 1962–1963 to around 86 per cent during the 1970s and early 1980s, and then declined to over 57 per cent during 1990–1991 to 1992–1993. Its share in the total cropped area rose again to almost 70 per cent during 1997–1998 to 1999–2000. In Haliyal taluk, also, the proportion of area under rice to the total cropped area rose from about 77.7 per cent during 1960–1961 to 1962–1963 to around 83–86 per cent during the 1970s and early 1980s. By the end of the 1990s its share has fallen to around 61 per cent of the total cropped area. This decline in the relative share of rice in the crop pattern in Uttar Kannada district and Haliyal taluk, may, apart from other factors, also be a preventive measure undertaken by farmers since rice is one of the crops that has to bear the brunt of attacks from wildlife such as wild elephants, wild boars, etc., as noted earlier. Interestingly, the share of fodder crops which occupied around 13–19 per cent of the total cropped area in the district and the taluk in the early 1960s has declined considerably and now claims only a negligible share in the total cropped area. This also has implications for biodiversity conservation since a reduction in paddy straw, fodder, etc., could induce greater pressure on forests and CPRs, and accelerate their degradation. The relative share of area under banana has also fallen in the district while that of sugarcane has improved slightly over the time periods under review. The relative share of area under betel nut, coconut and groundnut in the total cropped area of the district and taluk has improved. The proportion of area under non-foodgrains in the district and taluk has risen in the 1990s. Thus, the forgoing gives an overview of the shifts in the crop pattern in the selected districts and taluks. As noted earlier, the relative share of crops like rice, banana, etc., which are highly prone to attacks from wildlife such as wild elephants and boars have declined in some areas. This may be a preventive measure undertaken by farmers to reduce losses arising from damage to these crops caused by wildlife. These are the external costs incurred by the farmers as a result of wildlife conservation.

Population pressure on natural resources

Population growth along with poverty, as noted earlier, are important factors contributing to the loss or decline of habitats and biodiversity in developing countries. The extent of population pressure on forest and other natural resources in our study region, and changes therein during the decennial periods from 1961 to 2001 are reviewed here. Table 2.4 presents the relevant data and shows that the population pressure (both total and rural population) per hectare of the total reporting area has consistently risen for India as a whole, Karnataka state and the three districts under review. Total population per hectare of reporting area for India as a whole was approximately 1.5 persons per ha in 1961 and rose to 3.4 persons per ha by 2001. Similarly for Karnataka, this figure rose from 1.3 persons per ha in 1961 to 2.8 persons per ha in 2001. Population pressure per hectare of reporting area is relatively higher in Mysore district compared to Kodagu and Uttar

Kannada districts. The total and rural population per hectare of total cropped area also shows a consistent upward trend for India as a whole, Karnataka, Mysore and Uttar Kannada districts. For instance, the rural population per hectare of total cropped area rose for India as a whole from 2.4 in 1961 to 3.9 persons in 2001. For Karnataka the same category rose from 1.7 in 1961 to 2.8 in 2001. The number of rural persons per hectare of cropped area has shown an upward trend (albeit not smooth) in Mysore, Uttar Kannada and Kodagu districts. Among these three districts the number of rural persons per hectare of cropped area is relatively higher in Uttar Kannada district, as compared to Mysore and Kodagu districts. The low proportion of cropped area in Uttar Kannada accounts for this. The population pressure on natural resources is seen to be greater in respect of forest resources and has shown a consistent upward trend. For India as a whole, the total number of persons per hectare of forest area rose consistently from 8.1 in 1961 to 14.9 in 2001; for Karnataka these figures were 8.8 and 17.2 respectively. The number of persons per hectare of forest area is higher in Karnataka as compared to the same for India as a whole, which signifies the intensity of pressure on the state's forest resources. For the three districts under review, the population pressure in terms of the number of persons per hectare of forest area has witnessed a consistent rise. The number of persons per hectare of forest area is relatively higher in Mysore when compared to the other two districts. But this does not necessarily imply that the forests in Kodagu and Uttar Kannada are subject to less pressure, since different interest groups and various types of human interventions have contributed to the degradation of the forest resources in these two districts, which are noted for the wealth and biodiversity of their forests. Thus the forgoing discussion shows that the population pressure on forests and other natural resources are increasing over time, and this trend is more conspicuous for Karnataka, and the three districts under review.

Table 2.4 *Population pressure on natural resources: For India, Karnataka and Kodagu, Mysore and Uttar Kannada districts (1961–2001)*

Years	India	Karnataka	Kodagu district	Mysore district	Uttar Kannada district
			Persons per ha of reporting area		
			Total		
1961	1.5	1.3	0.8	1.5	0.7
1971	1.8	1.6	0.8	1.7	0.8
1981	2.2	2.0	1.1	2.1	1.1
1991	2.8	2.4	1.2	2.5	1.2
2001	3.4	2.8	1.3	2.9	1.3
			Rural		
1961	1.2	1.0	0.7	1.1	0.6
1971	1.4	1.2	0.8	1.3	0.7

Years	India	Karnataka	Kodagu district	Mysore district	Uttar Kannada district
1981	1.7	1.4	1.0	1.5	0.8
1991	2.0	1.6	1.0	1.8	0.9
2001	2.4	1.8	1.2	2.0	0.9
Persons per ha of total cropped area					
Total					
1961	2.9	2.2	3.2	3.5	5.3
1971	3.3	2.7	3.0	3.9	7.2
1981	3.9	3.5	3.3	4.4	9.1
1991	4.5	3.8	3.2	5.7	9.4
2001	5.4	4.3	3.8	5.4	10.6
Rural					
1961	2.4	1.7	2.8	2.6	4.4
1971	2.7	2.0	2.5	2.9	6.0
1981	2.9	2.5	2.8	3.2	6.8
1991	3.4	2.6	2.7	4.0	7.1
2001	3.9	2.8	3.3	3.7	7.6
Persons per ha of forest area					
Total					
1961	8.1	8.8	2.4	5.4	0.8
1971	8.6	10.1	2.8	6.4	1.0
1981	9.9	12.2	3.4	7.8	1.3
1991	12.4	14.6	3.6	9.4	1.5
2001	14.9	17.2	4.1	10.6	1.7
Rural					
1961	6.7	6.9	2.1	4.0	0.7
1971	6.9	7.7	2.4	4.8	0.8
1981	7.5	8.7	2.9	5.6	1.0
1991	9.2	10.1	3.1	6.6	1.1
2001	10.8	11.4	3.5	7.3	1.2

Source: Population data – Statistical Abstracts of India (various issues), Central Statistical Organisation, Ministry of Statistics and Programme Implementation, Government of India; Census of India (various issues), Registrar General of India, New Delhi and Census of Karnataka, Directorate of Census Operations, Karnataka, Bangalore, Land Use data – Indian Agricultural Statistics, Volumes I and II, Directorate of Economics and Statistics, Ministry of Agriculture, Government of India, New Delhi; Karnataka Statistics at a Glance, Directorate of Economics and Statistics, Government of Karnataka, Bangalore

Livestock pressure on natural resources

Livestock are a major factor contributing to the degradation of forests, and Common Property Resources (CPRs). In a number of tropical countries such as in Latin America, financial incentives have been given to divert forests to livestock ranching. The number of livestock maintained by rural communities in many developing countries is often beyond the carrying capacity of the region, and this coupled with the 'tragedy of commons' syndrome has contributed to biodiversity loss through degradation of forests and CPRs. The extent of livestock pressure on forest and other land resources in our study region are reviewed here. Table 2.5 presents information on the extent of livestock pressure per unit area of total reporting area, total cropped area and forests in our study region, compared to the same for all-India and Karnataka between 1961 and 1997. Since livestock are composed of different types of animals, and age groups, we have converted them into standardized animal units using the conversion factors suggested by Mishra and Sharma (1990).[1] Livestock censuses are conducted in India on a quinquennium basis and hence these data are presented for the quinquennium years between 1961 and 1997, the last year for which published data are available. Although the data are not perfectly comparable due to changes in definition and methodology of collection, they will help to give us a broad overview of the extent of livestock pressure on the forests and other natural resources in our study region. As evident from Table 2.5, for India as a whole the livestock population measured in standardized animal units per hectare of total reporting area has shown an increasing trend between 1961 and 1997. It rose from about 0.8 in 1961 to 1.2 in 1997 for India as a whole. For Karnataka, there has been a slow but slight increase in the extent of livestock per hectare of reporting area from 0.7 in 1961 to 0.9 in 1997. Among the three districts covered in our study, the livestock pressure relative to the total reporting area seems to have fallen (although not evenly) in Kodagu district and remained more or less constant in Mysore districts, whereas in Uttar Kannada district it has risen slightly over the periods under review. For instance, between 1961 and 1997, livestock pressure in terms of standardized animal units per hectare of reporting area fell from 0.8 to 0.4 in Kodagu district, and from 0.9 to 0.8 in Mysore district; whereas in Uttar Kannada district it rose from 0.3 to 0.5 respectively. The livestock population in standardized animal units per unit area of total cropped area for India as a whole hovered around 1.5 between 1961 and 1982, and rose to 1.9 in 1997. For Karnataka, it rose from 1.3 in 1961 to 1.4 in 1977, thereafter it fell steadily to 1.2 in 1990 and again rose to around 1.4 by 1997. While in Kodagu and Mysore districts the livestock pressure per hectare of total cropped area more or less declined over the periods under review, in Uttar Kannada an increasing trend is visible. Interestingly among the three districts under review, the extent of livestock pressure per unit area of total cropped area is comparatively higher in Uttar Kannada district. For instance, according to the Livestock Census for 1997, the livestock pressure in standardized animal units per hectare of total cropped area was 3.8 in Uttar Kannada compared to 1.6 in Mysore and 1.2 in Kodagu districts. Also the extent of livestock pressure relative to the total cropped area is (with stray exceptions) relatively higher in these three districts (except in recent years for Kodagu district) compared to the average for Karnataka state and India as a whole.

Table 2.5 *Livestock pressure on natural resources: For India, Karnataka and Kodagu, Mysore and Uttar Kannada districts (1961–1997)*

Years	India	Karnataka	Kodagu district	Mysore district	Uttar Kannada district
		Livestock (standardized animal units) per ha of geographical area			
1961	0.8	0.7	0.8	0.9	0.3
1966	0.8	1.2	0.4	0.9	0.4
1972	0.8	0.7	0.8	0.8	0.4
1977	0.8	0.7	0.6	0.8	0.4
1982	0.8	0.8	0.4	0.9	0.4
1990	0.9	0.8	0.5	0.8	0.4
1997	1.2	0.9	0.4	0.8	0.5
		Livestock (standardized animal units) per ha of total cropped area			
1961	1.5	1.3	3.2	2.1	2.7
1966	1.5	1.3	1.7	2.2	3.1
1972	1.5	1.3	2.5	2.0	3.6
1977	1.5	1.4	1.7	1.8	3.7
1982	1.5	1.3	1.2	2.0	2.7
1990	1.6	1.2	1.3	1.6	3.4
1997	1.9	1.4	1.2	1.6	3.8
		Livestock (standardized animal units) per ha of forest area			
1961	4.3	5.0	2.4	3.2	0.4
1966	3.8	5.0	1.3	3.6	0.5
1972	3.8	4.8	2.3	3.1	0.5
1977	3.7	4.9	1.7	3.0	0.5
1982	3.8	4.5	1.3	3.3	0.7
1990	4.3	4.8	1.4	3.0	0.5
1997	5.2	5.4	1.2	3.1	0.6

Source: Statistical Abstracts of India (various issues), Ministry of Statistics and Programme Implementation, Government of India, New Delhi; Indian Livestock Census (various issues), Department of Animal Husbandry and Dairying, Ministry of Agriculture, Government of India, New Delhi; Basic Animal Husbandry Statistics 2002, Department of Animal Husbandry and Dairying, Ministry of Agriculture, Government of India; Quinquennial Livestock Census (various issues), Directorate of Animal Husbandry and Veterinary Services, Government of Karnataka, Bangalore

The table also sheds light on the extent of livestock pressure on forest resources. For India as a whole, livestock pressure in terms of standardized animal units per hectare of forest area steadily declined from 4.3 in 1961 to 3.7 in 1977 and then rose again to 5.2 in 1997. The number of livestock in standardized animal units per hectare of forest area is relatively higher in Karnataka as compared to the average for India as a whole during all the Livestock Census years. For instance, in 1961, Karnataka reported the number of livestock in standardized animal units per hectare of forest area to be 5, compared to 4.3 for all-India; in 1997 this figure for Karnataka was 5.4 compared to 5.2 for all-India. The livestock number per hectare of forest area seems to have declined (although this trend is also not even) in Kodagu and Mysore districts, whereas in Uttar Kannada it rose consistently from 0.4 in 1961 to 0.7 in 1982, and again fell to 0.6 in 1997. A decline in the livestock number per unit area of forest area does not necessarily imply that pressure on the forests of this region has declined. This trend, apart from reflecting the changing composition of the livestock, may also be in response to growing scarcity of fodder due to degradation of forests and CPRs in these districts. As noted earlier, the proportion of permanent pastures and grazing lands to the total reporting area in Kodagu district has declined sharply from 12.2 per cent during 1960–1961 to 1962–1963 to just 2.9 per cent during 1997–1998 to 1999–2000. In absolute terms, however, the number of livestock in standardized animal units per hectare of forest area is relatively high in Mysore and Kodagu districts as compared to Uttar Kannada district. Thus, in 1997, Mysore reported over 3 standardized animal units of livestock per hectare of forest area as compared to 1.2 for Kodagu and only 0.6 for Uttar Kannada. Overall, Karnataka reports relatively greater magnitude of livestock pressure per unit of forest area as compared to the same for India as a whole. Among the three districts under review, Mysore reported relatively greater pressure of livestock per hectare of forest area in comparison to Kodagu and Uttar Kannada districts. Although, comparatively, the livestock number per unit of forest area is low in Uttar Kannada as compared to in Mysore and Kodagu districts, a rising trend in livestock pressure per hectare of forest area is observed over the three decades from 1961 to 1997. The forgoing discussion gives an idea of the various factors exerting pressure on the biodiversity of our study region.

Status of biodiversity in the Western Ghats biodiversity hotspot

To assess the status of biodiversity, one may adopt an ecosystem-based approach or a species-based approach or a combination of both approaches. Under the former, the health of the ecosystem is assessed in terms of certain parameters such as forest and vegetative cover, hydrological regimes, etc. Under the species-based approach, the health of the ecosystem is evaluated by examining the status and population trends of different wildlife species and especially species categorized as endemic, endangered, threatened, keystone, flagship or umbrella species, such as elephants, tigers, leopards. In the following, the status of biodiversity in the Western Ghats region is assessed in terms of the extent and quality of forests and the status and trends in the population of endangered wildlife species, such as royal Bengal tigers, leopards, Asian elephants and other selected wildlife species.

Status and changes in the vegetative cover of forests

One way of assessing the status of biodiversity in the Western Ghats region and Karnataka state in particular, as stated earlier, is to analyse the status of forests, particularly the extent of forest cover and changes over time as well as the quality of the forests. Based on satellite imagery data, the Forest Survey of India (FSI) publish the State of India's Forests every two years. This provides information regarding the forest cover across states and up to district level and also gives details about forest types, that is dense forests (those forests with crown density of over 40 per cent), open forests (forests with crown density between 10 and 40 per cent), scrubs (those with crown density of less than 10 per cent) and mangroves. Information regarding the forest cover and forest types and changes between 1995 and 2001 for India, Karnataka and five other Western Ghat states as well as for selected districts of Karnataka falling within the Western Ghats belt are presented in Table 2.6. Interestingly, India as a whole and the six Western Ghat states including Karnataka report an increase in the forest cover between 1995 and 2001. More significant, however, is that while for India as a whole the dense forest cover has increased (from 55.1 per cent to 57.7 per cent) between 1995 and 2001, Karnataka has reported a decline in the dense forest cover (from 67.2 per cent to 65 per cent) and a substantial increase in the area under open forests (from 20.3 per cent to 26.9 per cent). However, the latest FSI report for 2003 indicates that the dense forest cover in the country as a whole has shrunk by 26,245km^2 between 2001 and 2003, although the overall green cover has increased marginally by 2795km^2 or 0.4 per cent (News item: 'Lost – 26,000km^2 of forests', *Indian Express*, 20 July, 2005). Mining projects, industrial development, encroachments and fellings were the factors cited for this decrease in the dense forest cover. It is also stated that interpretational correction of remote sensing data explains this loss. According to the 2003 FSI report, Karnataka continued to record a decline in the dense forest cover. Table 2.6 further shows that not only has the forest cover declined in districts such as Uttar Kannada, Shimoga and Kodagu but also the dense forest cover in these districts has reduced substantially over the period 1995–2001. Although the forest cover in Mysore and Dakshin Kannada districts has recorded an upward trend, the area of dense forest has declined slightly, while the area under open forest and scrub has risen between the years 1995 and 2001. The above trends have serious implications for biodiversity in the region and shed light on the extent of degradation of forest and biological resources in the state. Among the Western Ghat states, while Karnataka and Kerala reported a decline in dense forest cover between 1995 and 2001, Gujarat, Goa, Maharashtra and Tamil Nadu reported an increase. However, the 2003 FSI report indicates that in addition to Karnataka and Kerala, Gujarat and Maharashtra also reported a loss in dense forest cover between the forest assessment years of 2001 and 2003 (News item: 'Forest Surveys: Cover up, but density down', *Times of India* – online 22 July, 2005). This has disturbing implications for the Western Ghats biodiversity hotspot and if these trends continue, it will sound

Table 2.6 *Changes in forest cover and forest types between 1995 and 2001 for India, states of India, and districts of Karnataka falling within the Western Ghats region*

Country, State and districts	Forest assessment year	Total forest area (including scrubs) in km²	Forest area as % of geographical area	Forest types as % of total forest area			
				Dense forest	Open forest	Mangrove	Scrub
India	1995	699,407	21.3	55.1	35.6	0.6	8.7
	2001	722,856	22.0	57.7	35.8	–	6.5
Western Ghat States							
Gujarat	1995	14,967	7.6	42.6	35.2	4.6	17.7
	2001	17,560	9.0	49.4	36.9	–	13.7
Goa	1995	1266	33.2	78.6	19.9	0.2	1.3
	2001	2095	56.6	85.2	14.8	–	0.0
Maharashtra	1995	51,093	16.6	50.2	35.3	0.3	14.2
	2001	53,619	17.4	57.6	30.9	–	11.5
Kerala	1995	10,419	26.8	81.1	18.1	0.0	0.8
	2001	15,631	40.2	75.3	24.2	–	0.5
Tamil Nadu	1995	20,572	15.8	45.8	40.5	0.1	13.6
	2001	24,662	19.0	50.7	36.4	–	12.9
Karnataka	1995	37,011	19.3	67.2	20.3	0.01	12.5
	2001	40,236	21.0	65.0	26.9	–	8.1
Districts of Karnataka							
Kodagu*	1995	3392	82.7	96.7	1.8	0.0	1.5
	2001	3010	73.4	86.6	13.3	0.0	0.1
Mysore*	1995	3668	30.7	49.9	44.5	0.0	5.6
	2001	3957	33.1	48.2	45.7	0.0	6.1
Uttar Kannada*	1995	7865	76.4	94.0	5.4	0.01	0.6
	2001	7808	75.9	83.3	16.7	0.0	0.01

Country, State and districts	Forest assessment year	Total forest area (including scrubs) in km²	Forest area as % of geographical area	Forest types as % of total forest area			
				Dense forest	Open forest	Mangrove	Scrub
Belgaum	1995	1813	13.5	50.5	9.1	0.0	40.4
	2001	1629	12.1	51.3	20.1	0.0	28.6
Chikmagalur	1995	3469	48.2	85.0	10.9	0.0	4.1
	2001	3605	50.1	85.1	13.5	0.0	1.4
Dakshin Kannada	1995	3647	43.2	75.9	24.0	0.0	0.07
	2001	4719	55.9	74.7	25.3	–	0.04
Dharwad	1995	924	6.7	43.1	36.1	0.0	20.8
	2001	1169	8.5	47.0	40.6	0.0	12.4
Hassan	1995	1311	19.2	65.1	13.7	0.0	21.2
	2001	1421	20.8	74.1	19.1	0.0	6.8
Shimoga	1995	5092	48.3	78.8	17.9	0.0	3.3
	2001	4509	53.2	69.1	30.1	0.0	0.8

Notes: * districts included in the study

Western Ghat States – These are the states of India within which the Western Ghats biodiversity hotspot lies.

Districts of Karnataka – These are the districts of Karnataka State within which the Western Ghats biodiversity hotspot lies.

Dense forests – those with crown canopy cover of 40% and above; Open Forests – those with crown canopy cover of 10% to below 40% and scrubs are those with crown canopy cover of below 10%.

Source: For 1995 – State of Forest Report 1995, Forest Survey of India, Ministry of Environment and Forests, Dehra Dun, India. For 2001 – Forest and Wildlife Section, www.indiastat.com

the death knell of the hotspot which is considered to be one of the eight hottest biodiversity hotspots in the world, as noted earlier.

Status and changes over time of the population of endangered species

Another indicator of the status of biodiversity is to examine the status and changes over time of the population of endangered or threatened wildlife species. State forest departments in India collect wildlife census estimates (wildlife population estimates to be more precise) for selected wildlife species in India across states every four or five years. Such wildlife population estimates are available for some endangered wildlife species such as tigers, elephants and leopards. Although state forest departments call these wildlife censuses, they are in fact only estimates of wildlife population, since it is impossible to enumerate or count all animals as is done in population censuses. Wildlife population numbers are usually estimated on the basis of pug marks (of big cats), block count and waterhole count methods, line transect methods, etc. In very sophisticated cases camera trappings or photographic capture–recapture methods are also used to estimate the population of big cats. Box 2.1 lists the various techniques used to conduct a wildlife census. These estimates will give a rough idea of the status of biodiversity especially of selected wildlife species and changes in their numbers over time. Table 2.7 presents the wildlife population estimates for tigers, elephants and leopards for India and six Western Ghat states (and also Andhra Pradesh) between 1972 and 2001–2002 for selected years. These statistics illustrate that in the case of tigers there was an improvement in their numbers in Karnataka between 1972 and 2001–2002 (from 102 to 401 tigers) whereas for the whole of India, although the tiger population increased from about 1827 in 1972 to 4334 in 1989, thereafter the numbers fluctuated and declined to 3642 in 2001–2002. In the other states such as Andhra Pradesh, Kerala, Maharashtra and Tamil Nadu the tiger population seems to have risen up to the mid/late 1980s, or early 1990s, and thereafter has more or less remained stagnant or declined. Thus, although trends up to the 1980s or early 1990s seemed to offer a ray of hope that conservation efforts initiated in India under Project Tiger from 1972 had helped to reverse the alarming decline of tiger population in India recorded earlier (with the tiger population of India plummeting to less than 2000 from the 40,000 estimated at the turn of the 20th century), recent trends are quite disturbing. In fact, wildlife experts such as Bittu Sahgal opine that the actual number of tigers in India is just half of that indicated by the wildlife census. In the case of elephants and leopards, the data show that overall there is an improvement in their numbers for India as a whole, although provisional estimates of the 2001–2002 Wildlife Census suggest that the population of elephants has declined slightly compared to the 1997 Census figures. The southern states of Karnataka, Kerala and Tamil Nadu, with a sizeable population of elephants, report an increase in their numbers between the census years 1993 and 1997, but thereafter their numbers have dwindled or remained stagnant. While the population of leopards seems to have increased in Gujarat and Karnataka between the census years 1984 and 1997, in other states their numbers seem to have increased initially and thereafter fallen, although these trends are not continuous. The data suggest that the population of these endangered species has improved partly due to conservation efforts, but the threats faced by these wild animals is far from removed, as is evident from the continued poaching of these animals, seizure of wildlife products such as tiger and leopard skins, ivory, etc., habitat loss, a flourishing illegal trade in wildlife products, etc. For instance, a press release dated 7 April, 2003 by the Ministry of Environment and Forests, Government of India (MoEF), notes that during 1999–2002 the poaching of 404 leopards, 181 elephants, 129 tigers, 51 rhinos and 3 lions were reported in the country. The highest levels of tiger poaching were reported from Uttar Pradesh (47), followed by Maharashtra (27), Madhya Pradesh (17), West Bengal (15) and Andhra Pradesh (7). Elephant poaching was highest in Karnataka (55 cases) followed by Orissa (29), West Bengal (25), Tamil Nadu (23) and Kerala (14). Uttar Pradesh state again reported the highest levels of leopard poaching at 250, followed by Tamil Nadu (28), Madhya Pradesh (26), Himachal Pradesh (24). These figures pertain only to recorded cases of poaching, and the actual level of poaching is likely to be much higher than is suggested by the official figures. Another report by the Wildlife Protection Society of India recorded the death of 719 tigers and 2474 leopards between 1994 and 2004 (see Thapar, 2005). This clearly shows the extent of the threat faced by wildlife and the need for sustained measures to conserve India's rich and varied wildlife.

Box 2.1 Wildlife Census Techniques

1. *Sample count*: Under this method a pre-determined portion of a park is searched, usually a number of distinct small areas. The wildlife population recorded or estimated in the sample area is then extrapolated to arrive at a figure for the whole park area. The sample units need to be representative of the total population and hence need to be selected carefully. Sample counts are less convincing but can give biologically and economically more efficient results than a total count.

2. *Total count*: Under this method the entire park or reserve area is searched and all animals seen are recorded. However, a disadvantage of this method is that the larger the area to be covered under the wildlife census or the smaller the animal, the more difficult it is to search and record animals. It is also time consuming and requires more resources in terms of staff and finances. In addition, there is the risk of either under- or over- or even double-counting, due to animal movements during the census period.

3. *Roadside count*: This method is designed for surveys along tracks and roads, and can be used for walking/cycle patrols along tracks, and vehicles along roads. Within the study area, a number of tracks which can be covered regularly and which include representative areas of all habitats are to be chosen for monitoring. These tracks need to be monitored a number of times at regular intervals. Each trip acts as a sample and consequently samples may differ greatly. Here, the data are best presented as averages. This method is frequently used for monitoring bird populations.

4. *Dung count*: Animal dung is considered to be a reliable indicator of animal presence and (has been) frequently used to estimate animal abundance. In certain situations, dung counts can lead to actual population estimates, but there are many assumptions to be met. The first criterion is the correct identification of dung from different species, and the second is the recognition and separation of different groups of droppings. The best way to ensure accurate dung identification is to keep a selection of pellets/droppings of each species in a transparent bag. These pellets should be collected when an animal is seen defecating. This needs to be used as a reference for comparison in the field. Transect samples are preferred as they are easily extended to cover a larger area and they run across micro-habitat diversity. Transects or quadrats should be large enough to allow most samples to have one or two dung groups at least. With low density populations, transects may have to be 50 or 100m long. For elephants, transect width could be doubled as droppings are easy to locate. The whole habitat unit should be searched. Base-line transects should run across the whole area. Line transect surveys require observers to move along straight trails called 'transects', counting animals seen on either side. Additionally using range finders and compasses, the observer measures the distance and angle from the transect to the animals seen (Karanth and Nichols, 2000).

5. *Pugmark count*: The pugmark technique has been used to count large carnivores such as tigers in India since 1969. The first all-India census of tigers in 1972 used this technique. The census is based on recording several distinguishable morphological features of the tiger's footprints or pugmarks, because studies have shown that each tiger in a defined area has a 'unique' pugmark signature which makes it possible to distinguish individual tigers in the forest. The overall shape of the pugmark helps in determining the gender. The smallest unit of survey and census is the forest beat, also called the counting unit. Tigers (or big cats) mostly walk along a well defined network of forest roads, paths, wildlife trails, stream banks. Like other wild animals they choose well-beaten paths and frequent water points. A census participant, therefore, must have thorough knowledge of such features within his area, that is counting unit. The hind feet prints are considered to be important in determining the gender of the tiger. Pugmark data, when collected and analysed, can yield more information than simple population size alone, such as age composition, adult gender ratio of the population, longevity of individual animals, habitat use patterns, etc.

6. *Waterhole census*: The waterhole census technique is widely used to count large animals when they visit waterholes. This technique is used when water sources are not numerous and widely scattered in the area. The best time to conduct a waterhole census would be at the height of the dry season when water is the limiting factor. The dry season is also considered to be appropriate for all types of census. A prior survey should locate all the waterholes in the census area. Simple access to the water points should be opened and a machan/hide constructed. The machan/hide should be far away from the waterhole so that animals are not deterred from using the waterhole. It is recommended that a census period during a full moon should be chosen, and the census should continue for a full 24 hours. This method will help in deriving an index of animal pressure. A large population will have more animals drinking than a small population. If a population increases in size, the number of animals seen drinking will increase. Data from successive years can be compared to show trends in population size provided conditions remain constant. It is assumed that there is a linear relationship for each animal species between the number of animals seen drinking per time period and the number of animals in the area.

7.   *Camera trapping (photographic capture–recapture)*: This method was tried in India
      by Ullas Karanth from 1995 to record the presence of tigers in selected parks/
      sanctuaries in India. The method combines camera trap photography to identify
      individual tigers with theoretically well founded capture–recapture models. Individual
      tigers are identified by studying the differences in stripe patterns (Karanth and Nichols,
      2000). This technique is considered to be a reliable scientific method to count tigers
      (and other big cats/carnivores). A camera trap consists of a small transmitter located
      on the side of any trail used by tigers. It emits an electronic beam aimed at a receiver
      placed at the opposite side of the trail, with the receiver connected to the cameras.
      When a tiger (or big cat/carnivore) walks along the trail and interrupts the electronic
      beam, it takes its own picture, activating the two cameras. Usually it is not possible
      to count all animals and hence a census which means total count is rarely feasible.
      The camera trapping method is recommended in an area with a relatively high
      density of big cat/carnivore population. Sampling a tiger population, for instance,
      through the capture–recapture method is used to estimate the number of tigers in
      the areas without photo-capturing all the tigers. Tiger numbers in Nagarhole National
      Park based on this method are presented in Chapter 4. The method is especially
      recommended in high priority, well protected and high animal density reserves.

Source: Appayya, 2001, pp155–169.

Table 2.7 *Status and changes in estimates of wildlife population (number) for
selected states and India between 1972 and 2001–2002*

States and wildlife species	Wildlife census year						
	1972	1979	1984	1989	1993	1997	2001–2002
Tiger (*Panthera tigris*)							
Andhra Pradesh	35	148	164	235	197	171	192
Gujarat	8	7	9	9	5	1	Nil
Goa	—	—	—	2	3	6	5
Karnataka	102	156	202	257	305	350	401
Kerala	60	134	89	45	57	79	71
Maharashtra	160	174	301	417	276	257	238
Tamil Nadu	33	65	97	95	97	62	60
INDIA	1827	3015	4005	4334	3750	3836	3646
Elephant (*Elephas maximus*)							
Andhra Pradesh					46	57	73
Karnataka					5500	6088	5838
Kerala					3500	5737	5737*
Tamil Nadu					2400	2971	2971*
INDIA					25,541	29,010	28,274
Leopard (*Panthera Pardus*)							
Andhra Pradesh			—	301	152	138	NA
Gujarat			498	702	772	832	NA

Goa	10	18	31	25	NA
Karnataka	238	283	455	620	NA
Kerala	—	27	16	16	NA
Maharashtra	380	580	417	431	NA
Tamil Nadu	189	119	138	110	NA
INDIA	4747	6767	6828	7787	NA

Notes: NA = not available.
* Figures for elephant populations for 1997 are repeated for 2001–2002.
Data for 2001–2002 tiger and elephant populations are provisional.

Source: Forest and Wildlife Section, www.indiastat.com

Table 2.8 sheds further light on the status of selected wildlife species over the census years 1977 to 1997–1998/2001–2002 for Karnataka state. The table shows that the population of endangered species such as tigers, leopards as well as that of prey populations such as spotted deer, wild boar, Indian bison in Karnataka has improved over the census periods under review. In the case of elephants, while their population increased consistently over the census years 1977 to 1997–1998,

Table 2.8 *Status and changes in estimates of wildlife population (number) of selected species in Karnataka for the period 1977 to 1997–1998/2001–2002*

Wildlife species	1977	1979	1989	1993	1997–1998	2001–2002
Elephant	1187	1195	4420	5980	6185	5835
Tiger	26	39	257	305	395	401
Leopard	29	42	283	455	817	
Sloth bear	22	41	—	—		
Spotted deer	1834	—	—	—	25,850	
Sambar	302	—	—	—	4998	
Wild boar	289	—	—	—	15,760	
Wild dog	149	139	—	—	—	
Langur	1512	—	—	—	—	
Barking deer	88	—	—	—	—	
Fox	—	—	—	—	957	
Indian bison (Gaur)	307	505	5470	—	8484	

Notes: The figures for elephants and tigers differ slightly (except 1979 for tigers where it is quite large) from that presented in Table 2.7 and may be due to provisional estimates or unrevised estimates presented in the Annual Reports of the Karnataka Forest Department.
Figures for elephants and tigers for 2001–2002 are taken from www.indiastat.com.

Source: Annual Reports of Karnataka Forest Department, Bangalore (relevant issues); Forest Statistics, 1987 and 1997, Karnataka Forest Department, Bangalore; for figures for 2001–2002, Forest and Wildlife Section, www.indiastat.com

thereafter as per 2001–2002 census estimates their numbers have decreased, as noted earlier. Leaving aside the question of whether the elephant population in Karnataka is declining or not, what is of more concern is the sex ratio of elephants. Usually it is the adult male elephants which are the target of poachers. Their tusks command a premium in the illegal international wildlife trade. The sustainability of the elephants also hinges upon a favourable male to female ratio. According to available evidence, the ratio of male to female adult elephants in Karnataka appears to have declined between the census years 1993 and 2001–2002. While the male to female adult elephant ratio in 1993 was about 1:2.6 this has deteriorated to 1:3.5 according to the 2001–2002 Wildlife Census. It is, however, lamentable to note from Table 2.8 that wildlife census data of a number of species, especially prey populations such as deers, bisons, wild boars, etc. are not being continuously collected. This poses problems for conservationists and planners, especially since the survival of endangered species such as tigers and leopards also critically depends upon the availability of an adequate prey population.

Table 2.9 furnishes information about the number, density and sex ratio of elephants across different forest divisions of Karnataka state as given in the 2002 Elephant Census. The table illustrates that Bandipur Tiger Reserve, Nagarhole National Park, Cauvery and Biligiri Rangana Temple (BRT) wildlife sanctuaries report a good concentration of elephant populations with the density in the range of 1.1–2.3 elephants per square kilometre of forest area. Overall for the state, the density of elephant population is $0.8/km^2$ of forest area. The sex ratio (adult male to adult female) of elephants varies widely across different forest divisions, ranging from 0:1 to 1:9. In the major national parks and sanctuaries this ratio ranges between 1:2.7 in Nagarhole National Park and 1:9 in the Cauvery Wildlife Sanctuary.

The discussion above has not considered the reliability of the wildlife census data. There are doubts in certain quarters about the reliability of the data and whether the forest officials are fudging the data in order to present a rosy picture of the wildlife situation in the country in order to ward off inconvenient questions and avoid alarm in Parliament, State Assemblies, and especially the public domain. This is because considerable funds, including those from international donor agencies, have been channelled to conservation projects. As stated earlier, wildlife experts such as Bittu Sahgal feel that the actual number of tigers in India is just half of that indicated by the wildlife census data. Valmik Thapar, another wildlife expert, echoes a similar or even gloomier view of the status of tigers in India in an aptly titled piece on: 'The Dying Roar-Tiger, tiger burning bright; only in forests of government files', published in the 26 February, 2005 issue of the *Indian Express* (Thapar, 2005). The case of missing tigers in the Sariska Tiger Reserve in Rajasthan reported by the *Indian Express*, a national daily, made national headlines and evoked concern among many, including the Indian Prime Minister who ordered an enquiry and also convened a meeting of the National Wildlife Board on 17 March, 2005 to review the tiger situation in India. Following a public outcry, a team from *Down to Earth*, an environmental monthly published by the

Table 2.9 *Number, density and sex ratio of estimated elephant population in Karnataka by forest divisions: Elephant census 2002*

Serial no.	Division	Estimated mean number of elephants	Number of elephants recorded			Sex ratio AM:AF	Mean density of elephants number per km²
			Total	Adult males (AM)	Adult females (AF)		
1.	Bandipur TR	1975	1919	157	711	1:4.5	2.3
2.	Nagarahole NP	1143	1241	154	419	1:2.7	1.8
3.	Cauvery WLS	807	519	20	180	1:9	1.6
4.	BRT WLS	594	401	14	107	1:7.6	1.1
5.	Kollegal	355	36	2	18	1:9	0.3
6.	Bhadra WL	300	160	28	40	1:1.4	0.6
7.	Brahmagiri WLS	117	32	7	5	1:0.7	0.7
8.	Madikeri TT	86	42	11	13	1:1.2	0.2
9.	Hunsur TT	73	75	18	33	1:1.8	0.7
10.	Mysore	72	109	17	55	1:3.2	—
11.	Bannergatta NP	71	106	22	40	1:1.8	0.7
12.	Hassan	56	60	7	9	1:1.3	0.2
13.	Virajpet	51	25	3	10	1:3.3	0.2
14.	Madikeri WL	49	24	6	10	1:1.7	0.3
15.	Nugu WLS	27	53	12	18	1:1.5	0.8
16.	Karwar	17	3	2	1	1:0.5	0.1
17.	Dandeli	17	4	2	0	2:0	0.02
18.	Mandya	14	26	3	14	1:4.7	—
19.	Belgaum	10	18	5	9	1:1.8	—
20.	Chikamagalur	5	5	2	2	1:1	—
21.	Haliyal	—	2	1	1	1:1	—
22.	Yellapur	—	2	0	1	0:1	—
	Karnataka	5838	4862	493	1696	1:3.7	0.8

Notes: The estimated mean number and density of elephants is based on block count method. To compute the sex ratio, the estimates of elephant population are based on the pooled results based on water hole and block count methods.
NP = National Park; TT = Territorial; TR = Tiger Reserve; WL = Wildlife Division; WLS = Wildlife Sanctuary

Source: Southern India Elephant Census 2002 – Report to the Karnataka Forest Department, Asian Elephant Research and Conservation Centre, Indian Institute of Science, Bangalore, July 2002

Delhi-based NGO, Centre for Science and Environment, visited the Sariska Tiger Reserve and met local villagers and forest officials. The local villagers confirmed fears that there are no visible signs of the presence of tigers in the reserve although local forest officials dispute this. The responses of the villagers to the queries of the *Down to Earth* team are quite revealing, with comments such as: 'How can tigers be spotted? They were killed to satiate official greed'; 'lax attitude of the forest officials killed the tigers', etc. Most indicting was the statement of a youth: 'They (i.e. forest officials) turn 1 tiger into 5!' Forest officials have their stock responses, such as that they are understaffed, inadequately armed to combat poachers, face non-cooperation and interference from the local community, etc. However, these statements imply that the situation of tigers (and other endangered species) is grimmer than is indicated by the wildlife census data. In fact, an enquiry by the Central Bureau of Investigation (CBI) instituted by the Government of India confirmed that there were no tigers left in the Sariska Tiger Reserve due to poaching. In response, the Government of India appointed a Tiger Task Force headed by Sunitha Narain, Director of the Centre for Science and Environment to enquire into the tiger situation and recommend measures to improve tiger conservation in India.

Our experiences during the course of this study have strengthened these doubts, especially when trying to obtain wildlife census data from some State Forest Departments, although this is neither classified nor confidential information. For instance, despite a personal visit to the Kerala State Forest Department headquarters at Thiruvananthapuram, Kerala State, I could not readily obtain the data. Finally after sending letters and reminders to the Principal Chief Conservator of Forests and the Chief Wildlife Warden, the wildlife census data from 1983–1997 for selected species were sent to me. But there were notable omissions in the data. According to the communication from the Conservator of Forests (Wildlife), Kerala dated 6 September, 2002, while 76 tigers were reported in the 1993 census year, and 73 tigers in the 1997 census year, for earlier census years the cells were interestingly left blank. However, information presented to the Indian Parliament in response to a question (Rajya Sabha unstarred question No.3780 dated 25.04.2003, see www.indiastat.com/forest and wildlife) as reported by an Indian Statistical website, suggested that while 134 tigers were reported in Kerala in the 1979 census, the figure reduced to 89 tigers in the 1984 census, 45 tigers in the 1989 census, and 57 tigers in the 1993 census (not 76 as furnished to us). In comparison with 1979 census figures, this would indicate that the population of tigers in Kerala has almost halved. It appears that by omitting the earlier data in the communication to us, the state forest department might have wanted to cover up the fact that the tiger population in Kerala State has declined substantially despite conservation efforts. Furthermore, there are similar doubts about some of the other data. For instance, according to the information furnished by the 1993 wildlife census, the population of Malabar giant squirrels, an endangered species, was estimated at 1384, four years later the 1997 census figures suggested that their population had increased by 46 times to reach 63,474! Quite apart from worrying about the veracity of these figures, how exactly the wildlife census officials recorded and estimated Malabar giant squirrels in the tropical forests is a mystery. Similarly the population of Nilgiri langur, another endangered species, was estimated at 2987 in 1993 and four years later their population increased almost eight fold to 24,890! Our experience in obtaining wildlife census data from the Tamil Nadu State Forest Department was no better. After letters and reminders, the 1997–1998 wildlife census data for several species was sent, but the photocopy of the data sheet was mostly illegible and hence we were unable to use these data. However our experience with the Karnataka State Forest Department was quite different to that in Kerala and Tamil Nadu. A Karnataka State forest official in charge of an important tiger reserve was honest enough to admit that if one were to see how the wildlife census data are being collected and recorded, one would know how credible they are. All these points serve to strengthen doubts about the reliability of the wildlife census data and might imply that forest officials may be fudging the data to present a rosy picture of the wildlife situation in India, especially of endangered species such as tigers, leopards and elephants. While it is commendable that India recognized the need and importance of collecting wildlife census data for tigers as early as 1972, and of other species such as leopards and elephants subsequently, there is now a need to review and strengthen the system of collecting wildlife census data. In order to improve the credibility of the data, it is vital that experts, including representatives of the civil society especially environmental groups and NGOs, are associated with the actual collection of wildlife census data so as to minimize the potential for fudging. In this context, it is gratifying to note that well-known experts and scientists of the Asian Elephant Research and Conservation Centre of the Indian Institute of Science, Bangalore were associated with the design and conduct of the elephant census in South India in 2001–2002, but the actual collection and monitoring of data should not be left to forest officials alone. This would improve the credibility of the wildlife census data. Recently, an international team, alarmed by the drastic decline of the population of Siberian tigers, was deputed to conduct a census of Siberian tigers. In addition, it is also important that the data of all the selected species are recorded during the census years. In the case of endangered species – especially tigers, leopards and elephants – it may be desirable to collect data and monitor their numbers on an annual basis.

Summary

A review of the land use changes over the four decades from 1960–1961 to 1999–2000 shows that the area under cultivation in the study region has increased and this has largely come about through the diversion of land under permanent pastures and grazing lands, land under miscellaneous tree crops, etc. A reduction in pastures and grazing lands has implications for biodiversity conservation, since a reduction in such lands leads to greater pressure on natural forests. Although land use data suggest that the forest area has declined only marginally in the study area, this does not convey the true extent of forest degradation that has taken place in the study region. In fact satellite imagery data suggest that, in contrast to the picture for India as a whole, in Karnataka and the three study districts, the area under dense forest has reduced considerably within the short span of five years between 1995 and 2001, while the area under open forest has increased. Considering the importance of the Western Ghats region as one of the 25 biodiversity hotspots of the world, this decline in the dense forest cover has serious implications for the biodiversity of the region. Added to that, population and livestock pressure on forests and natural resources is increasing over time and this is a further matter of concern. This trend is more conspicuous for Karnataka and the three districts under review.

A review of crop pattern changes for the same period throws up interesting insights. The relative share of crops such as rice, banana, etc., which are highly prone to attacks from wild animals, especially wild elephants and boars, has declined in some areas. Apart from other factors, this may be a preventive measure undertaken by farmers to reduce losses arising from damage to these crops caused by wildlife. These are the external costs incurred by the farmers due to wildlife conservation. The area under plantation crops such as coffee, however, has expanded fast in Kodagu over the four decades from 1960–1961 to 1999–2000, aided by favourable prices and other factors. Higher coffee prices, apart from other factors, also encourage farmers to deforest and encroach on forestlands and illegally cultivate coffee crop, which is detrimental to biodiversity conservation, as will be discussed in Chapter 3.

Wildlife census data suggest that the population of endangered species such as tigers, elephants and leopards in India has improved over the last two or three decades, but recent trends indicate a decline in their numbers when compared to 1997 census data. Among the Western Ghat states one discerns different trends. While the census data indicate an improvement in the population of tigers in Karnataka, in Kerala, Maharashtra and Tamil Nadu their population reportedly increased from the 1970s up to the 1980s or early 1990s, and thereafter remained stagnant or declined. Elephant population in Karnataka, Kerala and Tamil Nadu appears to have increased between 1993 and 1997, but thereafter their numbers have remained stagnant or declined. In the case of leopards, while Gujarat and Karnataka reported an increase in their population between 1984 and 1997, other states such as Maharashtra and Tamil Nadu reported an increase up to the early 1990s and a decline thereafter. Recent trends that indicate a decline in tiger and elephant populations is a matter of concern, especially as they are considered to be umbrella or flagship species and thus act as an indicator of the health of the ecosystem as a whole. The decline in the ratio of male to female adult elephants observed in Karnataka is even more disturbing since this can affect the sustainability of the elephant population. Thus the decline in the dense forest cover, the population of endangered species such as tigers, elephants and the sex ratio of adult elephants, suggest that the biodiversity of the Western Ghats region is degrading despite conservation efforts. Continued poaching of wildlife and a flourishing illegal trade in wildlife products pose a great challenge to conservation. If doubts about the reliability of the Indian wildlife census data are true this would imply that the wildlife situation in India, especially of endangered species, is even more precarious than implied by the wildlife census data. Revamping and strengthening wildlife census operations, including putting in place appropriate checks to prevent the fudging of data, should be high on the agenda for wildlife conservation in India.

Note

1   The conversion factors for converting livestock into standardized animal units are as follows: Cattle: adult – 1.0 units; young – 0.6; Buffalo: adult – 1.25; young – 0.6; Goats – 0.25; Sheep – 0.2; Pigs – 0.10; Horses/Ponies – 2.67; Donkey/Mules – 1.33; and Camel – 1 unit (Mishra and Sharma, 1990).

3
Maldari – The Context of a Coffee Growing Village

Introduction

The conservation of biodiversity by declaring certain tracts of forests as protected areas precludes deriving benefits for the economy from alternate land use options of forests such as utilizing it for agriculture, animal husbandry, tourism, recreation, etc. Growing plantation crops such as coffee constitute an alternative land use option for tropical forests. Hence, in this chapter, the economic and other related aspects of biodiversity conservation in the context of a plantation dominant area are examined. Coffee growing is predominant in Kodagu district, which falls within the Western Ghat tracts of Karnataka State. In Maldari village in Kodagu district coffee is predominant, and there is a mix of coffee plantations of different sizes. Human–animal conflicts are conspicuous and the village is also close to the reserve forest which is the setting for our analysis.

Maldari village

Maldari village, selected for the in-depth study, is located in Virajpet taluk of Kodagu district. The village is roughly 25km from the taluk headquarters and 45km from the district headquarters. According to the 2001 Population Census, there are 510 households in the village with a total population of approximately 2059 persons; 50.3 per cent male and 49.7 per cent female. About 41.9 per cent of the village population belong to scheduled castes and tribes. The total geographical area of the village extends to roughly 2789ha, of which forest accounts for about 1011ha, that is over 36.2 per cent of the village's total area. The net area sown in the village is over 1602ha and the rest comprises uncultivable wastes, fallows, land put to non-agricultural uses, etc. Coffee and other plantation crops cover over 41.7 per cent of the total village area and over 72.5 per cent of the net sown area. About 86 acres are under sacred groves. Apart from coffee and other plantation crops, rice is also a major crop.

To select the sample households in Maldari, a stratified random sampling procedure was adopted, as stated in Chapter 1. A list of households in the village was obtained from the village panchayat office. This list was cross-checked and after eliminating those households which figured more than once in the list, we had a total frame of 374 households from which to select our sample. The households in the sample village were stratified based on their land holding size: small holdings (below 2.5 acres), medium holdings (2.5–5 acres), large holdings (5–10 acres) and very large holdings (10 acres and above). From each stratum, 30 per cent of the households were selected on a random sample basis. In total 125 households were selected for in-depth study. However, due to discrepancies between the data on land holdings of the sample households obtained from the village panchayat office and that canvassed directly from the respondents during the primary survey, some of the sample households shifted from one land holding group to another. Consequently in some land holding categories the number of sample households increased, while in others it decreased. Information on the distribution of the population and sample households in Maldari village is indicated in Table 3.1.

Table 3.1 *Distribution of population and sample households in Maldari village, Kodagu district, India*

Land holding class in acres	Population	Sample
Below 2.5	226	59
2.5–5	43	21
5–10	24	15
10 and above	81	30
Total	374	125

Note: 1 acre = 0.4047ha; the above land holding classes in ha are respectively as follows: below 1.03ha; 1.03–2.02ha; 2.02–4.05ha; 4.05ha and above.

Profile of the sample households

Socio-economic characteristics

The socio-economic characteristics of the sample households are analysed here. Table 3.2 indicates that the average size of the sample households is 5.1 persons. This varies inversely with holding size, ranging from 5.5 persons per household among the lowest strata of holdings to about 4.3 persons per household among holdings of 5 acres and above. For the sample as a whole the sex ratio – the number of females per 1000 males – is about 907, which is below the average for Karnataka State (964) and all-India (933), as per the Population Census for the year 2001. Interestingly small and large holdings report these sex ratios to be above the national average.

Table 3.2 *Average household size and sex ratio for the sample households in Maldari*

Land holding class in acres	Average household size (persons per household)	Sex ratio
Below 2.5	5.5	946
2.5–5	5.6	800
5–10	4.4	941
10 and above	4.3	897
Total	5.1	907

Note: Sex ratio is the number of females per 1000 males.

Table 3.3 *Distribution of migrants and non-migrants among the sample households across land holding classes in Maldari*

Land holding class in acres	Per cent of migrants to total sample households in each stratum	Per cent of non-migrants to total sample households in each stratum
Below 2.5	64.4	35.6
2.5–5	52.4	47.6
5–10	40.0	60.0
10 and above	20.0	80.0
Total	48.8	51.2

Migrants constitute over 48.8 per cent and non-migrants about 51.2 per cent of the total sample households selected for the study (Table 3.3). The proportion of migrants among the sample households varies inversely with farm size, ranging from 64.4 per cent among small holdings to 20 per cent among the very large holdings. Conversely, the proportion of non-migrants is highest among large land holdings and lowest among the small holdings.

Overall, literate household members constitute about 90.7 per cent of the sample household population, excluding children below 7 years, and 9.3 per cent are illiterate (Table 3.4). The proportion of illiterates is highest among the lowest strata of holdings and varies inversely with farm size. Conversely the proportion of literates varies directly with farm size. The proportion of those who have studied up to high school and above is relatively higher among large holdings, and is lowest among small holdings.

Approximately 63 per cent of the sample household population reported as working population, while the rest were either not in the labour force or were unemployed (Table 3.5). Over 28.6 per cent are cultivators. The proportion of cultivators to total household population varies positively with farm size ranging from 19.4 per cent among small holdings to over 36 per cent among holdings of 2.5 acres and above. Over 15 per cent of the sample household population are

Table 3.4 *Literacy status of the sample household population (excluding children below 7 years) by land holding classes in Maldari (in percentages)*

Land holding class in acres	Illiterate	Lower primary	Upper primary	High school	College, professional, etc.
Below 2.5	13.8	30.7	28.6	23.6	3.3
2.5–5	9.9	23.8	20.8	34.7	10.8
5–10	4.9	1.6	18.0	41.0	34.5
10 and above	–	2.5	16.5	25.6	55.4
Total	9.3	20.5	23.6	27.8	18.8

Table 3.5 *Occupational status of the sample household population by land holding classes in Maldari (in percentages of total household population)*

Land holding class in acres	Cultivators	Agricultural labourers	General labourer	Salaried/ employed people	Business	Others (including house-wives)	Not in labour force or unemployed
Below 2.5	19.4*	13.8	12.6	3.1	4	8.0	39.1
2.5–5	36.7*	2.6	6.8	3.4	4.3	11.2	35.0
5–10	37.9	–	1.5	12.1	1.5	15.2	31.8
10 and above	36.4	–	–	1.6	3.1	22.3	36.4
Total	28.1*	7.5	7.8	3.8	3.6	12.2	37.0

Note: * includes some households who report both cultivation and agricultural labour as their main occupation.

employed as agricultural labourers or general labourers. Those who report this as their prime occupation are concentrated among small holdings whereas it is nil among larger holdings. Overall, over 19 per cent of the household population report salaried employment, business, etc., as their main occupation.

Land characteristics

The average size of holdings for the sample households as a whole is about 8.3 acres per household (Table 3.6). This varies from 0.6 acres among holdings of below 2.5 acres to 27.5 acres among large holdings of 10 acres and above. As is evident from the table, land is very unevenly distributed among the sample under study. Holdings of below 2.5 acres, which constitute 47.2 per cent of the sample, account for only 3.4 per cent of the total area operated by all households, whereas

Table 3.6 *Particulars of land holdings of sample households by land holding classes: Maldari*

Land holding class in acres	Average size of operated area in acres per household	Total operated area		Irrigated area	Unirrigated area
		Acres	%	(as % to total operated area)	
Below 2.5	0.6	35.4	3.4	4.2	95.8
2.5–5	3.4	72.1	6.9	22.1	77.9
5–10	7.0	105.7	10.2	19.4	80.6
10 and above	27.5	825.3	79.5	43.5	56.5
All	8.3	1038.5	100	38.2	61.8

over 79 per cent of the operated area is concentrated among very large holdings, which account for 24 per cent of the sample households. The proportion of irrigated area to total operated area also varies positively with farm size. Over 38 per cent of the total area operated by the sample households is irrigated. While this percentage is quite low for small holdings (over 4.2 per cent) it exceeds 43 per cent among very large holdings.

Information about the legal status of the land holdings of the sample households and the source of acquisition of these holdings is furnished in Table 3.7. Overall, about a tenth of the operated area of the sample households is without secure legal titles. This proportion varies inversely with farm size ranging from over 47 per cent among small holdings to 3.3 per cent among very large holdings. Most of these areas without titles are encroached lands, and Table 3.7 seems to suggest that this phenomenon is concentrated among small holdings. Overall, about 14 per cent of the holdings of the sample households has been acquired through encroachments on forest and common land. This phenomenon is more conspicuous among smaller holdings. This may suggest that it is small farmers who have a greater tendency to encroach upon forest and common land as compared to other land holding groups. However, this masks reality, since a large part of the land area with legal titles and reported as purchased or inherited lands was originally encroached lands that have been regularized over time.

In fact, the data presented in Table 3.8 suggest that although in relative terms encroached lands account for a very large proportion (86.3 per cent) of the total area owned by small holdings, in absolute terms larger holdings have encroached a greater area than smaller holdings. While the average area encroached among small holdings is around 0.5 acres per household, it is over 9 acres per household among large holdings. However, three-quarters of the encroached lands have been regularized and this proportion varies positively with farm size. Thus, almost 87 per cent of the lands encroached by the large holdings is with secure title, whereas for other land holding categories this proportion varies from 39 to over 45 per cent. Most of the encroachments that have been regularized may have taken place

Table 3.7 *Legal status and source of acquisition of land holdings of sample households by land holding classes; Maldari, India*

Land holding class in acres	Legal status of operated area		Source of acquisition of ownership holdings				
	With title	Without title	Forest	Common land	Purchased	Ancestral, inherited, etc.	Total
	(as % to total operated area)		(as % to total owned area)				
Below 2.5	52.5	47.5	23.6	46.6	9.6	20.2	100
2.5–5	58.0	42.0	42.0	11.5	20.4	26.1	100
5–10	73.0	27.0	18.1	14.9	24.8	42.2	100
10 and above	96.7	3.3	2.4	3.4	64.5	29.7	100
All	90.1	9.9	7.4	6.6	55.6	30.4	100
	(935.9)	(102.6)	(76.6)	(68.9)	(577.7)	(316.7)	(1039.9)

Table 3.8 *Particulars of encroached land and their legal status for sample households by land holding classes, Maldari, India*

Land holding class in acres	Total encroached land		Per cent distribution of encroached land by legal status	
	Acres per household	As % to total owned area	With title	Without title
Below 2.5	0.5	86.3	44.9	55.1
2.5–5	1.9	59.7	39.6	60.4
5–10	2.4	33.0	45.2	54.8
10 and above	9.2	33.6	86.8	13.2
All	3.1	37.0	74.5	25.5

over the span of one or two generations or in the decades prior to the enactment of the Forest Conservation Act of 1980 which barred the diversion of forest land to non-forest uses and also requires state governments to obtain the Central Government's prior approval to permit such diversion. Thus forests have provided valuable services to the local community who have used these lands for agriculture, growing plantation crops, etc.

Around 90 per cent or more of the land operated by the sample households is under cultivation (Table 3.9). The remaining land is accounted for by fallows, waste lands and land under non-agricultural uses. It is interesting to note that about 0.8 per cent of the operated area among the large holdings is under private forests.

Coffee is the predominant crop, accounting for over 78 per cent of the total cropped area among the sample (Table 3.10). This proportion varies from over 69 per cent among small holdings to 80.8 per cent among very large holdings. Rice

Table 3.9 *Land use pattern of sample households by land holding classes in Maldari, India (in percentages of total land holdings)*

Land holding class in acres	Land use pattern					Total	
	Under cultivation	Fallows	Wastelands	Private forests	Under buildings/ non-agricultural uses	%	Land holdings in acres
Below 2.5	89.0	—	0.6	—	10.4	100	35.4
2.5–5	90.1	4.3	1.0	—	4.6	100	72.1
5–10	95.6	0.9	0.4	—	3.1	100	105.7
10 and above	93.1	3.7	0.2	0.8	2.2	100	825.3
All	92.9	3.3	0.3	0.7	2.8	100	1038.5

Table 3.10 *Cropping pattern of sample households by land holding classes in Maldari, India (in percentages of total cropped area in each size class)*

Land holding class in acres	Coffee	Rice	Pepper	Fruit trees	Coconut	Other crops	Total	
							%	Cropped area in acres
Below 2.5	69.5	26.3	1.0	—	—	3.2	100	31.5
2.5–5	53.5	39.8	0.9	0.5	0.1	5.2	100	64.8
5–10	75.5	17.3	1.6	1.4	0.1	4.1	100	101.0
10 and above	80.8	15.5	1.0	1.0	0.3	1.4	100	767.2
All	78.1	17.7	1.0	1.0	0.2	2.0	100	964.5

is the next most important crop grown by the sample households, accounting for about 17.7 per cent of the total cropped area. Households with land holdings of up to 5 acres report 26–40 per cent of their total cropped area to be under rice. Pepper, fruit trees, coconuts, etc., account for the remaining area cultivated by the sample households.

Coffee cultivation in Maldari

Coffee is the most important cash crop cultivated in Maldari, along with other crops such as pepper, coconut and citrus fruits. Since the present chapter is concerned with estimating the opportunity cost of biodiversity conservation in the context of alternative land use options of growing plantation crops, coffee, as the predominant plantation crop grown in our study area, is taken up for an in-depth analysis.

In our study region, two varieties of coffee are widely grown: arabica (*coffea arabica*) and robusta (*coffea canephora*). While arabica coffee is ideally grown at elevations of 1000–1500m, robusta coffee is usually grown at lower elevations of 500–1000m (Coffee Board, 2002). The robusta coffee plant is more bushy and has a larger canopy cover compared to arabica coffee. Although per acre yields of arabica coffee are less than that of robusta coffee, prices for arabica coffee are higher. For instance, statistics furnished by the Indian Coffee Board suggest that yields of arabica coffee averaged about 713kg/acre as against 1175kg/acre for robusta coffee during the year 2000–2001. Producer prices for arabica coffee were around 53 US cents per lb as against 29.5 US cents per lb for robusta coffee during 1999–2000 (Coffee Board, 15 February, 2002). Of the total area under coffee in India during 2000–2001, 48 per cent was under arabica coffee and 52 per cent under robusta coffee. Karnataka State alone, which is the setting for our study, accounted for 57.6 per cent of the total coffee area and 70 per cent of total coffee output of India during 2000–2001 (Coffee Board, 2002).

Of the 125 sample households, 106 households (84.8 per cent) are coffee growers; the remaining households grow other crops, or only have homesteads. Of the total coffee growers, around 58.5 per cent are cultivating only robusta coffee, 6.6 per cent only arabica coffee while 34.9 per cent of households cultivate both robusta and arabica coffee on their lands (Table 3.11). Across land holding groups, there are some interesting differences. Among small holdings below 2.5 acres, and holdings of 5–10 acres, the majority of the households (71.4 and 66 per cents respectively) grow only robusta coffee. The proportion of sample households who grow both robusta and arabica coffee increases with farm size (although this trend is not smooth), whereas the proportion of households who grow robusta coffee only on their land varies inversely with holding size, although this decreasing trend is not continuous.

Information on the density of coffee plants among our sample households is furnished in Table 3.12. The average number of coffee plants planted per acre is

Table 3.11 *Per cent distribution of sample households cultivating different varieties of coffee by land holding classes in Maldari*

Land holding class in acres	Per cent of households cultivating			Total	
	Robusta coffee only	Arabica coffee only	Both robusta and arabica coffee	%	Number of households
Below 2.5	71.4	4.3	14.3	100	42
2.5–5	47.4	5.2	47.4	100	19
5–10	66.7	Nil	33.3	100	15
10 and above	43.3	Nil	56.7	100	30
All	58.5 (62)	6.6 (7)	34.9 (37)	100	106

Note: Figures in parentheses are the number of sample households in the respective columns.

Table 3.12 *Density of coffee plants grown by sample households in Maldari by land holding classes (average no. of plants per acre)*

Land holding class in acres	Density of robusta	Density of arabica	Density of small plants	Overall density
Below 2.5	236	67	133	435
2.5–5	234	77	39	349
5–10	344	81	75	501
10 and above	304	203	25	532
All	303	18	34	517

about 517, comprising of an average of 303 plants of robusta, 18 plants of arabica and 34 small plants that are not yielding. The number of coffee plants per acre more or less increases with the size of holding. While in the case of robusta, the density increases from 236 plants per acre among small holdings to 304 plants per acre among large holdings, in the case of arabica the plant density increases from 67 plants per acre among the lowest strata to 203 plants per acre among holdings of 10 acres and above.

Cost of coffee cultivation

The cost of coffee cultivation among the sample households is examined here. As the respondents were not able to furnish information about the cost of coffee cultivation separately for arabica and robusta, the estimates are presented for the coffee crop as a whole. The main costs incurred for coffee are establishment costs and recurring costs. Since a breakdown of the establishment and recurring costs for coffee in terms of discounted values is presented in a later discussion, here the costs of material inputs, labour and other costs (undiscounted values) are presented. Information about the cost of material inputs such as seeds, chemical fertilizers, farmyard manure and pesticides, etc., used for coffee cultivation by the sample households is shown in Table 3.13. Taking all farmers together it is seen that the cost of seeds, including the transport charges, for coffee cultivation was roughly Rs1798.8 per acre. The bulk of the seed costs reported here are incurred in the initial year when the coffee plantation is established and the remaining amount is due to replantings. The sample households applied about Rs2350.3 worth of chemical fertilizers per acre annually, Rs389.8 worth of farmyard manure per acre and about Rs294 worth of pesticides per acre. Chemical fertilizers, followed by seeds accounted for the major proportion of material inputs used for coffee cultivation, followed by farmyard manure and pesticides. Overall the farmers incurred costs of over Rs4906 per acre on material inputs for coffee cultivation. These costs were relatively higher among holdings of 5 acres and above as compared to other land holding groups.

Table 3.13 *Cost of material inputs used for coffee cultivation by sample households in Maldari by land holding classes (Rs per acre)*

Land holding class in acres	Seeds (including transport charges)	Chemical fertilizers	Farmyard manure	Pesticides	Transport charges for fertilizers/ farmyard manure	Total
Below 2.5	1953.4	1739.8	389.1	114.3	106.3	4302.9
2.5–5	1317.0	1542.6	443.4	85.9	148.7	3537.6
5–10	1660.2	3231.6	810.6	125.9	137.9	5966.2
10 and above	1833.5	2298.5	337.0	328.4	61.2	4858.6
All	1798.8	2350.3	389.8	293.9	73.3	4906.1

The labour costs incurred for coffee cultivation include making renovation pits, contour drains, fertilizer applications, plant protection operations (spraying pesticides against leaf diseases and sucking insects), pruning of coffee bushes, drying, etc. Generally the coffee plants begin to yield from the fourth year, although they attain maturity and give economic yields from the sixth year and have a lifespan of around 50 years. In the present study, those plants that were planted from 1995 onwards were considered to be young plants or those in the pre-bearing stage.

Information on the labour costs for coffee cultivation by crop operations incurred by the sample households is presented in Table 3.14. Overall, the sample households incurred an expenditure of over Rs6909 per acre towards labour costs (including the imputed value of family labour) for coffee cultivation. These costs are around Rs3503 per acre among small holdings of below 2.5 acres and vary inversely with farm size up to holdings of 10 acres and above, where they rise steeply to over Rs7600 per acre. Crop operations like opening and closing pits, coffee picking, planting and pruning of coffee bushes, the application of fertilizer, manure, etc., (in that order) incur the major labour costs for coffee in the study area. Labour costs for opening and closing pits amounted to over Rs4096 per acre, while coffee picking after the crop starts yielding from the sixth year costs about Rs1593 per acre annually.

Another important cost incurred by the sample households in the study area is irrigation. Of the total cost incurred on irrigation, the major share is the cost of installing the irrigation system. The sample households have installed their systems at different times, so, in order to get comparable figures, we also enquired about the replacement cost of the irrigation investments made. The major sources of irrigation in the study area are bore well, tank and open well. The main source of irrigation for almost 46.4 per cent of the sample households is tank irrigation followed by bore wells for 28.6 per cent of the households, and the rest by open wells.

The households, on average, incurred over Rs3187 per acre installing an irrigation system at the time of the installation (Table 3.15). They are also incurring

Table 3.14 *Labour costs for coffee cultivation incurred by sample households in Maldari by land holding classes (Rs per acre)*

Land holding class in acres	Opening/ closing pits	Planting	Making contour drains	Application of fertilizers, manure, etc.	Pruning coffee bushes
Below 2.5	949.0	793.6	228.0	238.7	86.3
2.5–5	957.4	479.1	112.2	223.8	452.7
5–10	622.6	381.4	94.4	258.4	263.5
10 and above	4741.0	348.4	44.2	349.2	372.4
All	4096.1	366.7	55.9	332.8	358.2
	Coffee picking	Drying	Other (e.g. supervision)	Total labour costs	
Below 2.5	1009.2	163.4	35.3	3503.5	
2.5–5	953.2	128.1	137.9	3444.4	
5–10	1458.9	122.8	24.9	3226.9	
10 and above	1654.1	39.4	52.6	7600.3	
All	1593.0	54.0	52.7	6909.4	

Note: Labour costs includes wages paid for hired labour plus the imputed value of family labour.

Table 3.15 *Average cost of irrigation investment for sample households by land holding class in Maldari (Rs per acre)*

Land holding class in acres	Cost of irrigation investment		Yearly operation and maintenance cost
	at the time of installation	at replacement cost	
Below 2.5	988.0	1552.6	—
2.5–5	2685.6	5135.3	377.5
5–10	2667.9	4966.9	615.0
10 and above	3391.7	6490.0	773.0
All	3187.0	6072.5	703.1

costs of over Rs703 per acre for its operation and maintenance every year. In terms of replacement costs, irrigation investments can be costed at over Rs6072 per acre. Broadly speaking, the cost of irrigation investment among the sample households both at initial and replacement costs varies positively with farm size.

Another important cost incurred by the coffee growing households is on fencing to protect the coffee estate from wild animals and grazing cattle. There are fences constructed of iron posts and iron wire and also wooden fencing. One or two households have also installed solar powered electric fencing which is capital intensive, and is mainly to protect against attacks from wild animals such as elephant and boar. According to a coffee planter who had invested in solar powered electric fencing during 1999–2000, the cost was around Rs150,000/km length of

Table 3.16 *Cost of fencing of coffee estates/farms by land holding classes in Maldari (Rs per acre)*

Land holding class in acres	Wooden fencing		Iron fencing		Solar fencing	Overall fencing cost	
	at initial cost	at replacement cost	at initial cost	at replacement cost	at replacement cost	at initial cost	at replacement cost
Below 2.5	417.8	4765.0	1305.2	3867.3	–	1722.9	8632.3
2.5–5	410.8	1894.5	694.0	1644.7	–	1104.8	3539.2
5–10	216.7	2303.7	350.1	1702.9	–	566.7	4006.6
10 and above	337.7	1560.0	166.6	456.8	636.1	504.3	2653.0
All	333.2	1768.3	260.7	782.4	505.6	593.9	3056.2

Note: Solar fencing refers to solar powered electric fencing.

electric fencing, which is beyond the reach of most farmers. In addition, there are no subsidies available to encourage the farmers to invest in electric fencing; the interest rates charged by banks on loans are also quite high and are a disincentive to any investment in electric fencing. The costs for these three types of fencing are examined separately. Table 3.16 indicates that the cost of fencing at replacement costs as reported by the farmers is an average of over Rs1768 and Rs782 per acre respectively for wooden and iron fencing. The sample households had incurred an average cost of about Rs505.6 per acre for electric fencing (Rs25,786 per acre for the two farmers in our sample who invested in electric fencing) at the time of fencing. The overall average cost of fencing at replacement costs, taking all farmers together, is over Rs3056 per acre. This varies inversely with farm size, from over Rs8632 per acre among small holdings to around Rs2653 among very large holdings. Almost 75.8 per cent of the sample households resorted to fencing to protect coffee and other crops from cattle and 24.2 per cent of households reported that it was to protect the crops from wild animals.

Other costs incurred by the sample households are land and plantation taxes, plus electricity and fuel charges for operating farm machinery, etc. The average amount of land and plantation taxes paid by the sample households was about Rs10 and Rs24.53 per acre respectively. Small holdings with less than 2.5 acres did not report any payment of plantation tax (Table 3.17). On average the sample households incurred an expenditure of about Rs96 per acre for electricity and fuel consumption.

Other costs incurred for coffee cultivation

The sample households in Maldari also incurred some additional costs for the cultivation of coffee mainly due to the damages caused by wildlife and defensive

Table 3.17 *Payment of taxes and electricity/fuel costs reported by sample respondents in Maldari by land holding classes (Rs per acre)*

Land holding class in acres	Average land tax	Average plantation tax	Electricity charges/ fuel costs
Below 2.5	25.9	—	—
2.5–5	9.5	5.6	—
5–10	10.3	15.6	56.8
10 and above	9.4	30.4	113.5
All	10.1	26.1	96.0

expenditures incurred to protect against wildlife. This could involve simply chasing the wild animals out of their estates by beating drums or bursting fire crackers to scare them. Alternatively, they may erect fences, and also undertake elephant proofing works such as digging trenches, etc. These expenditures are the external costs incurred by the farmers due to wildlife conservation. Since an analysis of these costs is undertaken in a later section, we will simply state here that these external costs due to damage caused by wildlife cost on average roughly Rs331.2 per acre, plus Rs196.5 per acre towards defensive measures against wildlife.

Coffee production and receipts

After having examined the costs incurred for the cultivation of coffee, we furnish below the per acre annual receipts from coffee in quantity and value terms. Table 3.18, which presents relevant information on the gross annual receipts from coffee reported by the sample households shows that, on average, the coffee growers in the study area obtained an annual yield of over 1088kg/acre from coffee. Annual yields from robusta coffee were conspicuously higher than from arabica coffee; that is, about 748.9kg and over 393kg/acre respectively. Overall, annual

Table 3.18 *Gross annual receipts from coffee in kgs and rupees per acre obtained by sample households in Maldari by land holding classes*

Land holding class in acres	Gross annual coffee output					
	Arabica	Robusta	Total	Arabica	Robusta	Total
	(Kgs per acre)			(Rupees per acre)		
Below 2.5	58.0	496.4	554.4	1005.8	12,050.9	13,056.8
2.5–5	81.0	550.9	631.9	1967.6	11,787.5	13,755.1
5–10	27.2	1076.1	1103.3	863.7	25,367.6	26,231.3
10 and above	395.9	725.7	1121.6	14,147.4	21,468.1	35,615.5
All	393.3	748.9	1088.2	12,050.7	21,273.9	33,324.6

coffee yields among the sample coffee growers varied positively with farm size, ranging from over 554kg/acre among small holdings to around 1121.6kg/acre among the very large holdings. In value terms, the annual receipts from coffee obtained by the coffee growers was over Rs33,324 per acre. This varied positively with farm size, ranging from about Rs13,056.8 per acre among small holdings to over Rs35,615 per acre among very large holdings.

The opportunity cost of biodiversity conservation

Since the present study seeks to assess the opportunity cost of biodiversity conservation in terms of the forgone coffee benefits, a comparative picture of the changes in coffee area and prices vis-à-vis forest area and timber prices in our study region and the net benefits from coffee are examined here. Coffee is the main competitor for land use in the study region, as noted earlier. For instance, in Virajpet taluk of Kodagu district where our sample village is located, the share of coffee in total cropped area rose from just 21.8 per cent during the triennium 1960–1961 to 1962–1963 to over 57 per cent during the triennium 1997–1998 to 1999–2000, as noted earlier. This has been brought about through a reduction in forest area and other land use categories such as area under permanent pastures and grazing lands as well as through crop substitution (Ninan et al, 2001; Ninan and Sathyapalan, 2005). An analysis of the behaviour of coffee area and prices in comparison with forest area and timber prices over the period 1960–1961 to 1999–2000 for Kodagu district and all India, as presented in Table 3.19, are quite revealing.

Over the 40 year period 1960–1961 to 1999–2000, while areas growing coffee registered a significant increase in Kodagu district, forest areas recorded negative trends. Both coffee and timber prices recorded significant increases during this period with timber prices rising faster than coffee prices. However, the period-wise trends are more revealing. During the post-1980 period, while areas growing coffee rose faster than in the earlier period, the forest area recorded a significant decline. More interesting, during the pre-1980 period coffee prices grew slower than timber prices, but in the subsequent period this trend was reversed with coffee prices rising faster than timber prices. Thus the economic incentive to grow coffee is quite strong. Higher coffee prices, apart from other factors, also encourage farmers and others to deforest and encroach on forest lands and illegally cultivate coffee, which is detrimental to biodiversity conservation (Ninan and Sathyapalan, 2005).

To assess the forgone coffee benefits, we need to compute the net benefits from coffee. Three alternative viability measures have been used for this purpose: net present value (NPV), benefit–cost ratio (BCR), and internal rate of return (IRR). In the study area, two varieties of coffee, arabica and robusta, are grown, as noted above. Although per acre yields of arabica coffee are less than those of

Table 3.19 *Trends in coffee and forest area and coffee and timber prices during 1960–1961 to 1999–2000: For Kodagu district and all India*

Period	Kodagu district (India)			All-India		
	Coffee area	Forest area	Ratio of coffee to forest area	Coffee price	Timber price	Ratio of coffee to timber price
Pre-1980	2.67*	−0.15^{ns}	2.93*	5.64*	9.06*	−3.48*
Post-1980	3.10*	0.00003*	3.13*	12.16*	6.71*	5.46*
Overall period	2.74*	−0.0001^{ns}	2.77*	7.97*	10.70*	−2.74*

Notes: Overall Period: 1960–1961 to 1999–2000; Pre-1980 period: 1960–1961 to 1979–1980; Post-1980 period: 1980–1981 to 1999–2000.
* = significant at 1 per cent level of significance; ns – not statistically significant even at 10% level. The year 1980 marked a watershed in forest conservation in India, when the Government of India enacted the Forest Conservation Act of 1980, which states that diversion of forests to non-forest uses is banned, and further states that those seeking to divert forests to non-forest uses need to seek the prior approval of the Central Government. Hence in order to discern trends, we have also tried to analyse the pre- and post-1980 period trends.

Source: Data on coffee growing area are taken from *Coffee Statistics* (various issues) and *Database on Coffee*, Coffee Board, Government of India (2002), Bangalore, India and data on forest area are taken from *Indian Agricultural Statistics*, Volume 2, Ministry of Agriculture, Government of India (various issues); data on coffee and timber prices are from Chandlok and the Policy Group (1990) and for subsequent years from *Index Number of Wholesale Prices*, Ministry of Industry, Government of India (various issues)

robusta coffee, the prices of arabica coffee are much higher than those of robusta coffee. The establishment costs of coffee include the cost of renovation pits, contour drains, planting and the cost of seedlings. In addition, there are fixed costs by way of irrigation investments and fencing costs. The recurring costs include material costs such as fertilizers, manure and pesticides, labour costs for applying fertilizers, manure and pesticides, repairs and maintenance, and supervision, etc. After coffee begins to yield (from the sixth year), there are recurring costs towards coffee picking, pruning coffee bushes and drying. Common costs such as irrigation and fencing investments, taxes, etc., have been apportioned in terms of the relative share of coffee in the gross sown area. There are also external costs incurred by the coffee growers by way of wildlife damage costs, and defensive expenditure incurred to protect against wildlife attacks. These external costs are assumed to arise during the entire lifespan of the crop. The benefits and costs are expressed in 1999 prices, and the lifespan assumed for coffee in the analysis is 50 years. The NPVs and BCRs have been computed at three discount rates: 8, 10 and 12 per cent. In addition, we have two sets of estimates, one excludes the external costs incurred by the coffee growers, and the other includes these external costs.

Table 3.20, which sheds light on the composition of coffee costs (discounted values at 12 per cent discount rate), shows that taking all farmers together, the establishment costs account for almost a fifth of the total discounted costs of coffee.

Table 3.20 *Composition of cost (discounted values at 12 per cent discount rate) of coffee cultivation in Maldari, India (for cash flows summed up over 50 years at 1999 prices)*

Cost components	Discounted costs at 12% discount rate (Rs per acre)	%
Establishment costs		
Opening and closing pits	3657.2	6.1
Cost of seedlings	1606.0	2.7
Planting costs	327.4	0.5
Making contour drains	49.9	0.1
Fencing costs	2129.5	3.5
Irrigation investment	4231.2	7.0
Subtotal	12,001.2	19.9
Recurring costs		
Chemical fertilizers	20,033.4	33.3
Farm yard manure	3329.9	5.5
Pesticides/plant protection measures	2440.9	4.1
Fertiliser and farmyard manure application	2763.7	4.6
Irrigation maintenance	4557.0	7.6
Electricity/fuel charges	622.3	1.0
Pruning of coffee bushes	1683.6	2.8
Coffee picking	7486.6	12.4
Drying and processing	253.6	0.4
Supervision	437.7	0.7
Taxes, etc.	234.7	0.4
Subtotal	43,843.4	72.8
External costs		
Wildlife damages	2750.5	4.6
Wildlife defensive expenditure	1631.1	2.7
Subtotal	4381.6	7.3
Grand total	**60,226.2**	**100**

Recurring costs, such as the value of material inputs and coffee picking account for about 72.8 per cent of the total discounted costs of coffee. External costs account for about 7.3 per cent of the total discounted costs of coffee.

The disaggregated data by land holding classes reveals some interesting differences. Establishment costs account for a higher proportion (22.2 per cent) of the total discounted costs of coffee among small holdings of below 2.5 acres, as compared to other land holding categories (Table 3.21). This is largely due to capital indivisibilities resulting in higher costs per unit area among small holdings.

Table 3.21 *Composition of cost (discounted values at 12 per cent discount rate) of coffee cultivation across land holding classes in Maldari, India (for cash flows summed up over 50 years at 1999 prices)*

Land holding class in acres	Establishment costs		Recurring costs		External costs		Total discounted costs	
	Rs/acre	%	Rs/acre	%	Rs/acre	%	Rs/acre	%
Below 2.5	9820.0	22.2	27,853.2	62.8	6669.3	15.0	44,342.5	100
2.5–5	6696.1	15.2	30,394.1	69.1	6915.7	15.7	44,005.9	100
5–10	8510.5	13.4	51,059.1	80.3	4010.8	6.3	63,580.4	100
10 and above	12,817.4	20.9	44,385.2	72.4	4110.5	6.7	61,313.1	100
All	12,001.4	19.9	43,843.3	72.8	4381.6	7.3	60,226.3	100

Recurring costs are relatively higher among larger holdings of 5 acres and above. This is due to the fact that larger holdings are better endowed and tend to use greater quantities of capital inputs such as chemical fertilizers, farmyard manure, pesticides, etc. Interestingly, the external costs, that is wildlife damage costs and defensive expenditures to protect against wildlife attacks account for around or over 15 per cent of the total discounted costs of coffee among those households with holdings up to 5 acres as against over 6 per cent among holdings with more than 5 acres. This is partly because small holdings are located along the forest fringe where the intensity of attacks from wild animals is greatest.

Table 3.22 presents the NPVs, BCRs and IRRs for coffee by land holding categories. Taking all farmers together the NPVs and BCRs from coffee excluding or including these external costs are quite high and significant. Excluding external costs, these NPVs range between Rs100,800 to Rs194,900 per acre, and between Rs96,400 to Rs188,500 per acre when external costs are also included. The BCRs range between 2.8 and 3.4 excluding these external costs, and from 2.6 to 3.2 when these external costs are included. Across land holding categories too these NPVs and BCRs are positive and high, both excluding and including the external costs. Even after including external costs, the IRRs from coffee for different land holding categories are 16.6–23 per cent. A sensitivity analysis of the net benefits from coffee under alternative assumptions revealed that even if expected coffee benefits were to decrease by 20 per cent, and costs were to rise by 20 per cent, the NPVs, BCRs and IRRs from coffee are still quite high and significant, with the IRRs ranging between 19.5 and 20.1 per cent (see Table 3.23). This implies that the opportunity cost of biodiversity conservation in terms of coffee benefits forgone is quite high. The estimates presented above should be considered as a lower bound of the benefits forgone by the coffee growers since coffee is grown along with several other crops such as pepper, citrus fruits, etc.

The above findings are in line with those of other researchers who pointed to the high opportunity costs of biodiversity conservation (e.g. Norton-Griffiths

Table 3.22 *Net present values, benefit–cost ratios and internal rates of return from coffee excluding and including external costs in Maldari, India (for cash flows summed up over 50 years at 1999 prices)*

Land holding class in acres	Net present value in 000 Rs/acre			Benefit–cost ratio			IRR %
	8%	10%	12%	8%	10%	12%	
			(discount rates)				
Excluding external costs							
Below 2.5	54.7	36.1	23.7	2.0	1.8	1.6	18.2
2.5–5	59.6	40.3	27.6	2.1	1.9	1.7	20.1
5–10	129.7	90.1	63.7	2.5	2.3	2.1	21.9
10 and above	212.1	151.0	110.2	3.6	3.2	2.9	23.3
All	194.9	138.5	100.8	3.4	3.1	2.8	23.2
Including external costs							
Below 2.5	44.9	28.1	17.0	1.7	1.5	1.4	16.6
2.5–5	49.4	32.1	20.6	1.8	1.6	1.5	18.2
5–10	123.8	85.3	59.7	2.3	2.1	1.9	21.3
10 and above	206.0	146.1	106.1	3.4	3.0	2.7	23.0
All	188.5	133.3	96.4	3.2	2.9	2.6	22.9

Note: External costs – wildlife damage costs and defensive expenditure to protect against wildlife attacks

and Southey, 1995; Pearce and Moran, 1994). Jyothis (2002), who estimated the forgone benefits of rubber cultivation in the Periyar Tiger Reserve in Kerala State, observed that the NPVs from rubber cultivation were quite high. The NPVs from rubber for cash flows summed over 25 years at 12 per cent discount rate was above Rs236,000 per acre. Even if output were to decline by 20 per cent, the NPVs from rubber were still high (Rs140,000 per acre). Jyothis's estimates, however, have not accounted for the external costs attributable to wildlife while estimating the net benefits from rubber cultivation in the Periyar Tiger Reserve area. A detailed review of estimates of the values of alternative uses of forested land, such as cattle ranching, growing agricultural and plantation crops, etc., presented in SCBD (2001a) are quite revealing. Although these studies are strictly speaking not comparable in terms of the methodology used, alternative land uses covered and the forest sites studied, yet they seem to suggest that the NPVs of the alternative uses of forest land show wide variation across countries and land uses. For cattle ranching the NPVs were in the range US$68–1622/ha, for agricultural crops US$1440–2255/ha and for plantation crops and tree growing US$184–4281/ha (SCBD, 2001a). It thus appears that it is primarily the non-market and unpriced benefits of tropical forests which provide the economic justification for biodiversity conservation.

Table 3.23 *Sensitivity analysis of net benefits from coffee under alternative assumptions in Maldari, India (for cash flows summed up over 50 years at 1999 prices)*

Assumption	Net present value in 000 Rs/acre			Benefit–cost ratio			IRR %
	8%	10%	12%	8%	10%	12%	
			(discount rates)				
	Excluding external costs						
Full expected benefits, net of costs	194.9	138.5	100.8	3.4	3.1	2.8	23.2
Assuming 20% *increase* in benefits	249.9	179.3	132.1	4.1	3.7	3.4	24.3
Assuming 20% *decrease* in benefits	140.0	97.7	69.4	2.8	2.5	2.2	21.7
Assuming 20% *increase* in costs	210.9	151.6	111.9	2.9	2.6	2.3	24.5
Assuming 20% *decrease* in costs	179.0	125.4	89.6	4.0	3.6	3.3	22.0
Assuming 20% *decrease* in benefits, and 20% *increase* in costs	124.1	84.6	58.3	2.3	2.1	1.9	20.1
	Including external costs						
Full expected benefits, net of costs	188.5	133.3	96.4	3.2	2.9	2.6	22.9
Assuming 20% *increase* in benefits	243.4	174.1	127.7	3.8	3.5	3.1	24.0
Assuming 20% *decrease* in benefits	133.6	92.4	65.1	2.6	2.3	2.1	21.2
Assuming 20% *increase* in costs	205.7	147.4	108.4	2.7	2.4	2.2	24.2
Assuming 20% *decrease* in costs	171.3	119.1	84.3	2.9	2.6	2.3	21.5
Assuming 20% *decrease* in benefits, and 20% *increase* in costs	116.3	78.3	53.0	2.1	1.9	1.7	19.5

Note: External costs – wildlife damage costs and defensive expenditure to protect against wildlife attacks.

External costs

Local communities are the ones most affected by the costs of conservation (Shyamsundar and Kramer, 1996, 1997). As noted earlier, coffee growers incur costs of conservation due to damage caused by wildlife, and expenditure to pre-

Table 3.24 *Particulars of external costs (wildlife damage costs and defensive expenditures to protect against wildlife) incurred by coffee growers during 1999–2000: Maldari, India*

Land holding class in acres	Wildlife damage costs	Wildlife defensive expenditures	Total external costs	Total* external costs (discounted values at 12%)	Total external* costs (discounted values) as % of total discounted costs of coffee cultivation
	(Rs/acre)			(Rs/acre)	
Below 2.5	671.8	131.3	803.1	6669.3	15.0
2.5–5	631.5	201.2	832.7	6915.7	15.7
5–10	332.5	150.4	482.9	4010.8	6.3
10 and above	290.2	204.8	495.0	4110.5	6.7
All	331.2	196.5	527.7	4381.6	7.3

Note: * discounted values for cash flows summed over 50 years.

vent this. On average these external costs were Rs527.7/acre during the reference year (Table 3.24).

These external costs were higher among smaller holdings up to 5 acres, as noted earlier. This is because many small holdings are located either near or within the forest boundary where the intensity of wildlife attacks is more pronounced. On average, these external costs (discounted values) account for about 7.3 per cent of the total discounted costs of coffee and goes up to 15 per cent or more among smaller holdings of up to 5 acres. However, as noted already, the net benefits from coffee even after including these external costs are positive and high among all land holding categories.

In order to give an incentive to local communities to conserve biodiversity the State, that is the Forest Department, has a mechanism to compensate local communities for damages caused by wildlife. However, as is evident from Table 3.25, the transaction costs of claiming this compensation are too high and act as a disincentive to the local community to support biodiversity conservation efforts.

The table shows that there is no perfect correspondence between the proportion of households reporting wildlife damages and those who filed claims for compensation. While 38.4 per cent of the households reported damages caused by wildlife during 1999–2000, only 22.4 per cent of these households filed claims for compensation. The proportion of households reporting wildlife damages more or less varies positively with farm size. If we take note of the previous five years, it is seen that more than half of the sample households reported damages caused by wildlife. This proportion varies from over 25 per cent among small holdings of below 2.5 acres to around or over 90 per cent among holdings of 5 acres and above.

Table 3.25 *Particulars of compensation claimed for wildlife damages and transaction costs incurred to claim compensation by sample households during 1999–2000: Maldari, India*

Land holding class in acres	Per cent of sample households reporting wildlife damages		Per cent of sample households who filed claims for compensation	Amount of compensation	
	Last 5 years	During 1999–2000		Claimed	Received
				(Rs per reporting household)	
Below 2.5	25.4	11.9	5.1	1833	350
2.5–5	66.7	57.1	28.6	7167	20
5–10	93.3	66.7	26.7	5125	125
10 and above	90.0	63.3	50.0	16,733	1167
All	56.0	38.4	22.4	11,429	685

Land holding class in acres	Transaction cost for claiming compensation			Total[1] expenditure per Rupee of compensation realized
	No. of trips made per reporting household	Cost of time in terms of income forgone*	Total expenditure Rs/reporting household	
Below 2.5	7.3	735	450	3.4
2.5–5	6.3	877	1392	13.4
5–10	4.7	1540	1175	21.7
10 and above	4.1	2239	1504	3.2
All	5.0	1163	1320	3.6

Notes: * Assuming that one trip to the local forest office requires one human days work
1 Total expenditure here includes total expenses actually incurred plus cost of time in terms of income forgone for trips made to pursue the compensation claims.

The proportion of those who filed claims for compensation ranged from over 5 per cent among small holdings to around 50 per cent among large holdings of 10 acres and above. High transaction costs, ineligibility to receive compensation due to insecure titles to property, etc., are among the factors cited by some households as to why they did not file claims for compensation. The average amount of compensation claimed was Rs11,429 per reporting household. The amount actually received at the time of the survey was only Rs685 per reporting household (i.e. 6 per cent of the total amount claimed). However, given the general tendency to inflate compensation claims in the expectation of getting more compensation, it is quite possible that the amount claimed by the sample households towards wildlife damages may be on the high side. The State Forest Department have a set procedure to verify a compensation claim once an application is filed by an affected party. The local forest officials make an on-the-spot verification to assess the damages and, based on their report, decide on the amount of compensation to be paid in accordance with Forest regulations. Even so, it is distressing to note that to obtain compensation of Rs685 per reporting household, the coffee grower incurred an average expenditure of Rs1320 plus an average of five trips per reporting household, each valued at Rs1163 in terms of their forgone income to visit the local forest office to pursue their compensation claim. In other words, for every rupee of compensation actually realized, the coffee grower spent Rs3.6. Interestingly, while very large holdings spent Rs3.2 per rupee of compensation realized, among holdings of less than 10 acres these expenditures were considerably higher at Rs3.4–21.7 per rupee of compensation actually realized, which suggests that the costs of conservation borne by smaller holdings in this respect is much more than larger holdings. However, it may be noted that small farmers in particular, get tangible benefits such as non-timber forest products (NTFP) which is an incentive for conservation. Although we have not estimated the NTFP benefits appropriated by the sample households of Maldari from the reserve forests, the next chapter presents results of a sample survey of tribals living within and on the periphery of the Nagarhole National Park (close to Maldari village) which revealed the high dependence of the tribals on the reserve forests for NTFPs.

There are other external costs incurred by the sample households. During our field survey some farmers stated that they had stopped cultivating paddy (rice) during the last few years due to the frequent attacks and damage caused by wildlife, especially wild elephants and boar for whom paddy, apart from other crops like banana and tuber crops, are a favourite target. Out of 22 acres of paddy fields left fallow by our sample households, 15 acres (8.8 per cent of the paddy fields or 1.4 per cent of the total land holding) was left fallow to cope with wildlife attacks. The forgone rice output from these paddy fields was estimated at Rs900 per sample household per annum or Rs108.3/acre. These also constitute the social costs of wildlife conservation. When estimating the net benefits of coffee, these external costs were not included since these costs pertain to paddy. Moreover, it is also not proper to assume that these farmers will leave their paddy fields fallow for 50 years, the time horizon assumed by us for estimating the net benefits from coffee, and it is most likely that they will put these lands to alternate uses later on. This finding confirms that the decline in rice area observed in Kodagu district discussed in Chapter 2 is, apart from other factors, also a preventive measure undertaken by farmers to cope with the damages caused by wildlife to the paddy crop. According to some farmers, one reason why the frequency of wildlife attacks on farms and coffee estates has increased is that, apart from habitat loss, the buffer that traditionally used to be maintained between the coffee estates and forests has been encroached for growing coffee and other crops with the result that wildlife attacks on farms and coffee estates has increased in intensity over time.

The local community's perceptions and attitudes towards the environment and biodiversity conservation

As the villagers in Maldari village are incurring losses due to attacks by wildlife on their crops, it is important to elicit their views regarding biodiversity conservation and wildlife protection. This is important while soliciting the participation of the local people in measures for the conservation of biodiversity. For instance, Kotchen and Reiling (2000) observe that those with strong pro-environmental attitudes are more likely to be supportive of environmental conservation and provide legitimate yes/no responses in contingent valuation surveys, while those with weaker attitudes are more likely to protest hypothetical contingent valuation scenarios. We elicited the views of the villagers on the importance of environmental issues, asking whether biodiversity loss is an important environmental issue, about the importance of avoiding biodiversity loss at any cost and finally discussing the importance of conserving biodiversity.

The structure of the schedule used for eliciting the attitudes of the respondents in Maldari towards the environment and biodiversity conservation is indicated below. The first few questions in the schedule related to eliciting their attitudes towards environmental issues in general. After having elicited their attitudes towards environmental awareness, we dealt with the questions relating to their awareness of biodiversity loss and the importance of its conservation. Then the specific issue of elephant conservation was posed, since elephants are a keystone and vulnerable species in Asia and our study region, as noted earlier. Also the village is on the migration path of the elephants, known as elephant corridors, and the villagers reported their vulnerability due to frequent attacks on crops and property by elephants and other wild animals such as wild boar. Considering that the villagers are under constant threat from attacks by wild animals, it is very important to know whether they have any positive attitude towards, for example, elephant conservation. To obtain more reliable answers, we enlightened the respondents about the status of elephants in Asia and South India in particular, and then asked them whether they think it is important to conserve the elephants in such a situation.

- *According to the IUCN's Species Survival Commission's Asian Elephant Specialist Group, there are only 20,000 to 24,000 elephants surviving in India. In the Southern states of India (Karnataka, Tamil Nadu and Kerala) there are about 6000 elephants only. According to the Zoological Survey of India these animals are vulnerable in their status. Due to illicit killing for tusks the proportion of male elephants is declining. In this situation do you think it is important to conserve our wild elephants?*

The respondents were asked to exercise their option and indicate their 'Yes' or 'No' answers to the above question. We probed further in order to find out the reasons for both answers. From those who answered 'yes', the reasons for elephant conservation as perceived by the respondents were elicited: we presented the respondents with a set of six reasons as to why elephants need to be conserved and asked them to react and state the importance of the reason in their opinion. The reasons were then ranked in the order of importance as stated by the respondents.

Next we introduced to the respondent a hypothetical programme to improve elephant conservation.

> *The elephants require certain kind of habitat in order to survive. In recent years this habitat has been increasingly threatened due to different forms of human activities in the periphery of the forest. In order to arrest many of these activities, we have to educate ourselves. Moreover, there is a need for promoting participatory forest protection in the fringe area of the forest. To ensure the existence of elephants in the Western Ghats for the future generation (say your kith and kin), if a reliable organization were to take up such a programme, would you be willing to participate with them.*

For those respondents who agreed to cooperate with the elephant conservation programme, we provided three institutional set-ups to choose from for implementing the proposed conservation programme: (i) a decentralized governmental organization, (ii) a non-governmental organization and (iii) willingness to be involved irrespective of the institutional set-up. For all three institutional alternatives, the respondent's willingness to pay in cash or the willingness to pay in terms of spending time for participatory elephant conservation activities was estimated. Finally, from those who were not willing to cooperate with the participatory conservation programme, we asked their reasons. In addition, information about their socio-economic characteristics was also collected.

It is heartening to note that a majority of the households responded positively towards these questions. As is evident from Table 3.26, only a very few households expressed indifferent attitudes towards these questions. Almost 99.2 per cent of the households agreed that it is important to conserve biodiversity and 97.6 per cent agreed that environmental issues are very important and need to be addressed seriously. Around 90 per cent of the households agreed that biodiversity loss is an important environmental issue. About 88 per cent of the respondents expressed the opinion that biodiversity loss should be avoided at any cost. However, 12 per cent of the respondents did not concur with this and expressed their indifferent attitude or said that avoiding biodiversity loss at any cost is not an important issue for them.

It is significant to note that the overwhelming majority of households belonging to all land holding groups reported a positive attitude towards environmental issues in general, and biodiversity conservation in particular.

After presenting the issues concerning biodiversity conservation before the respondents, we concentrated on the specific reasons for its conservation. For this we considered the respondents who responded positively towards the need for the conservation of biodiversity. We presented them with a set of reasons justifying

Table 3.26 *Attitude of the sample respondents in Maldari village towards environmental/biodiversity conservation issues (in percentages)*

Issues / Land holding class in acres	Attitudes: Important	Not important or indifferent	Total
Environmental issues			
Below 2.5	96.6	3.4	100
2.5–5	95.2	4.8	100
5–10	100.0	–	100
10 and above	100.0	–	100
Total	97.6	24.3	100
Biodiversity loss			
Below 2.5	81.4	18.6	100
2.5–5	90.5	9.5	100
5–10	100	–	100
10 and above	100	–	100
Total	89.6	10.4	100
Avoidance of biodiversity loss at any cost			100
Below 2.5	81.4	18.6	100
2.5–5	90.5	9.5	100
5–10	93.3	6.7	100
10 and above	96.7	3.3	100
Total	88.0	12.0	
Conservation of biodiversity			
Below 2.5	100.0	–	100
2.5–5	95.2	4.8	100
5–10	100.0	–	100
10 and above	100.0	–	100
Total	99.2	0.8	100

biodiversity conservation such as: the existence of biodiversity keeps ecosystems stable and functioning; it has ritual and cultural value in our lives; biodiversity has aesthetic and recreational value; we have to conserve it for future generations; we may find new uses for biodiversity in the future; and it is a major source of livelihood for many of us. At first we asked the respondents to react to these various reasons for the conservation of biodiversity and state whether these reasons are important or not, and finally we asked them to rank the reasons for biodiversity conservation in order of importance as perceived by them. Table 3.27 presents the ranks assigned by the sample households towards the important reasons for biodiversity conservation.

Of the 125 sample households, 120 responded positively regarding the role of biodiversity in keeping the ecosystem stable and functioning, followed by 116 households who considered its importance as a source of livelihood and 114 households stated that it is important to preserve biodiversity for the sake of future generations. When we considered the percentage of respondents who assigned the top three ranks to the various reasons for the conservation of biodiversity,

Table 3.27 *Ranking of reasons for biodiversity conservation stated by the sample households in Maldari*

Reasons	Rank 1	Rank 2	Rank 3	Rank 4	Rank 5	Rank 6	Total
Keeping ecosystem stable and functioning	31 (25.8)	38 (31.7)	26 (21.7)	13 (10.8)	7 (5.8)	5 (4.2)	120 (100)
Ritual and cultural value in our lives	7 (8.9)	6 (7.6)	9 (11.4)	14 (17.7)	25 (31.6)	18 (22.9)	79 (100)
Aesthetical and recreational value	3 (3.9)	4 (5.3)	9 (11.8)	26 (34.2)	19 (25.0)	15 (19.7)	76 (100)
Important for future generations	45 (39.5)	34 (29.8)	27 (23.7)	3 (2.6)	4 (3.5)	1 (0.9)	114 (100)
Important for developing new products in future	2 (2.0)	25 (24.5)	32 (31.4)	28 (27.5)	11 (10.8)	4 (3.9)	102 (10)
Important as a source of livelihood	32 (27.6)	11 (9.5)	14 (12.1)	19 (16.4)	19 (16.4)	21 (18.1)	116 (100)

Note: Figures in parentheses are percentages of row totals

the most highly rated were the following. Around 93 per cent of the respondents assigned first, second or third rank to the importance of conserving biodiversity for future generations, 79.2 per cent for the ecosystem functions of biodiversity, followed by 49.2 per cent for its livelihood functions. The other reasons were considered by the respondents to be of secondary importance. Thus, for the villagers in Maldari, the primary importance for conserving biodiversity is for the sake of future generations, for keeping the ecosystem stable and functioning, and as a source of livelihood.

It is interesting to note the responses of the villagers on the question of elephant conservation. In spite of all the damage caused to their crops by elephant attacks, 94.4 per cent of the households agreed that it is important to conserve the wild elephant (Table 3.28).

We tried to explore the reasons why they consider the conservation of elephants important. We presented the respondents with various reasons for elephant conservation and asked them to state whether these reasons are important

Table 3.28 *Attitude of the sample households in Maldari towards the conservation of elephants (in percentages)*

Land holding class in acres	Important	Not important or indifferent	Total
Below 2.5	94.9	5.1	100
2.5–5	90.5	9.5	100
5–10	93.3	6.7	100
10 and above	96.7	3.3	100
All	94.4	4.0	100

or not in their opinion. We asked the respondents to rank in order of importance those reasons that they considered important.

Of the various reasons presented, most of the respondents reacted positively (Table 3.29). Only a very few showed an indifferent attitude towards elephant

Table 3.29 *Attitude of the sample households in Maldari towards elephant conservation issues (in percentages)*

Land holding class in acres / Reasons	Attitudes: Important	Not important	Indifferent	Total
Elephants are beautiful animals				
Below 2.5	91.5	3.4	5.1	100
2.5–5	85.7	—	14.3	100
5–10	93.3	6.7	—	100
10 and above	80.0	13.3	6.7	100
Total	88.0	5.6	6.4	100
It has its own right to exist				
Below 2.5	94.9	—	5.1	100
2.5–5	90.5	—	9.5	100
5–10	100.0	—	—	100
10 and above	93.3	—	6.7	100
Total	94.4	—	5.6	100
It has educational value				
Below 2.5	15.3	79.7	5.0	100
2.5–5	38.1	47.6	14.3	100
5–10	60.0	33.3	6.7	100
10 and above	70.0	23.3	6.7	100
Total	37.6	55.2	7.2	100
Useful for domestic work				
Below 2.5	88.1	6.8	5.1	100
2.5–5	85.7	—	14.3	100
5–10	93.3	—	6.7	100
10 and above	86.7	10.0	3.3	100
Total	88.0	5.6	6.4	100
We may find new uses for elephants in the future				
Below 2.5	49.2	45.8	5.0	100
2.5–5	76.2	9.5	14.3	100
5–10	80.0	13.3	6.7	100
10 and above	60.0	33.3	6.7	100
Total	60.0	32.8	7.2	100
It has spiritual value in our lives				
Below 2.5	30.5	61.0	8.5	100
2.5–10	38.1	47.6	14.3	100
5–10	66.7	20.0	13.3	100
10 and above	56.7	30.0	13.3	100
Total	42.4	46.4	11.2	100

conservation. It is interesting to note that over 94 per cent of the sample respondents emphasized the elephants' right of existence. Around 88 per cent emphasized the aesthetic value of elephants, that is that elephants are very beautiful animals and therefore need to be conserved. Similarly, around 88 per cent of the respondents stressed the use value of elephants for domestic work (for example, transporting logs or in temple rituals) as a justification for elephant conservation. About 60 per cent of the respondents emphasized their option value, that is that we may find new uses of elephants in future (e.g. in developing new drugs). Other reasons, such as elephants' spiritual and educational value were considered as relatively less important factors favouring elephant conservation.

The respondents were also asked to rank the reasons for conserving elephants in order of importance. Table 3.30 indicates that the maximum number of households, 118, emphasized the rights of elephants to exist, followed by 110 households which stressed their aesthetic value and usefulness for domestic work. About 74 households also emphasized their option value. Among the households who stressed the right of elephants to exist, about 96 per cent ranked this reason to support elephant conservation in the top three places. Between 83–86 per cent of households who stressed the aesthetic value and the usefulness of elephants for domestic work ranked these two reasons to justify elephant conservation in the top three.

Table 3.30 *Ranking of reasons stated by sample respondents in Maldari village for the conservation of elephants*

Reasons	Rank 1	Rank 2	Rank 3	Rank 4	Rank 5	Rank 6	Total
Elephants are beautiful animals	10 (9.1)	49 (44.6)	34 (30.6)	9 (8.2)	6 (5.4)	2 (1.8)	110 (100)
Elephants have their own right to exist	79 (67.0)	24 (20.3)	10 (8.5)	2 (1.7)	1 (0.8)	2 (1.7)	118 (100)
Elephants have educational value	1 (2.1)	5 (10.4)	7 (14.6)	10 (20.8)	14 (29.2)	11 (22.9)	48 (100)
Elephants are useful for domestic work	24 (21.8)	32 (29.1)	39 (35.4)	13 (11.8)	2 (1.8)	0 (0.0)	110 (100)
We may find new uses of elephants in future	1 (1.3)	5 (6.8)	11 (14.9)	44 (59.5)	12 (1.62)	1 (1.3)	74 (100)
The elephant has spiritual value	1 (1.9)	6 (11.3)	6 (11.3)	22 (41.5)	15 (28.3)	3 (5.7)	53 (100)

Note: Figures in the parentheses are percentages of row totals.

Valuing the local community's preferences for biodiversity conservation

Notwithstanding the disincentives and costs borne by the local community for biodiversity conservation, it is heartening to note that a majority of the sample households had a positive attitude towards biodiversity conservation in general and wildlife protection in particular. As seen earlier, when asked to rank the reasons for biodiversity conservation, a majority of the households (i.e. 36 per cent) assigned first rank to its importance for future generations, followed by its livelihood function (26 per cent), and its ecosystem functions (25 per cent). When asked to rank the reasons why elephants, a keystone and threatened species in the study region, need to be conserved, a majority of the households emphasized its right to existence, its aesthetic value, its livelihood functions and its option value. The contingent valuation method (CVM) has been widely used to value public goods such as biodiversity. What it really measures is people's value preferences for biodiversity conservation. Hence, an attempt is made here to estimate the local community's willingness to pay (WTP) for participatory biodiversity conservation. To this end, we provided two options for the respondents, one was the willingness to pay in cash and the other was the willingness to pay in terms of spending time on participatory elephant conservation. For the CVM study, the elephant was taken up for an in-depth case study, as stated earlier. Elephants have a significant impact on plant composition due to their large and varied diet, their physical impact on their surroundings, and their ability to move large distances (Mendelssohn, 1999). From the conservationist's perspective, this focus is rationalized by the frequently inseparable nature of the subject good from its biosphere and supporting species links. In other words, the purchase of a good offered in a CV exercise often implies purchase of a complementary bundle of biodiversity (Moran, 1994). In conducting the CVM survey all the guidelines suggested by the NOAA Panel (1993) in the US were taken into account (i.e. pre-testing of schedules, canvassing through personal interview, sufficient sample size, etc.). The respondents in the sample village were asked (using discrete choice method) to indicate the amount they were willing to pay in cash or the time they were willing to spend on participatory elephant conservation such as participating in environmental awareness campaigns, providing voluntary labour for elephant proof trenching, and forest fire protection measures, etc. Although elephant proof trenching is primarily undertaken to prevent the entry of wild elephants and other wild animals into coffee estates and agricultural lands, it also helps to prevent cattle owned by farmers and others from intruding into forests for grazing. The intrusion of cattle into protected areas also puts wild animals at risk of contracting communicable diseases such as rinderpest from domestic cattle. Interestingly Table 3.31 indicates that while only around 8.9 per cent of the sample households in Maldari were willing to pay in terms of cash, and 2.4 per cent in terms of both

Table 3.31 *Per cent distribution of sample households in Maldari indicating their willingness to pay or not to pay for participatory elephant conservation*

Land holding class in acres	Willingness to pay for participatory elephant conservation in terms of				Total	
	Cash only	Time only	Both cash and time	Not willing	%	No. of observations
			(% to total households)			
Below 2.5	6.8	84.7	—	8.5	100	59
2.5–5	4.8	85.7	—	9.5	100	21
5–10	6.7	86.7	6.7	—	100	15
10 and above	17.2	65.6	6.9	10.3	100	29
All	8.9	80.6	2.4	8.1	100	124

cash and time, over 80.6 per cent of the households were willing to pay in terms of spending time for participatory elephant conservation activities. This proportion ranges from 84.7 to 86.7 per cent among the households with holdings up to 10 acres and thereafter declines to around 65.6 per cent among those with holdings of 10 acres and above. About a quarter of the very large holdings are willing to pay in terms of cash only or both cash and time. Approximately 8 per cent of the sample households expressed their non-willingness to pay for participatory elephant conservation activities. The reasons behind these protest responses were: it is the duty of the government [to conserve elephants]; elephants are destroying our crops; elephants are a threat to human life; and preservation of elephants is not important to me. Of the total sample households, only 14 expressed their willingness to pay in terms of cash for participatory elephant conservation. On average the amount that these households were willing to pay was Rs555 per reporting household per annum. This figure was Rs170–767 per reporting household per annum across different land holding groups.

A majority of the sample households in Maldari expressed their willingness to pay in terms of spending time on participatory elephant conservation. To estimate the opportunity cost of time spent for participatory elephant conservation in terms of the income forgone, we used the monthly income as reported by the respondents in the survey. These were converted into a per day basis and then multiplied by the number of human days that the sample respondents were willing to spend on elephant conservation. Table 3.32 indicates that on average the sample households were willing to spend 25.8 human days per household annually for participatory elephant conservation. In terms of the income forgone calculated as stated above, this worked out to over Rs6000 per household per annum. This figure varied positively with farm size due to income differentials across different land holding groups.

There are no comparable estimates of the willingness to pay for conservation of wild Asian elephants in India against which we could assess our estimates. As

Table 3.32 *Willingness to pay in terms of spending time for participatory elephant conservation: Maldari, India*

Land holding class in acres	Willingness to pay in terms of time for participatory elephant conservation		Opportunity cost of time in terms of income forgone (Rs/household/annum)
	Hours per week per household	Human days per household per annum	
Below 2.5	3.8	24.8	2491.8
2.5–5	4.9	31.8	4435.1
5–10	3.7	23.8	7817.2
10 and above	3.8	24.4	13,346.3
All	4.0	25.8	6003.4

noted earlier, Dixon and Sherman (1990, 1991) estimated the option and existence values of wild Asian elephants in Khao Yai National Park, Thailand to Thai residents at about 122million Baht, (approximately US$4,700,000 (1990–1991 US$)). The Park users' average maximum willingness to pay was estimated at 181 Baht (or US$7) per park user. A more recent study by Bandara and Tisdell (2003), who estimated the willingness to pay for the conservation of wild Asian elephants in Sri Lanka by urban residents of Colombo, Sri Lanka, noted that they were willing to pay about Sri Lankan Rupees 1322 per annum over the next five years for the conservation of wild Asian elephants. While users (those urban residents who had visited national parks or sanctuaries), were willing to pay Rupees 1648.56 per annum over the next five years for the conservation of wild Asian elephants, for non-users (those urban residents who had never visited a national park or sanctuary), this figure was Rupees 995.52 per annum (Bandara and Tisdell, 2003). The study also noted that 62 per cent of the WTP estimate was attributable to non-use values of wild Asian elephants. However, our estimates and those of Bandara and Tisdell (2003) differ in two important respects. While our WTP estimates pertain to a local community; that of Bandara and Tisdell (2003) pertains to urban residents. Moreover, the payment vehicle in our case is in terms of the willingness to spend time for participatory elephant conservation, whereas in the Bandara and Tisdell study it is in terms of the willingness to pay in cash over the next five years. Another study by Jyothis (2002) estimated the willingness to pay for biodiversity conservation in the Periyar Tiger Reserve located in the Western Ghats region in Kerala State, India. Although the focus of the CVM survey here was on biodiversity conservation in general and royal Bengal tigers, an endangered and umbrella species, in particular, it may be noted that the Periyar Tiger Reserve is also an important elephant habitat in Southern India. This study estimated the local community's mean WTP for biodiversity conservation in the Periyar Tiger Reserve at Rs162.68 per household, and of urban residents of Kerala state at Rs128 per respondent (Jyothis, 2002).

The respondents were also asked to indicate their preferences and choose between three institutional alternatives while stating their willingness to pay in

Table 3.33 *Per cent distribution of sample households in Maldari indicating their preference for an institutional set up for participatory elephant conservation*

Land holding class in acres	Preferred institution for participatory elephant conservation			Total	
	DGO	NGO	Irrespective of the institutions	%	No. of observations
Below 2.5	94.4	5.6	—	100	54
2.5–5	84.2	15.8	—	100	19
5–10	40.0	46.7	13.3	100	15
10 and above	38.5	46.2	15.4	100	26
All	72.8	21.9	5.3	100	114

Note: DGO = decentralized government organization; NGO = non-governmental organization.

terms of spending time for participatory elephant conservation. These alternatives were the Decentralized Government Organisation (DGO), Non-Governmental Organization (NGO), and willingness to be involved irrespective of the institution. The responses stated by the sample households is indicated in Table 3.33, which reveals there is a clear preference for DGOs compared to other institutional alternatives among the sample households, with 72.8 per cent of the households indicating this preference for participatory elephant conservation. This proportion varies inversely with farm size ranging from over 94 per cent among small holdings of below 2.5 acres to 38.5 per cent among very large holdings with 10 acres and above. Approximately 22 per cent of the sample households preferred NGOs for participatory elephant conservation. Interestingly, among large holdings of 5 acres and above a relatively higher proportion of households preferred NGOs, when compared to other institutional alternatives.

To evaluate the variables influencing the respondents' 'Yes' or 'No' responses, a logit model was used. The definition and summary statistics of the variables used in the logit function are indicated in Table 3.34.

Table 3.34 *Definition and summary statistics of independent variables used in logit function*

Variables	Minimum	Maximum	Mean	Standard deviation
Land holding in acres	0.03	82.00	7.13	12.83
Household size	1.00	11.00	5.12	2.18
Settler (dummy variable where settler = 1; otherwise 0)	0.00	1.00	0.52	0.50
Age of respondent	15.00	86.00	44.38	13.62
Education of respondent	1.00	6.00	2.95	1.50
DGO (dummy variable where DGO = 1; otherwise 0)	0.00	1.00	0.68	0.47

Table 3.35 *Maximum likelihood estimates using logit model of willingness to pay (i.e. spend time) for participatory elephant conservation: Maldari, India*

Variables	Coefficient	Standard error	t-ratio
Constant	2.835***	1.480	1.916
Land holding	−0.042***	0.022	−1.894
Household size	−0.029ns	0.135	−0.213
Settler	1.398**	0.607	2.303
Age of respondent	−0.009ns	0.020	−0.464
Education of respondent	−0.452**	0.199	−2.270
DGO	1.016***	0.585	1.737
Likelihood ratio index	0.22		
Chi-squared (6)	24.94		
Per cent correct prediction	86.29		
Significance level	0.0003		
No. of observations	124		

Note: **, ***, indicates statistically significant at 5 and 10 per cent levels of significance respectively; ns = not statistically significant at the above levels of significance.

Table 3.35 which presents the maximum likelihood estimates of the parameters in the logit function suggests that land holding and educational levels are negatively and significantly related with the dependent variable. This indicates those with bigger land holdings are less likely to say 'Yes' to spending time on participatory elephant conservation, and that this is also true of people with more education. However, it may be noted that some of the big land holdings that indicated their inability to spend time on participatory elephant conservation, expressed their willingness to pay in terms of cash. As seen earlier, the (external) costs of conservation and transaction costs incurred by smaller holdings was higher than for larger holdings which explains why they are more likely to say 'Yes' to the WTP bid. Interestingly, the settler variable is positive and significant which indicates that settlers (unlike migrants) have a higher probability of saying 'Yes' to spending time on participatory elephant conservation. The results also show that there is a clear preference among the respondents for a DGO rather than other institutional alternatives to organize participatory conservation, possibly because respondents feel that transparency, accountability and a sense of participation is better under a decentralized government set-up. The estimated model is highly significant with a likelihood ratio test of the hypothesis that the 6 coefficients are zero based on a chi-square value of 24.94. The likelihood ratio index is 0.22 (analogue to R^2 in OLS) which is a good fit for cross sectional data. The per cent correct prediction is 86.29.

Summary

The opportunity costs of biodiversity conservation in terms of the coffee benefits forgone are quite high. Even after including external costs due to wildlife damage and expenditure on defensive measures against wildlife attacks, the net benefits from coffee for all land holding groups are high. The NPVs range from Rs17,000 to over Rs106,000 per acre at 12 per cent discount rate, and the IRRs range is 16–23 per cent. If expected benefits were to fall by 20 per cent and costs rise by a similar percentage the NPVs, BC ratios and IRRs from coffee are still quite high and significant, with the IRRs in the range 19.5–20.1 per cent. The study shows that the external costs incurred by the coffee growers due to wildlife conservation are quite significant and account for 7–15 per cent of the total discounted costs of coffee. Interestingly, smaller holdings incurred higher external costs than larger holdings. Although the state has been operating a scheme to compensate farmers for wildlife damage costs, the analysis shows that not only are the transaction costs to claim this compensation too high but also holdings below 10 acres proportionally incurred higher transaction costs for claiming the compensation, which acts as a disincentive to biodiversity conservation. The fact that coffee prices have risen faster since 1980 is a further disincentive to biodiversity conservation. Notwithstanding these disincentives, it is heartening to note that the local community had a positive attitude towards biodiversity conservation. They felt that biodiversity should be conserved due to its bequest value, ecosystem and livelihood functions and option value. Elephants – a keystone and threatened species in the study region – were taken as a case study to analyse the local community's attitude and value preference for biodiversity conservation. The existence value of elephants, their aesthetic and use value for domestic work were the reasons emphasized by the local community to justify elephant conservation. A majority of the respondents expressed their willingness to pay in terms of spending time for participatory elephant conservation. On average, the sample respondents were willing to spend 25.8 human days per household per annum on participatory elephant conservation. The opportunity cost of time in terms of their income forgone was estimated at over Rs6000 per household per annum. Most interesting is that the local community expressed a clear preference for decentralized government institutions to be involved in participatory biodiversity conservation. This suggests that a decentralized and participatory based strategy for biodiversity conservation promises to be more effective than other institutional alternatives.

4

Nagarhole – The Context of Tribal Villages Located Within and Near a National Park

Introduction

Tribal and indigenous communities have maintained a symbiotic relationship with forests from time immemorial. Not only their economic but also their social and cultural life has been centred around forests. Whether tribals, especially those who practice swidden or shifting cultivation, are the scourge of forests as argued by foresters, or are critical to conserving forest resources and biodiversity as contended by anthropologists and ecologists is a debatable point. While traditional approaches to conserving biodiversity and wildlife have sought to exclude tribals and local communities from conservation programmes, more recent approaches acknowledge their critical role and hence emphasize community-based conservation strategies (e.g. Emerton, 1999a). The case study taken up in this chapter, therefore, seeks to analyse the economic and other aspects of biodiversity conservation from the perspective of tribal communities living inside and on the fringe or periphery of a national park.

The specific national park selected for the case study is the Rajiv Gandhi National Park, or Nagarhole National Park as it is more popularly known, which is one of several wildlife parks and sanctuaries located in the bio-rich Western Ghat region of India. This national park is also one among seven national parks and sanctuaries in India covered under the India Eco-development Project (October 1996 to September 2001) funded by the World Bank. The commencement of the project was, however, delayed by two years and only began in 1998. Under the project, special efforts have been made to promote participatory-based biodiversity conservation (World Bank, 1996). These measures include offering support for the voluntary relocation of the tribal households residing in settlements within the national park to areas outside the national park boundary. The Government of India under the Centrally-sponsored Beneficiary Oriented Scheme for Tribal Development (BOTD) offered a generous rehabilitation package consisting of

5 acres of farm land and a dwelling house per family, drinking water facilities, agricultural inputs, a maintenance grant of Rs1000 per family per month during the transition period for 9 months, plus other benefits, to those tribal households living within the national park willing to relocate to rehabilitated settlements outside the national park limits. The Eco-development Project caused unrest among a section of tribals and NGOs who viewed the project with suspicion especially as it was felt that its implementation would result in the displacement of tribals living inside the national park to settlements outside the park. Although the World Bank Project document stipulated that such effort had to be strictly voluntary and that there would be no element of compulsion in this exercise, a section of the tribals still had misgivings about the project and the government's intentions. Biodiversity conservation strategies, therefore, also need to look into the social implications of conservation strategies, as well as the economic issues. The Nagarhole National Park where the Eco-development Project was implemented is, therefore, well suited for studying the economic and social aspects of biodiversity conservation from the perspective of tribal communities.

Apart from examining the uses and economic values derived by the tribal communities from the Nagarhole National Park, the study will also analyse the perceptions and attitudes of the tribals towards biodiversity conservation in general, and wildlife protection in particular, taking the case of elephants, a keystone and threatened species, in the study area for an in-depth study, for reasons stated in Chapter 3. In addition, the study will analyse the value preferences of the local tribal communities for biodiversity conservation by studying their willingness to accept the compensation (i.e. rehabilitation package) offered by the government and relocate outside the national park, and the socio-economic factors influencing their responses. The reasons why the tribals are not accepting the rehabilitation package are also examined. Before analysing our data, some background information and the importance of the Nagarhole National Park are presented in the next section.

Nagarhole National Park

The Nagarhole National Park, renamed as Rajiv Gandhi National Park in 1992 after the late Indian Prime Minister, was initially established as a game sanctuary in 1955 covering the 285km^2 forests around the Nagarhole settlement. Subsequently the Nagarhole Wildlife Sanctuary was enlarged by including the Mysore forests and was notified as a National Park in the year 1975. The park presently covers an area of 643.39km^2, with a core zone of 192km^2 and a tourism zone of 110km^2, and forms part of the 4500km^2 Nilgiri Biosphere Reserve. The Nagarhole National Park falls within Hunsur, H. D. Kote and Periyapatna taluks (administrative units below a district) of Mysore district, and Virajpet taluk of Kodagu district in Karnataka state. Of the national park's total area 354.95km^2

falls within Mysore district, and 288.44km² in Kodagu district (Appayya, 2001). The park is located between 11°50′–12°15′ north latitude and 76°0′–76°15′ east longitude. The national park is bounded in the north by the Kabini river, in the south by the Kabini reservoir (which demarcates Nagarhole National Park from the neighbouring Bandipur National Park, also in Karnataka state), in the south-west by the Wynad Wildlife Sanctuary in Kerala state, and in the west by coffee and cardamom plantations which separate the park from the Brahmagiri Wildlife Sanctuary in Kodagu district of Karnataka. The name of the national park derives from the combination of two words in the local Kannada language: '*Nagar*' meaning 'snake' and '*Hole*' meaning 'streams'. This stems from the fact that a number of serpentine streams flow through the national park and also one of the important rivers in the park is named Nagarhole. The Kakanaanakote forests located in the southern part of the park were also famed for being the exclusive hunting ground of the erstwhile Maharajas (Kings) of the princely Mysore state. In fact the spectacular *Khedda* (stockade) system of capturing wild elephants pioneered by a British officer, G. P. Sanderson, in the latter half of the 19th century was undertaken in the Kakanaanakote forests which now falls within the Nagarhole National Park. It is reported that between 1891 and 1971, 1902 elephants were captured through *Khedda* operations (Appayya, 2001).

The landscape of the national park is generally characterized by gentle slopes and shallow valleys. The altitude is in the range 701–959m. Rainfall in the area is 900–1200 mm and temperatures fall between 17° and 30°C. There are three broad seasons: the wet season or monsoons (June–September), the cool season or winter (October–January) and the hot season or summer (February–May). There are two main types of vegetation: moist deciduous forests found in the northern and western parts of the national park, and dry deciduous forests in the south-eastern part. There are also patches of semi-evergreen forests in the western sheltered parts of the national park, and teak plantations and scrub forests in the eastern part of the park. Another unique feature of this national park is the presence of numerous open grassy swamps locally known as *hadlus*, which attract wild animals for water and forage, especially during the summer months. The national park is endowed by several perennial and seasonal streams which drain into the major rivers of the park: Kabini, Lakshmana Teertha and Nagarhole (World Bank, 1996).

The Nagarhole National Park is considered to be one of the finest wildlife sanctuaries in India that is rich in flora and fauna. The national park also contains species on the endangered list such as the tiger (*Panthera tigris*) and Asiatic elephant (*Elephas maximus*). In fact in recognition of its importance as an elephant habitat, the Nagarhole National Park was included under Project Elephant initiated by the Government of India in 1991–1992, whereby special efforts were made to conserve important elephant habitats in India by giving financial, technical and scientific support to state governments. Similarly Project Tiger was initiated in India from 1 April, 1973, whereby special efforts were made to conserve tiger habitats and improve the tiger population in the country. In 2003 Nagarhole

Table 4.1 *Estimates of wildlife population of selected wildlife species in Nagarhole National Park according to the Wildlife Census for the years 1993–1994, 1997–1998 and 2001–2002*

Wildlife species	1993–1994	1997–1998	2001–2002
	Estimated approximate number		
Tiger	53	55	55–60
Leopard	15	–	25–30
Elephant	1448	1707	1500–1600
Wild buffalo (Indian bison)	368	1170	1000–1100
Spotted deer		1164	7000–8000
Sambar		96	300–325
Barking deer		61	
Wild sheep			60–65
Langur		352	700–750
Wild boar			900–1000

Source: For 1993–1994 and 1997–1998 figures, Appayya (2001). Wildlife Census 2001–2002, Deputy Conservator of Forests, Hunsur Wildlife Division, Government of Karnataka

National Park was also added to the list of National Parks and Tiger Reserves covered under Project Tiger. Other important wildlife species found in the Nagarhole National Park include predators such as leopard, Indian wild dog (Dhole or *Cuon alpinus*), sloth bear (*Melursus ursinus*), jackal (*Canis aureus*), hyena (*Hyaena hyaena*) and herbivores such as spotted deer (chital), sambar, barking deer, mouse deer (*Tragulus meminna*), four horned antelope (*Tetracerus quardricornis*), gaur (Indian bison, *Bos gaurus*) and wild boar (*Sus scrofa*). Wildlife population estimates of selected species for Nagarhole National Park collected during the Wildlife Census Years of 1993–1994, 1997–1998 and 2001–2002 indicate the diversity and richness of the fauna of the national park, and also a favourable predator–prey ratio (see Table 4.1).

According to the Deputy Conservator of Forests, Hunsur Wildlife Division that oversees the Nagarhole National Park (as stated to the author on 23 March, 2004 during an interview), the elephant density of the national park is roughly 2–3 elephants per km². It is also stated that the Nagarhole National Park has a favourable bull to female elephant ratio, with 1 bull per 3 female elephants. Research undertaken under the Karnataka Tiger Conservation Project using camera trappings over the period 1998–2001 estimated the density of tigers in the Nagarhole National Park to range between 7.8–15.2 tigers per 100km² as against 12 tigers per 100km² in the adjoining Bandipur National Park (in 1999), and similarly 3–4 tigers in Bhadra Wildlife Sanctuary during 1997 (Karanth et al, 2001). Estimates of tiger and prey densities in the Nagarhole National Park over the period 1998–2000 by Karanth et al (2001) are presented in Table 4.2 and also

Table 4.2 *Estimated density (mean values) of tigers and prey population in Nagarhole National Park during 1998–2000 made by the Karnataka Tiger Conservation Project*

Wildlife species	Scientific name	1998	1999	2000
		(Number of animals per 100km²)		
Tiger	*Panthera tigris*	7.8	13.2	15.2
		(1.48)	(2.09)	(2.53)
Prey population				
Chital (spotted deer)	*Axis axis*	3610	2800	4280
		(3.46)	(3.07)	(4.05)
Sambar	*Cervus unicolor*	410	550	530
		(0.59)	(0.65)	(0.69)
Muntjac (barking deer)	*Muntiacus muntjac*	520	260	320
		(0.55)	(0.38)	(0.45)
Gaur (Indian bison)	*Bos gaurus*	1130	960	420
		(2.06)	(1.51)	(0.77)
Wild pig (wild boar)	*Sus scrofa*	280	360	450
		(0.52)	(0.62)	(1.03)
Langur	*Presbytis entellus*	3210	3980	3340
		(2.49)	(3.01)	(1.79)
Bonnet monkey	*Macaca radiata*	430	600	450
		(0.89)	(1.15)	(0.68)
All prey	–	9590	9510	9790

Notes: Estimates of tiger population are based on camera-trap capture recapture surveys over the period 1998–2000; estimates of prey population are based on line transect surveys during the same period.

Figures in parentheses are the standard errors.

This research was undertaken as part of the Karnataka Tiger Conservation Project funded by Wildlife Conservation Society, New York and other NGOs in collaboration with the Karnataka State Forest Department.

Source: Karanth et al (2001)

seem to indicate a favourable predator–prey ratio in the park. The national park is also noteworthy for its rich avian species and reptiles. Over 250 species of birds, such as the blue-bearded bee eater, scarlet minivet, Malabar whistling thrush, adjutant stork and osprey, and reptiles such as the marsh crocodile, monitor lizard and rock python are found in the Nagarhole National Park.

The biodiversity of the national park is facing threats and immense pressure due to anthropogenic and other factors. According to government reports, the Nagarhole National Park has 54 tribal settlements inside the park, comprising 1568 families with a population of 6254 persons. The park is surrounded by 96 villages with a population of 66,507 in the fringe areas of the park up to a distance of 2km from the border and they also maintain a large (5000) population of cattle (Dyavaiah, 2000). According to the Deputy Conservator of Forests, Hunsur

Wildlife Division, under whose jurisdiction Nagarhole National Park falls, as of March 2004 there were 1668 families with a population of about 10,000 persons residing in 45 tribal hamlets inside the Nagarhole National Park limits. In addition, there is also a population of approximately 200,000 persons on the periphery within a 5km radius of the national park limits. The tribes of Nagarhole are *Jenu Kurubas* (honey gatherers), *Betta Kurubas* (hill tribes), *Hakki-Pikki* (bird trappers) and *Yeravas* (hill tribes). These tribes dwelling inside the park collect non-timber forest products (NTFPs) from the park and also supplement their income by working as seasonal labour on coffee estates, especially during the coffee planting and picking seasons, or for the forest department, and in a number of other areas of casual employment. For instance, the Deputy Conservator of Forests in charge of the Nagarhole National Park stated during an interview with the author on 23 March, 2004, that approximately 125 tribals were employed by the park authorities in anti-poaching groups, and another 350 tribals were employed seasonally during the summer months (approximately 90 days in a year) for fire protection work in the national park. In addition, the park authorities employed the tribals as Forest Watchers, and two persons per elephant to look after a number of tame elephants maintained by the park authorities. It is reported that about 90 per cent of the people residing in the villages on the fringe and periphery of the national park practise agriculture and some are even growing crops such as *ragi* (finger millet), rice, root crops, etc., and/or grazing their cattle inside the park. In short, the communities living inside the Nagarhole National Park and the villagers living around the park depend on the forest to meet their various livelihood needs. The villagers are also under constant threat due to attacks by wild animals on humans, livestock and crops.

This national park has witnessed tribal unrest after the formation of the park and the rehabilitation programme initiated thereafter. When the establishment of protected areas limit the traditional rights and access of the local population they have very little incentive to cooperate with biodiversity conservation measures. The India Eco-development Project mentioned earlier aims to conserve biodiversity by addressing both the impact of local people on the protected areas and the impact of the protected areas on the local people (World Bank, 1996). Thus the eco-development strategy has two main thrusts: improvement of protected area management and the involvement of local people. In doing so, it seeks to improve the capacity of protected area management to conserve biodiversity effectively, to involve local people in protected area planning and protection, to develop incentives for conservation, and to support sustainable alternatives to the harmful use of resources (World Bank 1996). The Eco-development Project was implemented in the Nagarhole National Park over the period 1997–1998 to 2001–2002 with a budget of Rs394.39 million (Dyavaiah, 2000). Under the terms of the Indian Wildlife (Protection) Act of 1972 settlements within a national park are considered illegal. Although there were around 1550 households in the Nagarhole National Park, up to June 2000 when our field survey was conducted, only 50 tribal households had accepted the rehabilitation package offered by the government and relocated to Nagapura Resettlement village outside the national park area. Subsequently another 154 tribal households living within the national park limits were rehabilitated making a total of 204 tribal households who had accepted the rehabilitation package offered by the government and relocated to five blocks of Nagapura village as of March 2002. The sample tribal households surveyed by us in Nagapura are now identified as Nagapura Ist Block residents, whereas tribals who resettled in subsequent phases were relocated to IInd–Vth Blocks of Nagapura Resettlement Village. While the Nagapura Ist Block settlement (our sample) is located about 3km from the national park boundary, the IInd–Vth Block settlements of Nagapura are located about 6–7km from the park boundary. In the context of biodiversity conservation efforts, it is important to examine the effectiveness of the eco-development strategy in conserving biodiversity in the Nagarhole National Park, and also in addressing the social concerns of the affected tribal people.

Tourist arrivals and revenues

The Nagarhole National Park generates both domestic and international tourism benefits. The park has two identified tourism zones, one on the eastern side of the park, and the other on the southern boundary where the state government operates a jungle lodge near the Kabini Reservoir. As stated earlier, the national park has a tourism zone of 110km^2.

Information about the tourist arrivals and revenue generated by way of visitor entry fees (including vehicle fare, and elephant ride charges, etc.) in the Nagarhole National Park over the 10 year period from 1993–1994 to 2002–2003 is furnished in Table 4.3. The table indicates that an overwhelming majority of the visitors to the national park are domestic tourists (i.e. Indians). Between the period 2000–2001 to 2002–2003 an average of 31,000 domestic tourists and 1700 foreign tourists per annum visited the Nagarhole National Park. The tourism revenue generated during the same period was on average Rs1.11 million per annum from domestic tourists and Rs0.14 million from foreign tourists. There is no consistent trend in the arrivals of foreign tourists to the park and revenues earned which varies widely from year to year. Taking the 10 year period from 1993–1994 to 2002–2003, it can be seen that domestic tourist arrivals to the national park have risen by 3.6 per cent per annum compared with 1.4 per cent per annum in the case of foreign tourists. While tourism revenues from domestic tourists rose by 7.9 per cent per annum, that from foreign tourists rose by 32.7 per cent per annum. Overall, during the 10 year period under review, tourism revenues generated from the national park grew at 9.7 per cent per annum. The benefits to the local community from tourism are, however, small and mostly come from the opportunity to work as labourers in the guest houses, etc. (World Bank, 1996).

Table 4.3 *Tourist arrivals and revenue (visitor entry fees, vehicle hire and elephant ride charges) from Nagarhole National Park in Karnataka, India during 1993–1994 to 2002–2003*

Year	Indians	Foreigners	Total no. of tourists	Entry fees collected from Indians	Entry fees collected from foreigners	Total amount collected
	(No. in thousands)			(in thousand rupees)		
1993–1994	31.5	1.4	32.9	640.4	15.9	656.2
1994–1995	13.9	2.0	15.9	568.7	15.1	583.8
1995–1996	27.8	1.0	28.8	625.6	17.5	643.1
1996–1997	23.7	3.0	26.7	575.1	8.4	583.5
1997–1998	34.2	0.4	34.6	609.7	48.9	658.7
1998–1999	34.6	2.2	36.8	751.0	501.2	1252.2
1999–2000	28.7	1.5	30.2	808.9	68.5	877.5
2000–2001	24.2	2.3	26.5	1206.8	61.4	1268.2
2001–2002	43.3	1.6	44.9	1186.6	143.2	1329.8
2002–2003	25.7	1.4	27.0	936.3	210.0	1146.3
Annual growth rates (%)	3.6	1.4	3.3	7.9	32.7	9.7

Source: Deputy Conservator of Forests, Wildlife Division, Hunsur, Government of Karnataka, 2003

Income and expenditure of park

The income and expenditure for the Nagarhole National Park including the Brahmagiri wildlife sanctuary, both of which fall under the jurisdiction of the Deputy Conservator of Forests, Hunsur Wildlife Division, for the period 1992–1993 to 1999–2000 is presented in Table 4.4. A separate break down of the income and expenditure for the Nagarhole National Park and the Brahmagiri wildlife sanctuary is not available. According to the Deputy Conservator of Forests, Hunsur Wildlife Division about 90 per cent of the income and 80 per cent of expenditure is accounted for by the Nagarhole National Park, and the rest by the Brahmagiri wildlife sanctuary. As can be seen from Table 4.4, while the average income generated by the Nagarhole National Park, including the Brahmagiri wildlife sanctuary, was around Rs2.10 million per annum, the average expenditure was roughly Rs30.55 million per annum. It is clear from the above that the national park is highly subsidized and the income generated by the park and sanctuary covers only a fraction of the actual expenditure. Although the income and expenditure are steadily rising, the increase in expenditure is greater than the increase in income. However, this analysis does not shed any light on the non-market and unpriced benefits of the national park, which are believed to be considerable. As our analysis in a latter section shows, the tribals of Nagarhole derive considerable NTFP benefits from the national park.

Table 4.4 *Income and expenditure of Nagarhole National Park (including Brahmagiri Wildlife Sanctuary) for the period 1992–1993 to 1999–2000*

Year	Income (million rupees)	Expenditure (million rupees)
1992–1993	0.77	7.83
1993–1994	2.21	25.39
1994–1995	2.57	23.48
1995–1996	1.97	16.70
1996–1997	2.50	18.63
1997–1998	1.53	20.82
1998–1999	1.62	51.12
1999–2000	3.65	80.43
Average	2.10	30.55

Note: According to the Deputy Conservator of Forests, Hunsur Wildlife Division, 90 per cent of the income and 80 per cent of the expenditure is accounted for by the Nagarhole National Park, and the rest by the Brahmagiri wildlife sanctuary.

Source: Office of the Deputy Conservator of Forests, Hunsur Wildlife Division, Karnataka Forest Department

Sample selection

The tribal communities of Nagarhole live in small hamlets and villages within the national park and on the fringes of the park. In order to have a sufficient sample size for our in-depth case study, a number of tribal villages and hamlets were purposively selected. There were three main categories of tribal communities: those living inside the national park; those living outside on the fringe of the park; and those living in the rehabilitated village, Nagapura, located outside on the periphery of the Nagarhole National Park. The tribal villages/hamlets were purposively selected to represent these three typologies of tribal settlements. Of the two tribal villages or hamlets located on the park fringe or periphery, one, Dammanakatte, is a non-rehabilitated village, whereas the other, Nagapura, is a rehabilitated village situated about 3km from the park boundary where the tribals who accepted the rehabilitation package offered by the government have been resettled from inside the Nagahole National Park under the Centrally sponsored 'Beneficiary Oriented Scheme for Tribal Development'. Although Dammanakatte is located within the park adjacent to the park boundary and the road connecting Hunsur town in Karnataka State with Mannanthavady in Kerala State which cuts through the park, as part of the effort to rationalize the park boundary, Dammanakatte is effectively treated as a tribal village falling outside the park, even though forest department maps continue to show the village as being located within the park boundary. Of the tribal villages/hamlets located inside the Nagarhole National Park, six were finally selected for the in-depth survey: Sunkadakatte, Kaimara,

Nannachi, Kolangeri, Ganagur and Majjigahalli. Of these tribal hamlets, while Sunkadakatte, Kaimara and Nannachi are located within the core zone of the Nagarhole National Park, the remaining three tribal hamlets are located outside the core zone. In order to have a sufficient sample size for our survey, cluster sampling was used whereby all the households within the selected tribal villages/hamlets were surveyed. As far as possible, all the tribal households available or present in the selected villages at the time of the survey were interviewed. A number of tribal households could not be included since they were not available or had gone out on employment to coffee estates. Finally, 100 tribal households from the three sets of tribal villages/hamlets were interviewed (Table 4.5). This included 41 of the 50 households in Nagapura, the rehabilitated village, 11 of 30 households in Dammanakatte village and 48 of 170 households in the tribal hamlets located within the national park. Thus, of the total sample of 100 households, 41 per cent were from Nagapura, 11 per cent from Dammanakatte and 48 per cent from the tribal villages/hamlets located inside the national park.

Table 4.5 *Distribution of sample households across different categories of tribal villages/hamlets inside and on the fringe or periphery of the Nagarhole National Park, Karnataka, India*

Tribal villages/hamlets	Total number of households	Number of sample households	Per cent of sample households selected to the total number of households
Nagapura (rehabilitated village on park periphery)	50	41	41.0
Dammanakatte (village on park boundary)	30	11	11.0
Villages located inside the National Park	170	48	48.0
Sunkadakatte	13	6	—
Kaimara	12	2	—
Nannachi	15	9	—
Kolangeri	30	2	—
Ganagur	60	22	—
Majjigahalli	40	7	—
All villages/hamlets	250	100	100.0

Notes: Of the six tribal villages/hamlets located within the Nagarhole National Park that were surveyed, while Sunkadakatte, Kaimara and Nannachi are located within the core zone of the park, the other three villages/hamlets are located outside of the core zone.
Although Dammanakatte is located within the park adjacent to the park boundary and the road connecting Hunsur in Karnataka with Mannanthavady in Kerala, in order to rationalize the park's boundary, the village is treated as falling outside the park, although Forest Department maps continue to show the village as being within the park limits.

Profile of the sample households

The sample households selected for our in-depth analysis from within and outside the Nagarhole National Park belong to different tribes such as *Jenu Kuruba* (90 per cent), *Betta Kuruba* (9 per cent) and *Yerava* (1 per cent). Information on the demographic characteristics of the sample tribal households is presented in Table 4.6. The average size of households for the sample tribal households of Nagarhole as a whole is 4.5. The average size of households is highest in Dammanakatte (5.4), followed by Nagapura (4.7), and lowest (4.1) among the tribal households residing inside the Nagarhole National Park. The sex ratio (i.e. the number of females per 1000 males) for the sample tribal households as a whole is 1158. This sex ratio is highest for tribal households residing within the national park (1200) and above 1100 for the sample tribal households in the two villages located outside the national park. The sex ratio for the sample tribal households is also well above the average for Mysore and Kodagu districts, which was around 965 and 996 respectively according to the Population Census of 2001.

If one compares the demographic characteristics of the sample tribal households with that of the sample households surveyed in Maldari, the coffee-growing village analysed in Chapter 3, one finds some interesting differences. While the average size of the sample tribal households of Nagarhole is lower than that of the sample households in Maldari, the sex ratio for the sample tribal households is not only much higher than that of the sample households in Maldari, but it is also above 1000. Workers constitute over 61 per cent of the population among the sample tribal households. This proportion varies from 58 per cent for tribal households residing in villages or hamlets within the national park to 61 per cent for the two villages outside the national park.

The majority of the tribals have low educational levels (Table 4.7). Over 35 per cent of the sample tribal household population are illiterate, followed by 42.3 per cent who have completed lower primary level education, 15.8 per cent who have completed upper primary education and only 6.2 per cent who have

Table 4.6 *Average size of households, sex ratio and the proportion of workers to total population of the sample tribal households of Nagarhole*

Tribal villages/hamlets	Average size of households	Sex ratio	Per cent of workers to total population
Nagapura (rehabilitated village on park periphery)	4.7	1104	64.4
Dammanakatte (village on park boundary)	5.4	1133	61.8
Villages located inside the National Park	4.1	1206	58.1
All villages/hamlets	4.5	1158	61.1

Table 4.7 *Educational status of sample tribal population of Nagarhole*

Tribal villages/ hamlets	People who have completed lower primary education	People who have completed upper primary education	People who have completed high school education	Illiterates
	(percentages to total household population)			
Nagapura (rehabilitated village on park periphery)	37.1	18.8	9.1	35.0
Dammanakatte (village on park boundary)	61.4	11.1	1.8	25.7
Villages inside the National Park	42.3	14.4	4.8	38.5
All villages/hamlets	42.3	15.8	6.2	35.7

completed high school education. Illiteracy is relatively higher (38.7 per cent) among the tribal households living inside the national park and is lowest (21.2 per cent) among the tribal households of Dammanakatte. The data for each village reveal that the sample tribal households of Dammanakatte are relatively better placed in terms of their educational status with over 61.4 per cent of tribals in Dammanakatte having completed education up to primary school level; these proportions are much lower for the other villages. However, the proportion of those who have completed upper primary and high school education is lowest among the tribal households of Dammanakatte. Although the percentage of people educated up to primary level is lowest in Nagapura, the tribals of Nagapura report highest proportion of people who have completed education up to upper primary (18.8 per cent) and high school levels (9.1 per cent). When compared with the sample households of Maldari, the tribals of Nagarhole have very poor educational levels, with over a third of the tribal population being illiterate compared with less than a tenth in the households of Maldari.

Over 61 per cent of the sample tribal household population of Nagarhole are workers. Detailed information on the occupational status of the working population of the sample tribal households is presented in Table 4.8. Since the sample tribal households are drawn from various tribal villages/hamlets located both inside and outside the Nagarhole National Park, it is important to examine their occupational patterns in detail. It is clear from the data that there are important differences in the occupational structure of the sample tribal households residing in the rehabilitated and non-rehabilitated tribal villages located outside the national park, and those residing inside the national park. While in the rehabilitated village, Nagapura, 27.1 per cent of the total working population are cultivators, in Dammanakatte, located on the park boundary, there are no cultivators and among the tribes living inside the park only 1.1 per cent of the total working population are cultivators. Other than cultivators, all other workers are labourers employed either by the forest department or as agricultural labourers. The majority of the

Table 4.8 *Occupational structure of workers among sample tribal households of Nagarhole (in percentages to the total number of workers)*

Tribal villages/ hamlets	Cultivators	Labourers for forest department		Plantation or agricultural labourers		Other workers	Total
		Daily wagers	Salaried	Coffee plantation	Other crops		
Nagapura (rehabilitated village on park periphery)	27.1	19.6	15.6	18.9	3.6	15.2	100.0
Dammanakatte (village on park boundary)	0.0	34.5	7.6	32.6	10.9	14.4	100.0
Villages inside the National Park	1.1	24.6	4.8	63.7	1.1	4.7	100.0
All villages/hamlets	11.7	23.7	9.6	41.7	3.2	10.1	100.0

workers in Dammanakatte work for the forest department as daily wagers (34.5 per cent) and as labourers on coffee estates (32.6 per cent). It is interesting to note that among the tribals living inside the national park, about two-thirds of the workers are employed as labourers on coffee estates, and about 29.4 per cent work as labourers for the forest department as either daily wagers or regular salaried employment.

Thus we can see that the occupational pattern differs across the tribal villages inside and outside the national park. It seems that the operation or ownership of land is an important factor determining the occupational structure of the tribals in Nagarhole. While in Nagapura all the households have 5 acres of land per household, 91 and 93.8 per cent of the sample tribal households in Dammanakatte and in the villages inside the park respectively were landless (Table 4.9). Nine per cent of the households in Dammanakatte operated less than 1 acre of land and in the villages inside the park, 6.3 per cent operated, though did not own, less than 1 acre of land inside the park. The average size of land holdings for the entire sample is 2.09 acres. The average is 5 acres in Nagapura and 0.09 and 0.06 acres respectively in Dammanakatte and in the villages within the national park. On average, around 1.8 acres were utilized for cultivation in Nagapura and another 3.2 acres were left fallow. In the other villages, only a negligible area was utilized for cultivation purposes. The major crops cultivated in Nagapura village were maize and ragi (finger millet), whereas vegetables were mainly grown as homestead farming. On average 0.75 acres was put under maize and ragi cultivation and another 0.01 acres under root crops and vegetables.

Table 4.9 *Average land holding under different uses and crops for sample tribal households of Nagarhole (in acres per household)*

Tribal villages/ hamlets	Average size of land holding	Average area utilized for cultivation	Average area of land currently fallow	Average area under maize and ragi	Average area under root crops and vegetables
Nagapura (rehabilitated village on park periphery)	5.0	1.80	3.20	1.80	0.00
Dammanakatte (village on park boundary)	0.09	0.00	0.09	0.00	0.00
Villages inside the National Park	0.06	0.02	0.04	0.0	0.02
All villages/hamlets	2.09	0.75	1.34	0.75	0.01

Wildlife damage costs

There are both benefits and costs attributable to conservation. For the tribals of Nagarhole the direct benefits from the Nagarhole National Park are in terms of appropriating NTFPs. The costs of conservation borne by the tribals, apart from the forgone benefits, also include the wildlife damage costs and defensive expenditures, if any, to protect against wildlife attacks. If the number of cases filed and compensation paid by the State Forest Department for wildlife damages in the Hunsur Wildlife Division is an indicator, wildlife damage costs are increasing over time. Degradation and fragmentation of wildlife habitats, apart from other proximate and fundamental causes explain this increasing trend in wildlife attacks on human settlements and habitation. As can be seen from Table 4.10 over the period 1993–1994 to 2002–2003, the amount paid as compensation towards wildlife damages by the Hunsur Wildlife Division, Karnataka State Forest Department has registered an annual growth rate of 13.2 per cent. During this period a total amount of Rs8.72 million or approximately an average of over Rs0.87 million per year has been paid by the State Forest Department following wildlife damage to crops, livestock and humans in this forest division.

Information regarding wildlife damage costs borne by the sample tribal households of Nagarhole and the transaction costs incurred for claiming compensation are presented in Table 4.11. The table illustrates the fact that about 15 per cent of the sample tribal households reported damage caused by wildlife during the year 1999–2000. The proportion of tribal households who reported wildlife damage was highest in Nagapura (over 29 per cent), followed by Dammanakatte and the tribal villages or hamlets located inside the national park. Since the tribals of Nagapura have larger areas under cultivation, the damage caused by wildlife was

Table 4.10 *Category-wise details of number of cases filed and compensation paid for wildlife damage in Hunsur Wildlife Division of Karnataka between 1993–1994 and 2002–2003 (Amount in million rupees)*

Year	Crop damage		Cattle death		Human injury		Human death		Total amount paid as compensation in million rupees
	No. of cases	Amount	No. of cases	Amount	No. of cases	Amount	No. of cases	Amount	
1993–1994	76	0.05	10	0.01		—	2	0.05	0.11
1994–1995	312	0.40	11	0.05	5	0.01	6	0.15	0.61
1995–1996	969	1.08	36	0.03	2	0.001	4	0.10	1.21
1996–1997	608	0.49	52	0.05		—	5	0.12	0.66
1997–1998	422	0.56	61	0.06	6	0.02	1	0.03	0.67
1998–1999	696	0.55	23	0.02	6	0.01	2	0.11	0.69
1999–2000	1001	1.24	70	0.07	3	0.01	3	0.05	1.37
2000–2001	1604	1.58	9	0.01	2	0.02	6	0.48	2.09
2001–2002	523	0.59	11	0.02		—		—	0.61
2002–2003	424	0.57	6	0.01	6	0.02	1	0.10	0.70
Total	6635	7.11	289	0.33	30	0.09	30	1.19	8.72
Average annual growth rate (%)	14.30		−7.04		1.48		−7.65		13.2

Note: The Nagarhole National Park, and the neighbouring Brahmagiri Wildlife Sanctuary fall within the jurisdiction of the Hunsur Wildlife Division of Karnataka State Forest Department.

Source: Deputy Conservator of Forests, Hunsur Wildlife Division, Government of Karnataka

more pronounced there. Overall, the tribal households incurred an average cost of over Rs101 per household per annum or Rs674.7 per reporting household per annum due to damage caused by wildlife during 1999–2000. These damage costs are highest, over Rs183 per household per annum, for the tribal households of Nagapura. Only the tribal households of Nagapura made attempts to obtain compensation for the wildlife damage. They made an average of 1.1 trips per reporting household and incurred a total expenditure of over Rs89 per reporting household to claim compensation from the local forest office. However, they did not obtain any compensation. In fact according to the Forest Department regulations governing payment of compensation for wildlife damages, only those who have secure land titles are eligible for compensation, and since the tribals of Nagarhole did not have any legal titles to the land that they were occupying or cultivating they were not eligible for any compensation. At the time of our survey, the tribals of Nagapura, the rehabilitated village, did not have secure titles to the land distributed to them as part of the rehabilitation package. Subsequently they were given titles (without the right of sale) to enable them to obtain loans, and so also became eligible to receive compensation for damage caused by wildlife. Under the terms of the Indian Wildlife (Protection) Act, 1972, human settlements within national park limits are illegal and hence the tribals of Nagarhole National Park become ineligible to receive compensation for damage caused by wildlife. This acts as a disincentive to the tribals to support conservation activities.

Table 4.11 *Wildlife damage costs incurred by the sample tribal households of Nagarhole and the number of trips and expenditure incurred for claiming compensation*

Tribal villages/ hamlets	Per cent of households who reported damages caused by wildlife during 1999–2000	Wildlife damage costs in rupees per reporting household	Trips made to claim compensation (Number per reporting household)	Expenditure for claiming compensation		
				In cash	Opportunity cost of time spent in terms of wages forgone	Total
				(Rupees per reporting household)		
Nagapura (rehabilitated village on park periphery)	29.3	626.7 (183.4)	1.1	45.8	43.3	89.2
Dammanakatte (village on park boundary)	9.1	500.0 (45.5)	—	—	—	—
Villages inside the National Park	4.2	1050.0 (43.8)	—	—	—	—
All villages/ hamlets	15.0 15*	674.7 (101.2)	0.9	36.7	34.7	71.4

Notes: Figures in parentheses are in terms of rupees per sample household.
Reporting households are the sample households who reported damages caused by wildlife.
* Figures are the total number of sample tribal households who reported damage caused by wildlife.

Tribal communities' dependence on forests for non-timber forest products

Like most forest communities, the tribal communities of Nagarhole depend on the Nagarhole National Park for a variety of goods and services, and especially for non-timber forest products (NTFPs). These NTFPs provide subsistence, income and employment for the tribals. They depend on the forests for their food and non-food needs, and collect a wide variety of NTFPs such as honey and honey wax, fuelwood, bamboo, wild edible fruits and nuts, wild edible tubers and green leaves, bush meat, medicinal plants, etc. Some NTFPs also have significant cultural value, as totems, incense, and other ritual items (www.cifor.cgiar.org). This section, therefore, analyses the uses and economic values derived by the sample tribal households of Nagarhole from the Nagarhole National Park. Before analysing our data, it would be useful to review the various cross-country estimates of the economic values of NTFPs as indicated by different studies and their limitations.

Economic value of NTFPs: A review

Estimates of the economic values derived from NTFP extraction show wide variation across regions, forest sites and communities. A review of 24 studies covering a cross section of countries by Godoy et al (1993) observed the net economic values from NTFP extraction to vary widely between US$1 and US$420/ha per year. The median value was around US$50/ha per year. A more recent review by Pearce and Pearce in a report entitled: 'The Value of Forest Ecosystems' published by the Secretariat of the Convention on Biological Diversity, Montreal (SCBD, 2001a) covering 36 cross-country studies noted the net economic values of NTFP extraction (i.e. for actual flows) to be in the range US$1–188/ha per year (see Table 4.12). These wide variations in the estimates of NTFP extraction are due to differences in the methodology and assumptions employed to estimate the economic value of NTFP extraction, the biological and economic diversity of areas studied, NTFP products valued, etc. It is also, however, not clear whether the estimates of economic values of NTFPs from different studies reported by Godoy et al (1993) and Pearce and Pearce in SCBD (2001a) are expressed in terms of constant US dollars to make them comparable, or in current prices. While the studies reviewed by Godoy et al (1993) were conducted at different points of time between 1981 and 1993, those considered by Pearce and Pearce in SCBD (2001a) were conducted between 1988 and 2000. This makes comparisons of the various estimates of economic values of NTFPs which belong to different time periods all the more difficult, in case they are not expressed in constant US dollars.

Godoy et al (1993), however, cite several limitations of the studies reviewed by them. First and foremost the studies failed to make a clear distinction between two types of quantities being valued, the inventory or stock quantity of the forest resource, and the flow that is the actual quantity of forest resources extracted. While some researchers have valued the inventory, and others the flow, still others have valued both (Godoy et al, 1993). The two are, of course, inter-related. Overharvesting of forest resources (actual flows) will affect the stock of forest resources, which in turn will impact on the potential flow of forest goods. Pearce and Pearce (SCBD, 2001a) make a clear distinction of the various estimates of NTFP values in terms of the stock of goods, potential and actual flows. While in terms of the stock concept, the gross or net benefits from NTFPs for a cross section of countries and regions varied from US$377 to US$787/ha per annum, in terms of the flow concept (potential or actual flows) the gross or net NTFP values ranged between US$0.3 and US$188/ha per annum (SCBD, 2001a). Godoy et al (1993) list further limitations of the studies reviewed by them. These studies are not clear as to whether the estimates provided by them are gross or net values. From an economic standpoint, it is the net economic value (i.e. gross value minus cost) which is relevant since it is this factor which provides the necessary incentive to extract NTFPs.

Furthermore, while most studies have either valued only the flora or only the fauna, a proper and full assessment of the economic values derived from NTFP extraction should value both the flora and fauna, and all possible items harvested from the forests. The price used to value the NTFPs is another issue that has received inadequate attention. It is suggested that while NTFPs which are marketed ought to be valued at the selling prices, those retained for consumption need to be valued at forest gate prices or local market prices. In the case of NTFPs that are not traded or for which prices are not available, the price of a close substitute may be used to value such NTFPs. Alternatively, what users of the products are willing to pay for the NTFP in question, as revealed through a contingent valuation survey is also recommended. Moreover, a proper economic valuation of NTFPs should correct for taxes and subsidies or use shadow prices including estimating the externalities of extracting NTFPs (Godoy et al, 1993). For instance, extraction of NTFPs such as honey, wild edible tubers and green leaves, tender edible bamboo shoots, etc., deprive wild animals of their food source; in turn this may lead them to search for alternative food sources in human settlements and habitations resulting in the animals causing damage to agricultural crops, property, livestock and at times even human life, which has accentuated man–animal conflicts. These externalities of NTFP extraction need to be accounted for while estimating the net benefits from NTFP extraction. In estimating the cost of NTFP extraction some researchers have used the country's official wage rate as an estimate of the unprotected rural wages. But a proper economic valuation should use the wages which people actually pay or wages prevalent at the local level (Godoy et al, 1993). Moreover, harvesting, consumption or sale of NTFPs occur at different time periods and hence discounting of the values derived from NTFPs is essential. The sustainability of NTFP extraction is another aspect which has been relatively neglected in the studies reviewed (Godoy et al, 1993; SCBD, 2001a).

As a further impediment, most studies are not clear as to what they mean by non-timber forest products. While some exclude fuelwood from the purview of NTFPs, others include it under NTFPs. Still others prefer the term 'non-timber forest resources' (NTFRs) (SCBD, 2001b). Furthermore, in their Annual Reports Indian State Forest Departments make a distinction between 'major' and 'minor' forest produce (MFPs). While major forest produce includes items such as timber, fuelwood (or firewood), bamboo, etc., minor forest produce includes most NTFPs. However, the use of the word 'minor' to distinguish NTFPs from major forest produce drew criticism, since it was noted that many of these so-called 'minor' forest products yield substantial revenues to the state, NTFP collectors and others. Moreover, many NTFPs are high value, internationally traded products such as brazil nut, rattan, palm heart, pine resin, maple syrup, mushrooms, etc. (Shanley et al, 2002). The Food and Agriculture Organization (FAO), for instance, notes that there are at present at least 150 non-wood forest products (NWFPs) that are significant in terms of international trade, including honey, gum arabic, rattan, bamboo, cork, nuts, mushrooms, resins, essential oils, and plant and animal parts for pharmaceutical products (www.fao.org). Their total value is estimated at US$11 billion a year (Simpson, 1999). There are still others who use the broader term 'non timber forest benefits' (NTFBs) which includes tangibles as well as non-tangibles, extractive values such as NTFPs, watershed and carbon sequestration services, and preservation values such as option and existence values (Bishop, 1998; Lampietti and Dixon, 1995).

The use of the terms wood and non-wood forest products is also not uncommon. The FAO, for instance, makes a distinction between wood and non-wood forest products (NWFP). While wood products includes all industrial woods, fuelwood, charcoal and small woods, NWFPs includes all forest products of plant and animal forest origin other than wood, as well as services derived from forests and allied land uses. The FAO cites several other inter-changeable terms such as byproducts of forests, non-wood goods and benefits, other forest products, secondary forest products and special forest products, to describe NTFPs (www. fao.org). Following an internal interdepartmental FAO meeting on definitions of NWFPs held in June 1999, the FAO adopted a working definition of NWFPs which states that 'Non-Wood Forest Products consist of goods of biological origin other than wood, derived from forests, other wooded land and trees outside forests'. However, it was acknowledged that while the term NWFP excludes all woody raw materials such as timber, chips, charcoal, fuelwood and small woods, etc.; NTFPs in contrast generally include fuelwood and small woods (www.fao. org).

The Center for International Forestry Research (CIFOR), Bogor states: 'NTFPs are any product or service other than timber that is produced in forests. They include fruits and nuts, vegetables, fish and game, medicinal plants, resins, essences and a range of barks and fibres such as bamboo, rattans, and a host of other palms and grasses ... different users define NTFPs differently, depending

Table 4.12 *Studies of the economic values of non-timber forest products*

Entity being valued/authors	Products	Site	US$ per ha per annum, gross of costs (G) or net of costs (N)	
			G	N
Stock of goods				
Peters et al, 1989	Flora	Iquitos, Peru	700	420
Batagoda, 1997	Trees, climbers, herbaceous	Sinharaja, Sri Lanka	622	377
Amour et al, 2000	Includes environmental services	Peten, Gautemala	787	
Potential flow				
Pinedo-Vasques et al, 1992	Flora (latex, fruits)	Iquitos, Brazil		20
Batagoda, 1997	Flora	Sinharaja, Sri Lanka		186
Actual flow				
Schwartzman, 1989	Flora	Amazon, Brazil	5	
Nations, 1992	Flora	Maya, Guatemala	10	
Nations, 1992	Flora	Amazon, Brazil	5–16	
Padoch and de Jong, 1989	Flora	Iquitos, Peru		18–24
Anderson and Ioris, 1992	Flora (some)	Combu Isl, Brazil	79	
Alcorn, 1989	Flora	Veracruz, Mexico		116
Chopra, 1993	Flora	India	117–144	
Gunatilleke et al, 1993	Flora	Sinharaja, Sri Lanka		13
Batagoda, 1997	Flora	Sinharaja, Sri Lanka		14
Grimes et al, 1994	Flora	Amazon, Ecuador (various plots)		77–180

Entity being valued/authors	Products	Site	US$ per ha per annum, gross of costs (G) or net of costs (N)	
			G	N
Balick and Mendelsohn, 1992	Flora (medicinal plants)	Belize	–	41–188
Mori, 1992	Flora (brazil nuts only)	Brazil	97	
Bojo, 1993	Flora + wood crafts/implements	Woodland, Zimbabwe	21	
Houghton and Mendelsohn, 1996	Fodder (leaves and grass)	Nepal		33–115
Ruitenbeek, 1988	Fauna (hunting)	Korup, Cameroun		1
Thorbjarnason, 1991	Fauna (caiman)	Venezuela		1
Wilkie, 1989	Fauna (hunting)	Zaire		1–3
Caldecott, 1988	Fauna (wildlife)	Sarawak, Malaysia		8
Batagoda, 1997	Fauna (hunting)	Sinharaja, Sri Lanka		2
Kramer et al, 1995	Flora and fauna	Mantadia, Madagascar	4	
Meinyk and Bell, 1996	Flora and fauna (food only)	Southern Venezuela		15
Campbell et al, 1995	Flora and fauna (wood, birds, fruit, mushrooms)	Zimbabwe		57–92
Ammour et al, 2000	Includes environmental services	Peten, Guatemala		30
Yaron, 2001	Flora and fauna	Mt Cameroun, Cameroun		6
Bann, 1997	Nuts, wild meat, rattan, etc.	Ratanakiri, Cambodia		
Gram, 2001	Fish, game, flora	Peruvian Amazon	9–17	19
Godoy et al, 2000	Fish, game, fuelwood, timber, plants (NB includes timber)	Honduras	18–24	
Mai et al, 1999	Bamboo, medicinal plants, fuelwood, fodder, rattan, food plants	Vietnam	123–154	27–55
Bennett and Robinson, 2000	Wildlife only	Various countries	0.3–3.2	

Bann, 1998b	Flora and fauna	Turkey	5
Mangrove systems			
Ammour et al, 2000	Various, including recreation	Nicaragua	
Actual flows			70
Sustainable flows			130

Note: All references in the table are cited in SCBDa.

Source: The Value of Forest Ecosystems, CBD Technical Series No.4, Secretariat of the Convention on Biological Diversity, Montreal, Canada, November 2001, p14; Reproduced with Permission from the Publisher (SCBDa)

on their interests and objectives.' At CIFOR, the emphasis is on understanding how people use forest resources, and on helping to improve the contribution these resources make to the livelihoods of the world's rural poor. Accordingly, CIFOR uses an inclusive definition of NTFPs – one that even encompasses wood products such as those used for wood carving or fuel (www.cifor.cgiar.org).

The Secretariat of the Convention on Biological Diversity (SCBD) notes that non-timber forest resources (NTFR) or non-timber forest products (NTFPs) is a 'catch-all' term which refers to all natural resources from forests, apart from sawn timber (SCBD, 2001b). Wickens (1991, see SCBD, 2001b) considered NTFPs to be 'all the biological material (other than industrial round wood and derived sawn timber, wood chips, wood-based panel and pulp) that may be extracted from natural ecosystems, managed plantations, etc., and be utilised within the household, be marketed, or have social, cultural or religious significance'. Chamberlain et al (1998, see SCBD, 2001b) define NTFPs as plants, parts of plants, fungi, and other biological material that are harvested from within and on the edges of natural, manipulated or disturbed forests. NTFPs may include fungi, moss, lichen, herbs, vines, shrubs or trees (SCBD, 2001b). Thus even international bodies are not consistent about what they mean by NTFPs. There is, therefore, no uniformity or consensus over the use of the term non-timber forest products. In our analysis non-timber forest products or NTFPs in short is taken to also include fuelwood, but excludes timber, sawn timber, etc.

Estimates of NTFP values

Keeping in view the above discussion, in our survey information was elicited on both the flora and fauna collected by the sample tribal households from the Nagarhole National Park, as well as marketing of NTFPs, prices realized, and quantities retained for self-consumption, etc. To estimate the economic values of the NTFPs collected by the sample tribal households, the selling prices quoted by the tribal households have been used to value those NTFPs such as honey and honey wax, gum, tree seeds, etc., that were marketed (including that portion retained for self-consumption); in those cases where the tribal households have not reported any price, the forest gate or local market prices have been used to value the NTFP. In the case of those NTFPs which are wholly retained for self-consumption such as fuelwood, fibre, etc., prices quoted by the tribal households, or in those cases where these were not furnished, the forest gate or local market prices have been used. For certain NTFPs like wild edible tubers, wild edible green leaves, wild edible mushrooms and bush meat for which prices are not available or known the price of a close substitute has been used to estimate the economic value derived from these NTFPs. In the case of medicinal plants where the tribal respondents were either unable or not willing to disclose the quantity of medicinal plants collected, and problems in valuing them, the opportunity cost of labour time spent for collecting medicinal plants has been used to value them. Although the most scientific method to value the NTFPs is to identify, count, weigh and measure them as they enter the village each day (Godoy et al, 1993) over all the seasons of the forest cycle, if not over the entire year, due to resource and time constraints most researches such as ours are based on single point time surveys, which rely on the recall method to estimate the quantity and value of the NTFPs collected and consumed or marketed. In doing so, care has to be taken during the survey so that no item is omitted or under- or overestimated as well as to account for the seasonal availability and collection of NTFPs. In our survey, a structured household questionnaire was used to collect details of NTFPs collected, consumed and/or sold by the tribal respondents. The respondents were asked to furnish details of all NTFPs listed therein and any others collected during the preceding 30 days; and in the case of certain NTFP food items which were items of almost daily use such as wild edible tubers and green leaves over the preceding week. These figures were then used to extrapolate and arrive at the economic values derived by the tribals from NTFP collection per year. Care has been taken, again, to account for the seasonal availability of most forest products (see Table 4.13). More details regarding the norms followed to estimate the economic values of NTFPs have been indicated in the relevant places below.

Details of NTFPs extracted and the economic values derived by the sample tribal households from the Nagarhole National Park are analysed below. First, details of individual NTFP items collected by the sample tribal households in terms

Table 4.13 *Seasons or months and duration of availability of selected non-timber forest products in Nagarhole National Park*

Non-timber forest product	Season/period available	Duration of availability
Honey	April–May	2 months
Gooseberry	October–December	2 months
Wild fruits and nuts		2 months
Wild edible tubers (*Ganasu*)		6–7 months
Wild edible green leaves (*Sappu*)		6–7 months
Wild edible mushrooms	Rainy season	2 months
Fuelwood	All months except rainy season	10 months
Bamboo and fibre		Once in a year
Gum	Summer season	2–3 months
Bark	Rainy season	2–3 months
Tree seeds	Summer season	2 months
Medicinal plants		As and when needed
Bush meat	Almost round the year	Harvesting infrequent due to stringent Wildlife Rules

Source: Primary Survey; Personal discussion with Deputy Conservator of Forests, Hunsur Wildlife Division, Karnataka

of the quantity collected, economic values derived, etc., for the three sets of tribal villages or hamlets and overall for all villages/hamlets is analysed. This is followed by an analysis of the gross and net benefits derived by the sample tribal households from all NTFPs as a whole.

NTFP benefits appropriated by tribals

Honey and honey wax

Honey and honey wax are among the important forest products collected by the tribes of Nagarhole. Honey is used both for home consumption and for sale. Information was collected on the time spent by the tribal households for collecting honey and honey wax, quantity collected, consumption and sales, and prices realized. To estimate the average value derived from the collection of honey and honey wax from the Nagarhole National Park by the sample tribal households in a year, we have used the prices reported by the sample tribal households or when this was not available the forest gate or local market price for valuing honey and honey wax. For honey, the prevailing average local market price was around Rs40/kg and for honey wax around Rs47/kg. Honey is a seasonal product and is mostly available during two months each year, in April and May. Therefore, while estimating the economic value derived in a year we have adjusted for the seasonal nature of the product.

Table 4.14 shows the average time spent and the economic values derived from collecting honey and honey wax by the tribal families per year from the Nagarhole National Park. Each tribal household, on average, collects around 13.8kg of honey and 3.8kg of honey wax in a year and the average time spent by the sample tribal households collecting honey and honey wax is about 16 hours per household in a year. The total value derived from the collection of honey and honey wax is around Rs635.3 per household per annum, of which the major part is accounted for by honey, around Rs492.6. Across villages, one observes interesting differences in the time spent and total value derived from the collection of honey/honey wax by the tribal households. The average time spent and the economic value derived from honey and honey wax collection by the tribal households residing within the national park is conspicuously higher when compared to households in the other villages. While the sample tribal households residing in the villages or hamlets located within the national park spent on average about 19.4 hours per household per annum collecting honey and honey wax, these figures were about 16.5 hours for Dammanakatte and the lowest, about 11.6 hours per household per annum among the tribal households of Nagapura.

The average quantity of honey collected by the sample tribal households residing in the villages located within the national park, and Dammanakatte on the park boundary was conspicuously higher (around 16.6 to 16.7kg per household per annum) than that collected by the tribals of Nagapura (about 9.6kg per household

Table 4.14 *Details of time spent, and quantity of honey and honey wax collected from Nagarhole National Park and the economic values derived by sample tribal households in hours, kg and rupees per household per year*

Tribal villages/ hamlets	Average time spent for collection (in hours)	Average quantity of honey collected (in kg)	Average quantity of honey wax collected (in kg)	Value of honey (in Rs)	Value of honey wax (in Rs)	Total value (in Rs)
Nagapura (rehabilitated village on park periphery)	11.6	9.6	2.7	387.6	153.3	540.9
Dammanakatte (village on park boundary)	16.5	16.6	9.1	377.3	102.0	479.3
Villages inside the National Park	19.4	16.7	3.5	608.7	143.1	751.8
All villages/ hamlets	16.0	13.8	3.8	492.6	142.7	635.3

per annum). In the case of honey wax the average quantity collected by the sample tribal households was highest for Dammanakatte, followed by the villages located inside the national park, and lowest for Nagapura. The economic values derived by the sample tribal households from collecting honey and honey wax was the highest for tribal villages or hamlets located inside the national park (about Rs751.8 per household per annum), followed by Nagapura (Rs540.9 per household per annum) and the lowest for Dammanakatte (Rs479.3 per household per annum).

Gooseberry

Another important forest product collected by the tribal households from the Nagarhole National Park is gooseberry (*Emblica officinalus*). Gooseberry is a seasonal fruit, which is available only during two months usually, between October and December each year. For estimating the yearly value, we have taken note of the seasonal nature of the availability of gooseberry. In this case we have also taken the prices reported by the tribal households, or in their absence the local market price of gooseberry, for estimating the value of gooseberry collected by the tribal households from the national park. The local market price of gooseberry was around Rs5/kg. Data on the average time spent for the collection of gooseberry were not separately available as most of the tribal households collect them while collecting fuelwood or other forest products. From the survey it was seen that the collection of gooseberry was mainly for domestic consumption for making pickles, although a few households collected it to sell to local traders. Only about 1 per cent of the sample tribal households reported the sale of gooseberry in the local market.

Table 4.15 *Details of gooseberry collected by the sample tribal households from Nagarhole National Park in kg and rupees per household per year*

Tribal villages/hamlets	Average quantity of gooseberry collected (in kg)	Total value derived (in Rs)
Nagapura (rehabilitated village on park periphery)	6.1	29.8
Dammanakatte (village on park boundary)	78.0	135.5
Villages inside the National Park	85.0	119.2
All villages/hamlets	51.8	84.3

Information regarding the collection of gooseberry and the economic values derived by the sample tribal households from Nagarhole National Park are presented in Table 4.15 which shows that the overall average quantity of gooseberry collected by the sample tribal household from the national park is about 51.8kg per household per annum and the economic value derived was around Rs84.3 per household per year. It is interesting to note that it is the sample tribal households residing in the tribal villages or hamlets located within the Nagarhole National Park and Dammanakatte on the park boundary that collected the highest quantity of gooseberry from the park (about 85 and 78kg per household per annum respectively), while the tribals of Nagapura, the rehabilitated village located on the park's periphery, collected the least. The economic values derived from collection of gooseberry from the park were highest for Dammanakatte and the villages inside the park, and lowest for Nagapura.

The tribal communities depend on the forest to a great extent for meeting their various food requirements. The different food items collected by the tribals from the National Park include *ganasu* (wild edible tubers), honey, *sappu* (wild edible green leaves), wild edible mushroom, wild meat or bush meat, wild edible fruits and nuts etc.

Wild edible fruits and nuts

The sample tribal households also collect a variety of wild edible fruits and nuts from the Nagarhole National Park such as Gare Kai (*Randia duematorium*), Nerale Kai (*Syzygium cumini*), Sagade Kai (*Schleiechera oleosa*), Seethapala Kai (*Annona squamosa*), Thotte Hannu (*caparis moonii*). These are available only for about two months each year during specific seasons. Table 4.16 indicates that the sample tribal households on average collected about 20.9kg of fruits and nuts per household per annum. The average quantity collected was highest (25.2kg per household per annum) for the villages located inside the national park, followed by Dammanakatte (21.8kg per household per annum) and lowest for Nagapura at 15.7kg per household per annum. Overall the economic values derived by the

Table 4.16 *Details of wild edible fruits and nuts collected by the sample tribal households from Nagarhole National Park in kg and rupees per household per annum*

Tribal villages/hamlets	Average quantity of wild fruits and nuts collected in kg	Total value (in Rs)
Nagapura (rehabilitated village on park periphery)	15.7	74.8
Dammanakatte (village on park boundary)	21.8	109.1
Villages inside the National Park	25.2	126.0
All villages/hamlets	20.9	103.2

sample households from the collection of wild edible fruits and nuts from the Nagarhole National Park were over Rs103 per household per annum. These values ranged between Rs74.8–126 per household per annum across the three sets of tribal villages or hamlets.

Wild edible tubers

Wild edible tubers or *ganasu* (*Dioscoria* sp.) as they are known locally is another important food item collected by the tribes from the forest. Information about the average quantity of *ganasu* (wild edible tubers) collected by the tribes from the Nagarhole National Park in a year, and the economic values derived are presented in Table 4.17. The average quantity of *ganasu* (wild edible tubers) collected by the sample tribal households as a whole is about 151.8kg per household in a year. The quantity of wild tubers collected from the national park by the tribal house-holds residing in villages or hamlets inside the national park is highest compared to that collected by the tribal households of the other villages. While the tribal households from the villages/hamlets inside the national park collected an average quantity of 172.7kg of wild tubers per household per year, these figures were over 135kg of wild tuber for tribals of Nagapura and about 123kg for tribals of

Table 4.17 *Details of ganasu (wild edible tubers) collected by the sample tribal households from Nagarhole National Park in kg and rupees per household per annum*

Tribal villages/hamlets	Average quantity of *ganasu* (wild edible tubers) collected (in kg)	Total value (in Rs)
Nagapura (rehabilitated village on park periphery)	135.1	334.2
Dammanakatte (village on park boundary)	122.9	307.3
Villages inside the National Park	172.7	431.7
All villages/hamlets	151.8	378.0

Dammanakatte. To estimate the value of the *ganasu* (wild tubers) collected by the tribals from the forest we have used the local market price of a close substitute, cassava or tapioca, a root crop. The price of tapioca in the local market was around Rs2.50/kg. *Ganasu* (wild edible tubers) are available for about 7 months each year and this factor has been taken into account while estimating the yearly value of *ganasu* collected by the tribals. This is to adjust for the peak monsoon season during which period there is no collection of *ganasu*. Overall for the sample the economic value derived by the tribals from collection of *ganasu* (wild edible tubers) was about Rs378 per household per annum. These values ranged between Rs307 and Rs431.7 per household per annum across the three sets of tribal villages or hamlets.

Wild edible green leaves, mushrooms and bush meat

The Nagarhole tribals also depend on the Nagarhole National Park for other food items such as *sappu* (wild edible green leaves), wild edible mushrooms and wild meat or bush meat. Table 4.18 illustrates that each tribal household collects an average quantity of 157.7kg of *sappu*, 15.2kg of wild edible mushrooms and 2.1kg of wild meat or bush meat in a year from the Nagarhole National Park.

To estimate the economic value derived by the tribal households from collecting *sappu* we have used the local market price of Rs2/kg. In the case of wild edible

Table 4.18 *Details of sappu (wild edible green leaves), wild edible mushrooms and wild meat (bush meat) collected by the sample tribal households from Nagarhole National Park in kg and rupees per household per year*

Tribal villages/ hamlets	Average quantity of *sappu* (wild edible green leaves) collected (in kg)	Total value of *sappu* (wild edible green leaves) (in Rs)	Average quantity of wild mushroom collected (in kg)	Total value of wild edible mushroom (in Rs)	Average quantity of wild meat (bush meat) collected (in kg)	Total value of wild meat (bush meat) (in Rs)
Nagapura (rehabilitated village on park periphery)	107.9	209.0	10.2	165.0	1.8	175.6
Dammanakatte (village on park boundary)	218.9	476.0	13.8	269.9	2.3	227.3
Villages inside the National Park	186.2	372.4	19.8	327.8	2.3	229.2
All villages/ hamlets	157.7	316.8	15.2	254.7	2.1	207.0

mushrooms the prices reported by the tribals, and in the case of those who did not state any price, the local market price of wild edible mushrooms which was about Rs16.58/kg was used to value the wild edible mushrooms collected by the tribals. In the case of bush meat since local market prices were not known or available, the price of a close substitute, mutton – around Rs100/kg – was used to value the bush meat collected by the tribals. In value terms the sample tribal households of Nagarhole collected *sappu* (wild edible green leaves) valued at over Rs316.8 per household per annum and similarly wild edible mushrooms valued at over Rs254.7 and bush meat at Rs207 per household per annum. In the case of wild edible mushrooms, the average quantities collected by the tribal households in a year ranged between 10.2kg per household in Nagapura and about 19.8kg per household for the villages located inside the park. Across the villages it can be seen that it is the tribal communities of Dammanakatte and the villages inside the national park who depend comparatively more on the national park for *sappu* (wild edible green leaves), wild edible mushrooms and wild meat (bush meat). While tribal households of Dammanakatte collected an average quantity of 218.9kg of *sappu* (wild edible green leaves) per household per year the amount for the villages located inside the national park was over 186kg and about 107.9kg for Nagapura tribals.

Fuelwood

Fuelwood is an important item collected by people and communities living within and near forests. This is true of Nagarhole as well where the local tribals and community depend on the national park to meet their fuelwood needs. The tribals collect fuelwood mostly for their own household consumption. To gather reliable data, the sample tribal households were asked to indicate the time spent and the quantity of fuelwood collected by them during the preceding seven days of the survey. In this case the respondents were able to recollect better the time spent, distance travelled and the quantity of firewood collected by them. These weekly data were extrapolated to derive monthly and then yearly data. While extrapolating and estimating the yearly data on fuelwood collected by the sample tribal households, we considered only 10 months in a year for this purpose since during the peak monsoon season the collection of fuelwood was almost impossible. For estimating the value of fuelwood collected by the sample tribal households from the national park we used the prices reported by the sample tribal households or the local market price which was around Rs0.85/kg. Table 4.19 shows the details of fuelwood collected, time spent and the economic value derived by the sample tribal households from fuelwood collection. It is interesting to note that in the case of Nagapura, the rehabilitated village on the park's periphery, only a third of the tribal households reported collection of fuelwood from the national park. The tribal households of Dammanakatte, located on the park boundary, and the Dammanakatte villages or hamlets located inside the national park collected their fuelwood needs from the Nagarhole National Park. For the sample as a whole,

Table 4.19 *Details of fuelwood collected by the sample tribal households from Nagarhole National Park in kg and rupees per household per annum*

Tribal villages/ hamlets	Per cent of households collecting fuelwood	Average time spent for fuelwood collection (hours per year)	Quantity of fuelwood collected (in kg)	Value (in Rs)
Nagapura (rehabilitated village on park periphery)	36.6	13.4	363.4	327.7
Dammanakatte (village on park boundary)	100	184.0	3600.0	3195.0
Villages inside the National Park	100	116.0	2979.6	2507.2
All villages/hamlets	74.0	81.4	1975.2	1689.3

74 per cent of the tribal households collected their fuelwood needs from the national park; the average time spent by them in a year for collecting fuelwood was 81.4 hours per household (i.e. about 10.2 human days per household per year). The tribal households of Dammanakatte reported the highest average time spent in a year for fuelwood collection (184 hours per household) followed by those residing in the villages or hamlets located within the national park (116 hours per household) and households in Nagapura reported the lowest times (13.4 hours per household).

The sample tribal households collected an average of over 1975kg of fuelwood per household per year from the Nagarhole National Park valued at around Rs1689 per household per year. A look at the data across villages reveals that the dependence of the tribal households of Dammanakatte on the national park for their fuelwood needs is the highest (3600kg per household per annum) followed by the tribals residing inside the park (over 2979kg), and the tribals of Nagapura showed least dependence (over 363.4kg). The economic values derived by the tribals from fuelwood collection from the national park varied from Rs3195 per household per annum in Dammanakatte to over Rs2507 for the tribal villages inside the national park and to just about Rs328 per household per annum for tribals of Nagapura. It is obvious from the above that in the case of the tribals who relocated from the Nagarhole National Park to Nagapura, the rehabilitated village on the park's periphery, there has been a sharp reduction in their dependence on the park for their fuelwood needs. The tribals of Nagapura now mostly depend on their own lands and community woodlots raised as part of the rehabilitation programme for meeting their fuelwood needs.

Bamboo and fibre

Bamboo is another important item collected by the tribes from the national park. Bamboo is mainly used as a construction material for constructing and maintaining the huts of the tribals. The tribals also collect the tender shoots of bamboo, which is edible, for self-consumption. For estimating the value of bamboo collected by the tribal households from the forest, we have used the local market price of bamboo which is about Rs40 per pole. The tender bamboo shoots were valued at Rs2/kg. Information on the average time spent by the tribals for collecting bamboo, and the average quantities of bamboo and tender bamboo shoots collected by each tribal household in a year and the economic values derived are presented in Table 4.20.

As evident, the tribal households spend on average 4 hours per household per year for collecting bamboo from the forest. The average quantity of bamboo collected from the national park by each tribal household is around 18.5 poles per year valued at roughly Rs740. Owing to their better access to the forest, it is the sample tribal households of Dammanakatte and the villages inside the national park who on average collected the highest quantity of bamboo per annum (22–24.7 poles per household per year) whereas the tribals of Nagapura collected the least (12.7). This is also due to the fact that since the houses of the tribals of Nagapura are tiled their requirement for bamboo is comparatively lower compared to the tribal households in the other tribal villages or hamlets. The economic value derived by the tribals through the collection of bamboo from the national park varies from over Rs509 for Nagapura to over Rs989 for Dammanakatte. On average the tribals also collect about 5kg of tender bamboo shoots per household per annum for their home consumption valued at Rs10 per household per annum.

Fibre is another product collected by the tribal communities from the forest which is used for hut construction and repair. Each tribal household collects on average 5kg of fibre from the national park in a year (Table 4.21). Interestingly in the case of fibre, the quantity collected by the Nagapura tribals is the highest (7.6kg per household per year) followed by the tribal households of Dammanakatte (5.3kg) and the least amount (2.7kg) is collected by those tribals residing inside

Table 4.20 *Details of bamboo collected by the sample tribal households from Nagarhole National Park (per household per year)*

Tribal villages/hamlets	Average time spent for collecting bamboo (in hours)	Average quantity of bamboo collected (in poles)	Average value (in Rs)	Average quantity of tender bamboo shoots collected (in kg)	Average value (in Rs)
Nagapura (rehabilitated village on park periphery)	3.8	12.7	509.3	6.9	13.9
Dammanakatte (village on park boundary)	4.5	24.7	989.1	3.9	7.8
Villages inside the National Park	4.0	22.0	880.0	3.7	7.3
All villages/hamlets	4.0	18.5	740	2.0	10.0

Table 4.21 *Details of fibre collected by the sample tribal households from Nagarhole National Park in kg and rupees per household per annum*

Tribal villages/hamlets	Average quantity of fibre collected (in kg)	Total value (in Rs)
Nagapura (rehabilitated village on park periphery)	7.6	226.8
Dammanakatte (village on park boundary)	5.3	158.2
Villages inside the National Park	2.7	81.9
All villages/hamlets	5.0	149.8

the park. To estimate the economic value derived by the tribals from the collection of fibre from the forest we have used the price of a close substitute, namely, thin coir rope. Coir rope costs Rs30 per kg. If we impute the price of thin coir rope to estimate the value of fibre collected by the tribals from the forest, the value derived by them is about Rs149.8 per household per year. This varies from over Rs81 to above Rs226 per household per annum across the three sets of tribal villages or hamlets.

Tree seeds

The tribal households of Nagarhole also collect seeds of certain trees such as Teak (*Tectona grandis*), Matti (*Terminalia tomentoza*), Honnge (*Pangamia pinnata*), Soapnut (*Acacia consina*), etc., for the Forest Department. For this the Forest Department pays an average price of Rs9 per basket of 10kg. The availability of tree seeds is season bound and mostly collected during the summer months of April and May. On average the households collect about 21.3kg of seeds in a year and realize a value of about Rs87.3 in a year (Table 4.22). The table clearly shows that it is the tribals living inside the national park who mostly engage in the collection of these seeds. The average quantity of tree seeds collected by them in a year is over 43kg per household, whereas for the tribals of Dammanakatte and Nagapura this figure is negligible.

Table 4.22 *Details of tree seeds collected by the sample tribal households from Nagarhole National Park in kg and rupees per household per annum*

Tribal villages/hamlets	Average quantity of tree seeds collected (in kg)	Total value (in Rs)
Nagapura (rehabilitated village on park periphery)	1.0	3.0
Dammanakatte (village on park boundary)	0.6	0.5
Villages inside the National Park	43.3	179.2
All villages/hamlets	21.3	87.3

Medicinal plants and gum

The tribal households of Nagarhole also collect medicinal plants from the forest to cure a variety of ailments and illnesses such as colds and fever, pain, stomach ailments, to heal wounds, etc. Estimating the value of medicinal plants collected by the tribals is not easy, partly because the tribals are unable or unwilling to disclose these details. However, they were able to indicate the average time spent by them per year for collecting medicinal plants. In the present study, in order to estimate the value of medicinal plants collected by the sample tribal households, we have taken into account the opportunity cost of time spent by them, collecting the medicinal plants. For this purpose the minimum wage that they have forgone by spending time for collecting the medicinal plants has been taken into account. The minimum wage if they worked on a coffee estate was Rs40. Table 4.23 presents the relevant data and indicates that on average the tribal households of Nagarhole collected medicinal plants valued at about Rs8.9 per household per annum. Across the three sets of tribal villages or hamlets these values ranged between Rs4.4 and about Rs13.6 per household per annum. Since the real value of the medicinal plants is not known to us, due caution needs to be observed while interpreting the value of medicinal plants based on the time spent by the tribals in collecting them.

The tribals also collect gum from the national park. The average quantity of gum collected was about 0.9kg per household per annum. The economic values derived by the tribes from collection of gum from the national park averaged about Rs26.5 per household per annum for the sample as a whole. As observed in the case of most other NTFPs, the average quantities collected by the tribal households of the rehabilitated village Nagapura were the lowest compared to the other villages located inside the park, or on the park boundary.

The above analysis shows that the tribal communities living both inside and outside the Nagarhole National Park depend on the national park for a variety of

Table 4.23 *Details of medicinal plants and gum collected by the sample tribal households of Nagarhole from the Nagarhole National Park in kg and rupees per household per annum*

Tribal villages/hamlets	Average value of medicinal plants collected (Rs)	Average quantity of gum collected (kg)	Total value of gum collected (in Rs)
Nagapura (rehabilitated village on park periphery)	4.4	0.2	4.4
Dammanakatte (village on park boundary)	13.6	2.2	54.7
Villages inside the National Park	11.6	1.2	38.9
All villages/hamlets	8.9	0.9	26.5

NTFPs. This includes both food and non-food items. Tribals collect NTFPs not only for direct consumption but also for exchange in the market.

A summary of the various use values appropriated by the sample tribal households from the Nagarhole National Park analysed earlier is presented in Table 4.24. These data indicate that fuelwood followed by honey, wild edible tubers, tree seeds and bush meat are the major items collected by the sample tribal households from the Nagarhole National Park.

Food and non-food NTFPs

Table 4.25 shows that the tribal communities living both inside and outside the Nagarhole National Park depend on the national park to meet their food and non-food requirements. Except in Nagapura, in the other tribal villages/hamlets the share of food items in the total value of NTFPs derived are less than from non-food items. While overall the total value of NTFPs derived per household is around Rs4690.8 per year, the share of food items is only about Rs1846.5 per household, whereas the value derived from non-food items exceeds Rs2844 per household. Although the dependence of the tribals of Nagapura on the national park for NTFPs is comparatively less than is the case for the other tribal villages/ hamlets, they still derive a considerable amount of value from the collection of various NTFPs from the park. A look at the data across the tribal villages reveals that the dependence of the tribals on the forest for NTFP food items is relatively more among the tribals living inside the national park, followed by the tribal households of Dammanakatte and is lowest among the tribals of Nagapura, the re-habilitated village. The dependence on non-food NTFP items is relatively higher among the tribal communities living in Dammanakatte which is on the fringe of the national park followed by the tribals living inside the national park and then the tribals of Nagapura. While the total value derived from non-food NTFPs is over Rs4513 per household per year in Dammanakatte and over Rs3841 among the tribals living inside the Nagarhole National Park, it is as low as over Rs1228 per household per annum among Nagapura tribals. The table indicates that the pattern of dependence of the sample tribal households on Nagarhole National Park for food and non-food NTFPs differs across the three sets of tribal villages/ hamlets. While tribal communities in some villages depend on the forest more for food items, in others the dependence for non-food items is more pronounced. The NTFPs collected by the tribals of Nagarhole are used for their household consumption as well as for sale in the market. The above analysis of the type and extent of forest uses by the tribal communities of Nagarhole indicates that the national park provides a major source of livelihood and has considerable use value to them.

Table 4.24 *Summary of the various use benefits appropriated by the local tribals of Nagarhole from Nagarhole National Park*

Benefits derived from Nagarhole National Park	Valuation method	Value of NTFP benefits derived by sample Nagarhole tribal households in Rupees per household per annum (1999 prices)	Time duration regarding the availability of forest products
Fuelwood	Market based valuation. The local market price of fuelwood was Rs0.85/kg at 1999 price.	1689.3	We considered only 10 month fuelwood collection in a year to derive the yearly value because during the peak monsoon the collection of fuelwood is almost impossible
Bamboo and tender bamboo shoots	Market based valuation. The price of bamboo in the local market was Rs40 per pole and of tender bamboo shoots Rs2/kg	750.0	They collect bamboo once in a year for repairing house/hut; and tender bamboo shoots for consumption
Honey and honey wax	Market based valuation. The price of honey was Rs40/kg and of honey wax about Rs47/kg in the local market	635.3	Honey is available only during the summer period (2 months in a year)
Wild tubers (*Ganasu*)	Market based valuation. The price of a close substitute, that is, cassava (tapioca) has been used for valuation. The price of tapioca was Rs2.5/kg in the local market.	378.0	Wild edible tubers are available for nearly 6–7 months in a year
Wild edible green leaves (*Sappu*)	Market based valuation. The price of a close substitute, that is, vegetable leaves in the local market has been used for valuation, Rs2/kg	316.8	Wild edible green leaves are available nearly 6–7 months in a year
Wild edible mushrooms	Market based valuation. The price of a close substitute, domestic mushroom, has been used for valuation. The price of mushrooms was about Rs16.58/kg in the local market.	254.7	Wild mushroom is available only for 2 months (monsoon time) in a year

Benefits derived from Nagarhole National Park	Valuation method	Value of NTFP benefits derived by sample Nagarhole tribal households in Rupees per household per annum (1999 prices)	Time duration regarding the availability of forest products
Wild meat (bush meat)	Market based valuation. The price of a close substitute, mutton, has been used for valuation. The price of mutton was Rs100/kg in the local market	207.0	Bush meat is available nearly 10 months, but hunting is only an occasional event due to wildlife rules
Fibre	Market based valuation. The local market price of the close substitute of fibre, thin coir rope, has been used to estimate the value. Value of thin coir rope was Rs30/kg at 1999 price	149.8	Fibre is collected once in a year for constructing/repairing houses or huts
Wild edible fruits and nuts	Market based valuation. The local market price was around Rs5/kg	103.2	Wild edible fruits and nuts are available for 2 months in a year
Tree seeds	Market based valuation. Forest department's price for tree seeds was Rs9 per basket of 10kg at 1999 price. One basket contains approximately 10kg of seeds	87.3	It is reported that in a year they collect tree seeds only in summer months of April and May
Gooseberry	Market based value. The local market price of gooseberry was around Rs5/kg	84.3	Gooseberry is available only 2 months in a year between October to December
Gum	Market based valuation. The average local market price of gum was around Rs30/kg	26.5	Mostly available during the summer season for about 2–3 months
Medicinal plants	Opportunity cost of labour time spent for collection has been used	8.9	As and when needed
TOTAL		4691.0	

Table 4.25 *Total value of non-timber forest product benefits derived by the sample tribal households of Nagarhole from the Nagarhole National Park in rupees per household per annum*

Tribal villages/hamlets	Value derived from non-timber forest products		
	Food items	Non-food items	Total NTFPs
	(Rupees per household per annum)		
Nagapura (rehabilitated village on park periphery)	1389.8	1228.8	2618.6
Dammanakatte (village on park boundary)	1910.0	4513.1	6423.2
Villages inside the National Park	2222.1	3841.8	6063.9
All villages/hamlets	1846.5	2844.3	4690.8

Marketing of non-timber forest products

The tribals of Nagarhole collect NTFPs not only for their subsistence needs but also for sale. Table 4.26 presents information on the marketing of NTFPs by the sample tribal households of Nagarhole and shows that almost 15 per cent of the total value of NTFPs is marketed. Among the tribals of Nagapura this proportion is almost 18 per cent, followed by the tribals residing within the national park (15.6 per cent) and it is lowest among Dammanakatte tribals (9.1 per cent). However, in value terms it is the tribals living inside the national park and Dammanakatte who realized a higher value from the marketing of NTFPs. While

Table 4.26 *Value of non-timber forest products marketed by the sample tribal households of Nagarhole in rupees per household per year*

Tribal villages/ hamlets	Honey	Honey wax	Gooseberry	Gum	Tree seeds (including nuts)	Bamboo and fibre	Total value of marketed NTFPs	Per cent of NTFPs marketed
Nagapura (rehabilitated village on park periphery)	275.1 (59.0)	145.7 (31.3)	3.2 (0.7)	— —	2.9 (0.6)	39.1 (8.4)	466.0 (100)	17.8
Dammanakatte (village on park boundary)	305.9 (52.6)	106.2 (18.3)	111.8 (19.2)	54.7 (9.4)	2.7 (0.5)	—	581.3 (100)	9.1
Villages inside the park	474.9 (52.3)	127.9 (14.1)	98.7 (10.9)	28.5 (3.1)	178.5 (19.6)	—	908.5 (100)	15.6
All villages/ hamlets	374.4 (54.2)	132.8 (19.2)	61.0 (8.8)	19.7 (2.9)	87.2 (12.6)	16.0 (2.3)	691.1 (100)	14.7

Note: Figures in parentheses are percentages of the total value of NTFPs marketed.

the tribal households from within the national park marketed NTFPs worth over Rs908 per household per year, the figures for the tribals of Dammanakatte and Nagapura were over Rs581 and Rs466 respectively. The table clearly illustrates that honey and honey wax, tree seeds and gooseberry are the important NTFPs marketed by the tribals of Nagarhole. Other NTFPs that are marketed include gum, bamboo and fibre. From the above, it is clear that the tribals of Nagarhole market a variety of NTFPs, both food and non-food items. Other NTFPs such as fuelwood, wild edible tubers and green leaves, wild fruits and nuts, and bush meat, etc., were collected solely for meeting their own consumption needs.

Gross NTFP benefits

To estimate the benefits or forgone benefits derived by the sample tribal households from Nagarhole National Park, the stream of NTFP benefits derived by the tribal households need to be converted into present value terms. For this purpose, the cash flow of benefits is summed up over a time period of 25 years. This does not seem unreasonable considering that even after more than 25 years after Nagarhole National Park was notified as a national park (in 1975), the tribals continue to appropriate NTFPs from the forests. This is also based on the assumption that the forest is used sustainably and there is no bar on the local tribals from limited use of the forest. In this case the cash flows will constitute the benefits derived by the tribals from Nagarhole National Park. However, as stated earlier, the Indian Wildlife (Protection) Act of 1972 prohibits any human use of national parks. In which case the cash flow of benefits estimated by us needs to be considered as the forgone benefits of biodiversity conservation borne by the tribals of Nagarhole. The cash flow of NTFP benefits derived by the sample tribal households from Nagarhole National Park are estimated using three alternative discount rates, at 8, 10 and 12 per cent in order to check the robustness of our estimates (Table 4.27). The forgone benefit of biodiversity conservation from NTFPs in present value terms (at 1999 prices) for the sample tribal households of Nagarhole was estimated at over Rs50,073, Rs42,578 and Rs36,790 per household at 8, 10 and 12 per cent discount rates respectively assuming a time horizon of 25 years (Table 4.27). While the present value of non-food NTFPs was estimated at over Rs30,362, Rs25,817 and Rs22,308 per household at 8, 10 and 12 per cent discount rates respectively assuming a time horizon of 25 years, these estimates for NTFP food items were over Rs19,711, Rs16,761 and Rs14,482 respectively.

Net NTFP benefits

In assessing the benefits derived by the sample tribal households from the Nagarhole National Park in the preceding section, we have not taken note of the costs incurred by the tribals for collecting NTFPs such as the cost of time spent, collecting NTFPs, other harvesting costs, if any, and so on. These need to be accounted for while estimating the benefits derived by the sample tribal households from the

Table 4.27 *Present value of non-timber forest products derived by the sample tribal households of Nagarhole from the Nagarhole National Park at 8, 10 and 12 per cent discount rates in rupees per household at 1999 prices for cash flows summed up over 25 years*

Tribal villages/hamlets	Discount rate %	Present value of benefits derived from non-timber forest products in rupees per household		
		Food items	Non-food items	Total NTFPs
Nagapura (rehabilitated	8	14,835.6	13,117.6	27,953.2
village on park periphery)	10	12,615.1	11,154.2	23,769.3
	12	10,900.2	9638.0	20,538.2
Dammanakatte (village	8	20,389.2	48,176.7	68,565.9
on park boundary)	10	17,337.5	40,965.9	58,303.4
	12	14,980.7	35,397.1	50,377.8
Villages inside	8	23,720.5	41,009.9	64,730.4
the National Park	10	20,170.2	34,871.8	55,042.0
	12	17,428.3	30,131.5	47,559.8
All villages/hamlets	8	19,711.3	30,362.4	50,073.7
	10	16,761.0	25,817.9	42,578.9
	12	14,482.6	22,308.3	36,790.9

Nagarhole National Park. To assess the costs incurred by the tribals for harvesting NTFPs, we have taken into account the time spent by them for collecting NTFPs. In estimating these costs we have taken note of the seasonal nature and duration of the availability and collection of different NTFPs. Further certain items are collected jointly, for example fuelwood and fodder, wild edible mushrooms, honey and wax, and wild tubers and *sappu* (wild edible green leaves), and this factor has also been taken into account when estimating costs in order to avoid double counting. The estimated time spent by the tribals for collecting NTFPs has been imputed at the minimum wage forgone by the tribals of working on nearby coffee estates; that is, Rs40 per human day. Using this information, the net present values (NPVs) of the NTFP benefits derived by the sample tribal households from Nagarhole National Park at 8, 10 and 12 per cent discount rates for cash flows summed up over 25 years at 1999 prices are presented in Table 4.28.

The NPVs of the NTFP benefits derived by the sample tribal households from the Nagarhole National Park are positive and significant. Taking all tribal households as a whole it is seen that the NPVs of total NTFP benefits realized by the tribals for cash flows summed up over 25 years at 1999 prices varies from over Rs42,426 per household at the 8 per cent discount rate to over Rs31,172 per household at the 12 per cent discount rate. Non-food items constitute the dominant share of NTFP benefits appropriated by the tribal households residing within the national park, and on the park's boundary (Dammanakatte), whereas among the Nagapura tribals the share of food items in total NTFP benefits is

Table 4.28 *Net present value of non-timber forest product benefits derived by sample tribal households of Nagarhole from Nagarhole National Park in rupees per household for cash flows summed up over 25 years at 1999 prices*

Tribal villages/ hamlets	Discount rate %	Net present value of benefits derived from non-timber forest products		
		Food items	Non-food items	Total
		(Rupees per household)		
Nagapura (rehabilitated village on park periphery)	8	12,908.9	12,052.0	24,960.9
	10	10,976.7	10,248.2	21,224.9
	12	9484.6	8855.1	18,339.7
Dammanakatte (village on park boundary)	8	17,342.1	37,865.8	55,207.9
	10	14,746.5	32,198.3	46,944.8
	12	12,741.9	27,821.3	40,563.2
Villages inside the National Park	8	20,321.9	34,094.2	54,416.1
	10	17,280.2	28,991.2	46,271.4
	12	14,931.2	25,050.2	39,981.4
All Villages/ hamlets	8	16,954.9	25,471.7	42,426.6
	10	14,417.1	21,659.3	36,076.4
	12	12,457.3	18,715.0	31,172.3

slightly higher than non-food items. If we look at the disaggregated data across tribal villages and hamlets it can be seen that the NPVs of NTFP benefits derived by the sample tribal households from the Nagarhole National Park at a 12 per cent discount rate ranges from over Rs40,563 per household in Dammanakatte to over Rs39,981 per household among the tribals residing within the park, and to over Rs18,339 per household among the tribals of Nagapura, the rehabilitated village outside the Nagarhole National Park. Access and human uses are disallowed in national parks, as stated earlier. However, local communities and others from the larger economy – such as poachers, commercial loggers – either overtly or covertly (and often in connivance with local forest officials and politicians) continue to appropriate various use benefits from national parks such as timber and non-timber forest products. If forests are used unsustainably this will impact on the benefits by reducing the expected benefits and also increase the costs of collection and harvesting, for example requiring more time to collect NTFPs, etc. One approach suggested by Markandya and Pearce (1987, see Godoy et al, 1993) to judge whether NTFP extraction rates are sustainable or not is to estimate the value of NTFPs after adjusting the cost of extraction by adding a depletion premium based on the expected rate of extraction. The alternative approach, which is attempted here, is to do a sensitivity analysis of the estimate of net benefits from NTFP extraction. A sensitivity analysis of the net benefits derived by the sample tribal households of Nagarhole using alternative assumptions presented in Table 4.29 indicates that if the expected benefits were to reduce by 25 per cent, and costs also rise by 25 per cent the NPVs of NTFP benefits appropriated by the sample tribal households of

Table 4.29 *Sensitivity analysis of the net present value of non-timber forest product benefits derived by the sample tribal households of Nagarhole from the Nagarhole National Park in rupees per household for cash flows summed up over 25 years at 1999 prices*

Assumption made	Discount rate %	Net present values of benefits derived from non-timber forest products		
		Food items	Non-food items	Total
		(Rupees per household)		
Benefits reduced	8	12,027.0	17,881.1	29,908.1
by 25%	10	10,226.9	15,204.8	25,431.7
	12	8836.7	13,137.9	21,974.6
Costs rise by 25%	8	16,265.7	24,249.1	40,514.8
	10	13,831.2	20,619.6	34,450.8
	12	11,951.0	17,816.7	29,767.7
Benefits reduced by	8	11,337.9	16,658.5	27,996.4
25%, and costs rise	10	9640.9	14,165.1	23,806.0
by 25%	12	8330.4	12,239.6	20,570.0
Benefits reduced by	8	5721.0	7845.2	13,566.2
50%, and costs rise	10	4864.7	6671.0	11,535.7
by 50%	12	4203.4	5764.2	9967.6

Nagarhole will reduce to over Rs27,996 per household at 8 per cent discount rate, over Rs23,806 per household at 10 per cent discount rate and over Rs20,570 per household at 12 per cent discount rate. If, however, the expected benefits were to reduce sharply by 50 per cent, and costs rise by a similar proportion, the NPVs will decline sharply to over Rs13,556 per household at 8 per cent discount rate, over Rs11,535 per household at 10 per cent discount rate and just around Rs9967 per household at 12 per cent discount rate.

NTFPs and sustainability

While the sensitivity analysis undertaken above enables us to see how the expected net NTFP benefits are affected if the NTFP benefits were to decline and/or cost of collection rise under alternative assumptions, these are hypothetical scenarios. Considering its importance, it may be useful to dwell a little more on the question of NTFPs and sustainability. As stated earlier, this issue has been a relatively neglected area of research. Godoy et al (1993) note that scholars are divided into three camps on this issue. While some (e.g. anthropologists) contend that indigenous communities manage NTFPs sustainably, others say that they do not, while a third group states that sustainability is the result of special conditions that must be identified in each case. For instance, anthropologists cite various practices by indigenous communities to manage forests sustainably, such as manipulating forest fallow areas to speed the growth of desirable plants and animals, establishing corridors and scattered gardens, and spacing human settlements to stimulate the reproduction of wildlife, mandating the hunting of one animal species to relieve hunting pressure on others, tabooing the killing of threatened animals, and forbidding hunting and fishing in depleted zones (cited in Godoy et al, 1993). However, whether NTFP extraction by tribals and indigenous communities is responsible for forest degradation, or whether commercial forestry and illegal logging, is also a debatable point.

Peters et al (1989), on the basis of a study in the Peruvian forests, suggest that NTFP extraction is compatible with forest conservation. To quote them: 'The results from our study clearly demonstrate the importance of non-wood forest products. These resources not only yield higher net revenues per ha than timber, but they can also be harvested with considerably less damage to forests. Without question, the sustainable exploitation of non-wood forest resources represents the most immediate and profitable method for integrating the use and conservation of Amazonian forests. Why has so little been done to promote the marketing, processing and development of these valuable resources?'

However, their argument that NTFP (plus timber extraction) values could exceed those obtained by land clearance and conversion to non-forest uses have largely been discredited. This is due to various reasons such as the poor design of the study, the findings of subsequent research, limitations in generalizing the findings of their study site to the entire forest, overlooking the fact that if the whole forest were to be exploited for NTFPs, the prices and hence profitability of NTFP production would decline, a failure to clarify whether the values in question relate to the stock of goods and services, or potential flows or actual flows, failure to account for post-harvest losses, and so on (SCBD, 2001a). Southgate (1996, see SCBD, 2001a) notes that quite a few extractive NTFP ventures have collapsed due to overexploitation. Arnold and Perez (2001) also contradict the view of Peters et al (1989) and suggest that commercialization of NTFPs will not only accelerate the denudation of forests but will also adversely affect the interests of the poor and indigenous communities who depend on forest resources for subsistence and income generation. Moreover, the selective nature of market demand, and the uneven distribution of resources of use value within forests, mean that with NTFP harvesting the resource can become altered and degraded, and therefore works against the ecological objective of conserving the profile of biological diversity present in the untouched forest (Arnold and Perez, 2001). In addition, certain NTFPs constitute food resources for wild animals and hence NTFP extraction by humans has negative externalities and must be accounted for while considering the sustainability of NTFPs.

A proper assessment about whether NTFP harvesting is sustainable and compatible with forest conservation requires a long-term study. Typically unsustainable uses of the forest will be reflected in terms of growing scarcities of NTFPs, a shift in harvesting from more prized to less preferred species, increasing costs of collection, etc. However, there is also the problem of attribution. Whether a decline in the availability of NTFPs can be attributed to overharvesting of NTFPs per se, or due to logging is difficult to say. In the case of Nagarhole National Park, as stated earlier, although the park was notified in 1975, the tribals of Nagarhole have continued to appropriate NTFP benefits even after 25 years, as our survey reveals. This may suggest that NTFPs are being harvested on a sustainable basis. However, it is equally possible that if tribals overharvest one part of the forest, they may shift operations to another unexploited part of the forest. According to local forest officials, parts of the eastern side of the park have turned into scrubs due to overharvesting of forest resources by tribals and other local communities. However, whether the local community is to be blamed for this, or whether illegal logging by timber poachers (who have been known to act in connivance with some local forest officials) is debatable. In fact in 2003 the Lok Ayukta (Ombudsman) of Karnataka State paid a surprise visit to the Nagarhole National Park and was shown (by tribals) areas within the park that had been illegally logged, although the local forest official had denied the same earlier. The question of NTFPs harvesting and sustainability, therefore, needs close observation and long-term scientific study in order to draw any meaningful conclusions.

NTFP benefits and externalities

In assessing the net benefits derived by the sample tribal households of Nagarhole from extraction of NTFPs from the Nagarhole National Park, one needs to account for the externalities of NTFP extraction. As stated earlier, extraction of NTFPs from the national park deprives the wild animals of their food sources, leading them to search for alternative food sources in human settlements and agricultural lands resulting in their causing damage to crops, property, livestock and humans. For instance, the harvesting of bamboo resources by tribals deprives wild elephants of an important food source. Similarly extraction of NTFPs such as wild edible tubers and green leaves, wild fruits and nuts deprives herbivores and other wildlife species of their main diet. Extraction of NTFPs thus gives rise to negative externalities in the form of wildlife damages to crops and the property of NTFP extractors and third parties. As noted earlier, the sample tribal households of Nagarhole reported wildlife damage costs of over Rs101 per household during 1999–2000. However, it is not only the sample tribal households (i.e. NTFP extractors) who are affected by the negative externalities of NTFP extraction but also third parties. In our study, for instance, the sample households of Maldari, the coffee growing village which is close to the Nagarhole National Park in Kodagu district, reported wildlife damage costs and defensive expenditures to protect against attacks from wildlife. It could be argued that NTFP extraction by the tribals of Nagarhole not only affected them but also third parties such as the growers of Maldari. These external costs need to be accounted for while estimating the net benefits from NTFP extraction. Table 4.30 presents the estimates of net NTFP benefits derived by the sample tribal households of Nagarhole both

Table 4.30 *Net non-timber forest product benefits excluding and including external costs*

Item	Net NTFP benefits		
	Excluding external costs[1]	Including external costs borne by sample tribal households (i.e. NTFP extractors)[2]	Including external costs borne by sample tribal households and third parties[3]
	Rupees per household per year		
Undiscounted values	3974.5	3873.3	−510.7
Discounted values at following discount rates:	Rupees per household (for cash flows summed up over 25 years at 1999 prices)		
8%	42,426.6	41,346.3	−4371.6
10%	36,076.4	35,157.8	−3717.3
12%	31,172.3	30,378.6	−3212.0

Notes: 1 External costs refers to wildlife damage costs and defensive expenditures to protect against wildlife attacks.
2 Net NTFP benefit is here calculated after deducting costs of extraction plus the external costs (wildlife damage costs) borne by the sample tribal households (i.e. NTFP extractors) from gross NTFP benefits.
3 Net NTFP benefits here is calculated after deducting costs as above plus the external costs (i.e. wildlife damage costs and defensive expenditures) borne by a third party, the sample households of Maldari, the coffee growing village, which is close to the Nagarhole National Park boundary in Kodagu district of Karnataka State.

excluding and including these external costs. It is interesting to note that even after including these external costs borne by the sample tribal households, that is the NTFP extractors, the net NTFP benefits are positive and high (over Rs3873 per household per year or over Rs30378 per household at 12 per cent discount rate). But most interesting is the fact that if the external costs borne by a third party (e.g. coffee growers of Maldari) are also added to the costs the net NTFP benefit turns negative (Rs −510.7 per household per year or Rs −3212 at 12 per cent discount rate for cash flows summed up over 25 years). It is thus clear that although from the perspective of the tribals, NTFP extraction yields positive and high returns, when the negative externalities of NTFP extraction borne by third parties are also taken into account the net NTFP benefits turn negative.

Estimate of NTFP benefits for Nagarhole National Park

In order to estimate the economic value of NTFPs appropriated from the Nagarhole National Park we need to extrapolate the benchmark values obtained from our survey and generalize for the park as a whole, as well as convert these values from per household to per ha terms. This also facilitates comparison of our estimates with those of other studies. However, in undertaking such an exercise one faces a number of problems. One is how far it is appropriate to generalize based on the benchmark values obtained from a small area of forest to wider areas or the entire forest. The benchmark values may not necessarily be typical of the entire forest. The second problem is that in order to estimate the NTFP values on a per hectare basis we need to know the park catchment area that is accessible and used by the tribals and local people for appropriating NTFPs. Typically NTFP values ought to be higher in more accessible forest areas, and lower in less accessible areas as the costs of extraction rise when higher distances need to be covered for extracting NTFPs. Pearce and Pearce (SCBD, 2001a) list other problems, such as that in a hypothetical world where the whole forest was exploited for NTFPs, prices and hence profitability of NTFP production should fall; failure to define whether the values in question relate to the stock of goods and services or their potential or actual flows; failure to account for post-harvest losses, etc.

In order to extrapolate the benchmark values and arrive at the estimated total value of NTFPs extracted by the population as a whole, we need information about the number of households within and on the periphery of the national park. According to the State Forest Department and the World Bank project document of the India Eco-development Project (World Bank, 1996) there are approximately 1550 households residing in tribal hamlets within the Nagarhole National Park and a population of about 66,507 persons on the periphery of the national park within a radius of 2km from the park boundary. Assuming an average household size of 4.5 persons (as per our survey results) this works out to roughly 14,779 households residing in the periphery of the national park. That makes a total of 16,329 households over which the benchmark values need to be extrapolated. However, NTFP extraction rates would vary across forest sites and regions and the benchmark values may not adequately reflect the NTFPs values appropriated by the population as a whole.

Another important question regards the park catchment area that is accessible and from which the tribals and locals extract NTFPs. This becomes more complicated when the villages and human settlements are not clustered or concentrated in any particular part of the national park or protected area but are spread widely across the park and its surroundings, as is the case in our study area. In the Nagarhole National Park there are tribal hamlets or settlements spread across the core and non-core zone of the park, and almost all around the park's periphery. Zeroing in on any particular figure to represent the park catchment area thus becomes all the more difficult. Keeping this in mind in our study, the NTFP values obtained from the tribal hamlets located within the Nagarhole National Park (including Dammanakatte located on the park boundary) have been used to extrapolate and generalize for the 1550 households living inside the national park limits. Although Nagapura village may not be typical of the villages on the periphery of the national park in the absence of any other alternative we have used the NTFP values of Nagapura to generalize for all the households on the periphery of the national park. Using the above procedure, the total NTFP values aggregated over all households living within and around the Nagarhole National Park works

Table 4.31 *Estimated net non-timber forest product benefits from Nagarhole National Park in rupees and US$ per hectare per year*

Assumed park catchment area as % to total national park area	Net NTFP benefits	
	Excluding external costs	Including external costs incurred by NTFP extractors
	Rupees per ha per year	
10	7492.1	7212.4
25	2996.8	2884.9
50	1498.4	1442.5
	US$ per ha per year	
10	174.0	167.5
25	69.6	67.0
50	34.8	33.5

Notes: Park catchment area refers to that proportion of the national park area that is assumed to be accessible and used by the households living within and on the periphery of the Nagarhole National Park for NTFP extraction.
External costs refers to wildlife damage costs.
The figures in Indian rupees have been converted into US dollar terms by using the exchange rate of 1 US$ = Rs43.0552 in 1999.

out to about Rs48.20 million (US$1.12 million) excluding external costs, and Rs46.40 million (US$1.08 million) when the external costs (i.e. wildlife damage costs) borne by the NTFP extractors is included. The external costs borne by coffee growers are not included due to the lack of information on the coffee growers in the park's vicinity. Moreover, these external costs will vary depending on the distance and location of the coffee estates from the park boundary, etc. These values then need to be converted to a per hectare basis.

Keeping in view the limitations mentioned earlier, a range of values is estimated based on alternative assumptions, namely that 10, 25 or 50 per cent of the national park constitutes the park catchment area from which the tribals and locals can access and harvest NTFPs. The NTFP values expressed in terms of rupees and US dollars per hectare per year are presented in Table 4.31. The table shows that the NTFP values after including the external costs borne by the NTFP extractors for Nagarhole National Park vary from over Rs1442 to Rs7212/ha per year or from US$33.5 to US$167.5/ha per year depending on the assumptions made regarding the park catchment area. Interestingly our estimates fall within the range of NTFP values of US$1–188/ha per year indicated by the various studies reviewed by Pearce and Pearce (SCBD, 2001a).

NTFPs' share in tribal household income

Non-timber forest products (NTFPs) provide subsistence, income and employment for tribal and local communities in forest regions, as noted earlier. This is true for the tribals of Nagarhole as well. Although NTFP values do not compete well with land conversion values, the importance of NTFPs lies in the role they play in supporting local community incomes (SCBD, 2001a). In the following, an attempt is made to assess the role of NTFPs vis-à-vis other sources in the household incomes of the sample tribal households of Nagarhole. Table 4.32 illustrates the contribution of NTFPs to gross household incomes for the three sets of tribal villages or hamlets and for all the villages as a whole. The share of NTFPs to gross household income is above 28 per cent. Forest employment accounts for almost 50 per cent of gross household income, and together with NTFPs account for over three-quarters of the gross income of the sample tribal households. The remaining quarter is accounted for by employment in coffee estates, cultivation, etc. This aggregate picture, however, masks the wide variations in the importance and role of NTFPs in household incomes across different tribal households. As is shown in the table, for the tribals who reside in villages inside the Nagarhole National Park, close to half of the household income is derived from NTFPs. In Dammanakatte too, located adjacent to the national park boundary, about 36 per cent of the household incomes of the tribal households accrues from NTFPs. In contrast, in Nagapura, the rehabilitated village located outside the periphery of the park, NTFPs account for around 12.5 per cent of household incomes. For the sample tribal households of Nagapura approximately three-quarters of the house-

Table 4.32 *Source-wise annual gross income of sample tribal households of Nagarhole in rupees per household*

Tribal villages/ hamlets	Source-wise gross income						
	Non-timber forest products	Forest employment		Coffee employment	Cultivation	Other	Total gross income
		Casual labour	Salaried				
Nagapura (rehabilitated village on park periphery)	2618.6 (12.5)	1498.5 (7.2)	13756.1 (65.8)	1737.3 (8.3)	1284.3 (6.2)	— —	20,894.8 (100)
Dammanakatte (village on park boundary)	6423.2 (35.7)	3298.6 (18.3)	6327.3 (35.2)	1763.6 (9.8)	172.7 (1.0)	— —	17,985.4 (100)
Villages inside the National Park	6063.9 (47.0)	1612.6 (12.5)	310.0 (2.4)	3271.0 (25.4)	773.5 (6.0)	862.5 (6.7)	12,893.5 (100)
All villages/ hamlets	4690.8 (28.1)	1751.3 (10.5)	6484.8 (38.8)	2476.4 (14.8)	916.9 (5.5)	414.0 (2.5)	16,734.2 (100)

Notes: Figures in parentheses are percentage distributions of gross income by source to total gross income.
'Other' includes income from petty business, teaching, etc.

hold income is accounted for by forest employment. Interestingly for the tribals from within the national park, employment on coffee estates is the next important source of income (over 25 per cent) after NTFPs, whereas for the tribals of Dammanakatte forest employment contributes more than 53 per cent of household income. In absolute terms, the income from NTFPs contributes between Rs6063 and Rs6400 per household for the tribals of Nagapura. The importance of NTFPs in the household income of tribals and local communities living within or near national parks and protected areas is thus obvious, and a factor that needs to be taken into account when formulating biodiversity conservation strategies.

Local tribal communities' perception and attitudes towards the environment and biodiversity conservation

The fact that the national park is a major source of livelihood for the tribal communities living inside and on the periphery of the national park poses a serious challenge for biodiversity conservation efforts. However, it is also well recognized now that successful conservation efforts require the support and cooperation of the local community. In the next section the perceptions and attitudes of the tribal communities regarding environmental issues in general and biodiversity conservation and wildlife protection in particular are analysed. This knowledge is very important for policy making.

Since the tribal communities in the study area derive various types of use values from the forest, any biodiversity conservation measure may be assumed to be disadvantageous for the community. With this in mind, we have tried to capture the attitudes of the tribal communities towards environmental issues in general and biodiversity conservation in particular.

The attitudes of the tribal communities towards environmental issues such as biodiversity loss, avoidance of biodiversity loss at any cost, and conservation of biodiversity was elicited and they were asked to express their opinion and state whether they considered these issues to be important or not, or say whether they are indifferent about these. Care was taken to administer the questions in a logically sequential way during the survey. Adequate information was imparted to the people before asking the specific questions. It is heartening to note that the tribal communities responded positively towards the questions posed on environmental issues. Almost 98 per cent of the sample tribal households responded that environmental issues and the conservation of biodiversity are important, while 2 per cent displayed an indifferent attitude towards that question (Table 4.33). However, on the issue of biodiversity loss and whether biodiversity loss should be avoided at any cost, the opinion of the tribal community differed. While around 90 and 91 per cent of the sample tribal households responded that the above two issues are important, 8 and 7 per cent, respectively, expressed indifferent attitudes. Also, 2 per cent of the sample of tribal households expressed the opinion that

Table 4.33 *Attitude of the tribal households of Nagarhole towards environmental/ biodiversity conservation issues (in percentages of total sample respondents)*

Issues	Attitudes	Important	Not important	Indifferent
Environmental issues		98.0	0.0	2.0
Biodiversity loss		90.0	2.0	8.0
Avoidance of biodiversity loss at any cost		91.0	2.0	7.0
Conservation of biodiversity		98.0	0.0	2.0

biodiversity loss and the avoidance of biodiversity loss at any cost are not important issues for them.

Since most of the tribal respondents expressed a positive attitude towards the environment and biodiversity conservation, we probed further in order to find out what values the tribals attach to biodiversity conservation. We presented to them six reasons that are considered to be important for biodiversity conservation and asked them to express their ranking of these reasons in order of importance for them. The reasons and their responses are given in Table 4.34. It is interesting to note that the important reasons stated by the sample tribal households of Nagarhole to support biodiversity conservation are as follows: it is an important source of livelihood for the tribes; it is important for future generations; it keeps the ecosystem stable and functioning; and it has ritual and cultural values in their lives. Around 97 tribal households responded to and considered the livelihood aspect of biodiversity conservation to be an important justification for conserv-

Table 4.34 *Ranking of reasons stated by the sample tribal households of Nagarhole for biodiversity conservation*

Reasons	Rank 1	Rank 2	Rank 3	Rank 4	Rank 5	Rank 6	Total
Keeping ecosystem stable and functioning	7 (8.0)	13 (14.9)	21 (24.1)	30 (34.6)	16 (18.4)	—	87 (100)
Ritual and cultural value in our lives	2 (2.8)	13 (18.6)	27 (38.6)	20 (28.6)	6 (8.6)	2 (2.8)	70 (100)
Aesthetic and recreational value	3 (4.4)	20 (29.4)	20 (29.4)	14 (20.6)	7 (10.3)	4 (5.9)	68 (100)
Important for future generations	4 (4.4)	34 (37.8)	13 (14.4)	9 (10.0)	23 (25.6)	7 (7.8)	90 (100)
Important for developing new products in future	0 (0)	4 (8.7)	6 (13.0)	7 (15.2)	8 (17.4)	21 (45.7)	46 (100)
Important for livelihood of tribes	81 (83.2)	8 (8.4)	4 (4.2)	2 (2.1)	2 (2.1)	—	97 (100)

Note: Figures in parentheses are percentages of row totals.

ing biodiversity. Of these 97 households, 83.2 per cent assigned first rank to this reason for conserving biodiversity. The second most important perceived reason for biodiversity conservation is that it is in the interest of future generations. Ninety households gave different rankings to this aspect of biodiversity conservation. However, most of them – 37.8 per cent – assigned second rank to this reason. The third most important reason expressed by the tribal respondents for conserving biodiversity was to keep the ecosystem stable and functioning. A majority of the tribal households (59 per cent out of 87 tribal households) assigned third and fourth placed rankings to this reason for biodiversity conservation. The fourth most important reason cited by the tribal respondents for biodiversity conservation is the ritual and cultural value that wildlife has in their lives. Seventy households gave differing rankings to these reasons; however, of these 70 tribal households, 38.6 per cent assigned third rank and 28.6 per cent assigned fourth rank to this reason for conserving biodiversity. The other reasons for biodiversity conservation, such as its option value and aesthetic and recreation value, were assigned lower ranks by the tribal respondents.

Having elicited the attitudes of the tribal respondents towards biodiversity conservation in general, we came to the specific issue of the conservation of elephants, a keystone, threatened species in the study area. The elephants pose a severe threat to lives, crops and property, and hence it was important to know the perceptions and attitudes of the local tribals towards elephant conservation.

We presented the following information in order to create adequate awareness among the tribal respondents about the status of elephants in India.

- *According to IUCN's Species Survival Commission's Asian Elephant Specialist Group, there are only 20,000 to 24,000 elephants surviving in India. In the Southern states of India (Karnataka, Tamil Nadu, and Kerala) there are about 6000 elephants only. According to the Zoological Survey of India these animals are vulnerable in their status. Due to illicit killing for tusks the proportion of male elephants are declining.*

After presenting this information, the tribal respondents were asked to express their opinion and state whether they consider the protection of elephants important or not. It is heartening to note that approximately 91 per cent of the sample tribal households responded positively and considered the conservation of elephants to be important.

The three important reasons cited by the majority of the tribal households for conserving elephants are (i) that elephants have their own right to exist; (ii) they are beautiful animals; and (iii) their usefulness for domestic work (Table 4.35). Among these three, the majority assigned first rank to the existence value of elephants followed by the beauty and recreational value of elephants and then the usefulness of elephants for domestic work such as transporting logs, use in temple

Table 4.35 *Ranking of reasons stated by the sample tribal households of Nagarhole for the conservation of elephants*

Reasons	Rank 1	Rank 2	Rank 3	Rank 4	Rank 5	Rank 6	Total
Elephants are beautiful animals	1 (1.1)	22 (24.2)	38 (41.8)	20 (22.0)	10 (11.0)	0 (0.0)	91 (100)
Elephants have their own right to exist	54 (59.3)	22 (24.2)	13 (14.3)	2 (2.2)	0 (0.0)	0 (0.0)	91 (100)
Elephants have educational value	0 (0.0)	0 (0.0)	0 (0.0)	2 (14.2)	1 (7.1)	11 (78.6)	14 (100)
Elephants are useful for domestic work	15 (18.3)	19 (23.2)	33 (40.2)	13 (15.9)	1 (1.2)	1 (1.2)	82 (100)
We may find new uses of elephants in future	0 (0.0)	3 (8.1)	5 (13.5)	13 (35.1)	16 (43.3)	0 (0.0)	37 (100)
The elephant has spiritual value	0 (0.0)	2 (2.8)	14 (20.0)	34 (48.6)	16 (22.9)	4 (5.7)	70 (100)

Note: Figures in the parentheses are percentages of row totals.

rituals. Other reasons for conserving elephants, such as their educational value, spiritual value and option value (in terms of finding new uses for the elephant in future), were assigned lower ranks. In fact only 14 out of the sample of 100 tribal households expressed the view that elephants need to be conserved because of their educational value. Similarly only 37 tribal households felt that elephants need to be conserved because of their option value. However, 70 per cent of the tribal households stated that elephants need to be conserved because of their spiritual value, although they assigned only third, fourth and fifth place rankings to this reason for elephant conservation. As is well known, among the Hindu pantheon of gods, the elephant god (Lord Ganesha) occupies a prime position, and worship of the elephant god is widespread among Hindus in India and elsewhere.

We have already referred to the rehabilitation programme taken up under the centrally sponsored Beneficiary Oriented Scheme for Tribal Development (BOTD), and the support for voluntary relocation under the World Bank aided India Eco-development Project in Nagarhole National Park. Some tribal families have already accepted the compensation and rehabilitation package offered by the government and moved out of the national park. However, there are still tribal families who dwell inside the park. To them we administered a contingent valuation survey to elicit their willingness to accept (WTA) compensation (i.e. the rehabilitation package offered by the government) and move out of the park. For that we presented them with the following situation.

- *The elephants require a certain kind of habitat in order to survive. In recent years this habitat has been increasingly threatened due to different forms of human activities in the periphery of our forests.*

To provide a better habitat for our wildlife including elephants are you willing to leave the national park and settle outside the forest by accepting the facilities offered by the government. You must be aware that some families settled outside the forest in Nagapura village. The government offered them 5 acres of land and constructed houses and extended other help to them to cope with the new situation. If the same package were offered to you, would you accept the offer?

The respondents were asked to exercise their option and indicate their 'Yes' or 'No' answer to the above statement. It is interesting to note that 72.9 per cent of the households expressed their readiness to accept the package to relocate outside the forest. However, 27.1 per cent of the tribal households stated that they are not willing to accept the rehabilitation package offered by the government.

In this context, it is very important to analyse the reasons stated by these tribal households for their non-acceptance of the rehabilitation package and relocate outside the Nagarhole National Park. Table 4.36 presents the details on the reasons cited by the tribal respondents for the non-acceptance of the rehabilitation package.

Table 4.36 illustrates that there are three important reasons for the tribals' reluctance to accept the rehabilitation package offered by the government. Of the 13 households who were not ready to accept the offer, 11 feared that their accessibility to the forest would be denied. Ten of the 13 households also feared that their livelihood would be affected and were worried about the difficulty in coping with the new surroundings.

Table 4.36 *Ranking of reasons stated by the sample tribal households of Nagarhole for not accepting the rehabilitation package offered by the government to relocate outside the Nagarhole National Park*

Reasons	Rank 1	Rank 2	Rank 3	Rank 4	Rank 5	Rank 6	Total
Preservation of wild animals is not important to me	0 (0.0)	0 (0.0)	0 (0.0)	4 (66.6)	1 (16.7)	1 (16.7)	6 (100)
Difficulty in coping with the new surroundings	2 (20.0)	2 (20.0)	3 (30.0)	1 (10.0)	2 (20.0)	0 (0.0)	10 (100)
Protest from the community leaders	1 (20.0)	0 (0.00)	1 (20.0)	2 (40.0)	1 (20.0)	0 (0.0)	5 (100)
Accessibility to the forest will be affected	3 (27.2)	4 (36.4)	2 (18.2)	1 (9.1)	1 (9.1)	0 (0.0)	11 (100)
Livelihood will be affected	3 (30.0)	2 (20.0)	4 (40.0)	1 (10.0)	0 (0.0)	0 (0.0)	10 (100)

Note: Figures in parentheses are percentages of row totals.

Valuing local tribal communities' preferences for biodiversity conservation

Although the government had initiated a programme for the rehabilitation of tribals living inside protected areas by offering a rehabilitation package to them to relocate outside of the protected areas, and the World Bank-funded India Eco-development Project also encouraged the voluntary resettlement of tribals to outside protected areas, out of 1550 households residing inside the Nagarhole National Park only 50 tribal households were rehabilitated up to June 2000, at the time of our survey. Subsequently, another 154 tribal households accepted the rehabilitation package offered by the government and relocated to Nagapura village outside the Nagarhole National Park limits. An obvious question that arises in this context is why many of the tribal households have not moved out of the forest.

Leaving aside the institutional hurdles in the rehabilitation programme, we tried to capture the reasons why they have not accepted the package offered by the government or what determines the probability of their accepting the compensation and rehabilitation package. To study this, we applied a contingent valuation survey. As is the case for any contingent valuation survey, the utmost care was taken in designing the questionnaire. Prior to the survey, a rapid appraisal of the tribal households was conducted. This was done to get a complete picture of the state of affairs in the area so that questions could be structured in a logically consistent way. The survey instrument was based on theoretical considerations, secondary data and pilot study. The discussions with village leaders, forest officials and NGOs helped to refine the questionnaire. A pre-test of the questionnaire was administered to a few tribal households in the national park. Motivated by the pre-test of the questionnaire, we concentrated on the willingness to accept (WTA) format of contingent valuation. The survey was administered during June 2000.

Since our sample also included those who were rehabilitated out of the forest, several considerations had to be made while framing the questions. The rehabilitated households are the ones who have already accepted the government's compensation package and moved out of the forest. Their future role in biodiversity conservation was assumed to be different from those who had not accepted the government's package. Therefore, we treated these two categories of respondents separately. The situation presented before the households who had not accepted the offer was given above. We asked the respondents to state whether they are ready to play a major role in biodiversity conservation by being willing to accept the rehabilitation package and leave the park in order to provide a better habitat for wildlife. The respondents were given a dichotomous choice of answering 'yes' or 'no' to the question. Here we discuss the probability of such households saying 'yes' or 'no' to the offered package.

To estimate the valuation function, the 'yes' or 'no' responses were regressed on a number of socio-economic variables. In addition to age, literacy status, sex and the household size of the respondents, we included variables to represent the income from NTFPs, income from coffee employment and forest employment, and whether the respondents were staying within the core zone of the Nagarhole National Park or outside the core zone. It was hypothesized that although the state or Forest Department would prefer that all human settlements within the national park should be relocated outside the park limits, official concern and pressure is more likely to be on those tribals residing within the core zone of the national park. Hence the attitude of the tribals residing within the core zone of the park may differ from the attitude of those residing in the non-core zone of the park. The summary statistics of the variables used to model the valuation function is given in Table 4.37.

We have estimated the valuation function using logit maximum likelihood estimation. The 'yes' or 'no' responses to the contingent valuation question were regressed on the socio-economic variables of the households, as stated earlier. The coefficients of the finally estimated valuation function that gave satisfactory and meaningful results are presented in Table 4.38.

The logit model explains the variations in the responses to the contingent valuation questions. How the probability of accepting the rehabilitation package is influenced by the explanatory variables is provided by the maximum likelihood logit estimates. Since the coefficients do not explain the marginal effects, the sign of the coefficients are more important. It is most interesting to note that the dum-

Table 4.37 *Summary statistics of the variables used in the logit function*

Variable	Minimum	Maximum	Mean	Standard deviation
WTA where Yes = 1; No = 0	0.00	1.00	0.78	0.42
Age of the respondent	14.00	71.00	33.71	12.23
Dummy for the sex of the respondent D = 1 for male, and D = 0 for female	0.00	1.00	0.69	0.46
Dummy for the literacy status of the respondent D = 1 for literate D = 0 for illiterate	0.00	1.00	0.68	0.47
Household size of the respondent	2.00	8.00	4.32	1.46
Dummy for households living inside and outside the core zone of the National Park D = 1 for households living inside the core zone of the park D = 0 for households living outside the core zone of the park	0.00	1.00	0.28	0.46
Income of the respondent from work in coffee estates and forest employment in rupees per year	0.00	51,600.00	8618.59	10,915.78
Net income from NTFPs in rupees per year	1055.00	15,690.28	5111.45	2991.34

Table 4.38 *Maximum likelihood estimates using logit model of willingness to accept compensation (rehabilitation package) by sample tribal households of Nagarhole National Park and relocate outside the park*

Variable	MLE coefficients	Standard error	t-ratio
Constant	−0.0834	1.869	−0.045
Age of the respondent	0.008	0.30	0.270
Dummy for the sex of the respondent D = 1 for male, and D = 0 for female	0.639	0.780	0.819
Dummy for the literacy status of the respondent D = 1 for literate D = 0 for illiterate	0.490	0.779	0.629
Household size of the respondent	0.040	0.326	0.123
Dummy for households living inside and outside the core zone of the National Park D = 1 for households living inside the core zone of the Park D = 0 for households living outside the core zone of the Park	−1.379***	0.736	−1.873
Income of the respondent from work in coffee estates and forest employment per year	−0.00006***	0.00003	−1.784
Net income from NTFPs marketed per year	0.003	0.002	1.342
Log likelihood value	−24.857		
LR Chi² (7)	12.51		
Significance level of Chi²	0.0849		
Pseudo R2	0.2011		
No. of observations	59		

Note: *** indicates statistically significant at 10 per cent level of significance.

my variable for households living inside or outside the core zone of the national park is negative and statistically significant. This implies that the probability of the respondent to say 'Yes' to the WTA question is less when the respondent is from the core zone of the national park. Furthermore, people having more income from employment in coffee estates and forest employment are less inclined to move out of the forest. This could be due to their fear about losing their employment on the coffee estates and in the forest if they are rehabilitated outside the forest and lose their accessibility to the coffee estates and the forest. Alternatively this indicates that they are not fully convinced about the viability of the economic activities that they could undertake after rehabilitation. Although the tribals derive considerable NTFP benefits from the national park, it is perplexing to note that the coefficient for the variable income from NTFPs has a positive sign. However, the coefficient was not statistically significant. It may, however, be noted that extraction of NTFPs from protected areas is illegal, which also may explain why the respondents are more concerned about losing the income from employment on coffee estates and in the forest in case they have to relocate outside the national park. Although the other variables such as sex and literacy status had the expected sign (i.e. positive) they were not statistically significant. The estimated model is highly significant with a likelihood ratio test of the hypothesis that the seven coefficients are zero based on a chi-square value of 12.51. The pseudo R^2 is 0.20 which is a good fit for cross-section data.

Summary

To sum up, the analysis indicates that the tribal households of Nagarhole derive considerable NTFP benefits from the Nagarhole National Park. They collect a diverse variety of food and non-food NTFPs. These NTFPs primarily meet their subsistence needs, but they also market NTFPs such as honey and honey wax, tree seeds, gooseberry, gum, bamboo and fibre. Other NTFPs such as wild edible tubers and green leaves, wild fruits and nuts, bush meat and fuelwood are harvested to meet subsistence needs. Excluding external costs (i.e. wildlife damage costs) the net NTFP benefits derived by the sample tribal households averaged over Rs3974 per household per year and including these external costs borne by the sample tribal households (i.e. the NTFP extractors) the net NTFP benefits are also quite high and significant at over Rs3873 per household per year. In present value terms, these net NTFP benefits excluding external costs was over Rs31,172 per household and including external costs over Rs30,378 per household at 12 per cent discount rate for cash flows summed up over 25 years at 1999 prices. However, when the external costs borne by third parties (i.e. coffee growers in our case) are also included, these net NTFP values turn negative (i.e. Rs −510.7 per household per year or Rs −3212 per household at 12 per cent discount rate for cash flows summed over 25 years at 1999 prices). In other words, although from the viewpoint of the NTFP extractors harvesting of NTFPs yield positive returns even after including the external costs borne by them, from the society's viewpoint this is not so. The estimated NTFP values (after including external costs borne by NTFP extractors only) appropriated from the Nagarhole National Park using alternative assumptions regarding the park's catchment area that is accessed by the tribals for harvesting NTFPs averages about Rs1442 to over Rs7212/ha per year or US$33.5–167.5/ha per year. The analysis shows that although the forgone benefits of NTFPs for the tribal communities are high, the tribal communities still have a positive attitude towards the conservation of Nagarhole National Park. The logit analysis shows that the probability of saying 'Yes' to the WTA question is less if the tribals are residing within the core zone of the national park, and also if they have higher income from employment on coffee estates or for the Forest Department.

5

Uttar Kannada: The Context of Agricultural cum Pastoral Villages Located Within and Near a Wildlife Sanctuary

Introduction

The next case study deals with agricultural cum pastoral villages located within and on the periphery of the Dandeli Wildlife Sanctuary in Uttar Kannada district of North Karnataka. The two villages selected are Kegdal and a hamlet of Badaganasirada in Haliyal taluk of Uttar Kannada. While Kegdal is located within the wildlife sanctuary, Badaganasirada is located outside, on the periphery of the sanctuary. An important difference between this case study and the one taken up in Chapter 4 is that while this case study pertains to a wildlife sanctuary, the previous one concerned a wildlife national park. The essential distinction between a national park and a sanctuary lies in the nature of access and uses permitted. In a national park, as per the Indian Wildlife (Protection) Act of 1972, all human uses are prohibited and illegal, in a sanctuary limited use is permitted for subsistence purposes. Moreover, unlike in the Nagarhole National Park where none of the sample tribal households had legal titles to the land that they occupied, in the Dandeli case most of the households residing within the sanctuary hold legal titles to their lands. This can be explained by the fact that the households of Kegdal obtained legal titles to the lands they operate prior to the formation of the Dandeli Wildlife Sanctuary. Before presenting more details of our study villages and the sample households, some background information of Uttar Kannada district and the Dandeli Wildlife Sanctuary is presented below.

Uttar Kannada district

Uttar Kannada district, the setting for this case study, is famed for its rich forest and wildlife resources. In fact the district has the largest single contiguous tract of humid tropical forests in Peninsular India (Gadgil, 1992). Buchanan, a naturalist in the employ of the British East India Company who travelled extensively in the district during 1800–02 has written detailed accounts of her rich forest and abundant wildlife (Gadgil, 1992). The district which is located at 13°52' to 15°30' North latitude and 74°05' to 75°5' East latitude extends to an area of 10,200km². The district is characterized by gently undulating hills rising rather steeply from a narrow coastal strip bordering the Arabian sea to a plateau at an average altitude of 500m rising to 600–860m.

Attracted by the rich forest resources of the district, the British and Dutch established trade stations on the West Coast of India to deal in forest products such as wild pepper, cardamom, teak and other hardwoods. Gadgil (1992) documents how assertion of state rights over forest resources and commercialization of forests accelerated the denudation of the district's forests. The reserve forests were dedicated to supply raw materials, primarily teak, to serve the colonial interests of ship building, railways and other construction. As a result, they were almost depleted of natural teak during the years 1800–1850; followed by depletion of other hardwoods especially *Terminalia* and *Lagerstroemia* species and conversion to monocultures of teak. Subsequently forest based industries to manufacture paper and plywood through a supply of cheap raw materials at below socially optimum levels further accelerated the degradation of forest resources. What is appalling is that the district was famed for the cultural traditions of the local people in nature conservation such as maintaining sacred groves and the communal management of reserves. Colonial rule, however, sounded the death knell of these traditions and wise practices in the use of forests and other natural resources. The post-independence period was marked by further acceleration of the commercialization of India's forests (Ninan, 1996). Establishment of hydroelectric and mining projects took a further toll of the district's forest resources. All these factors have had an adverse impact on the rich biodiversity of the forests here which harbour 1741 species of flowering plants and 403 species of birds (Gadgil, 1992). As discussed in Chapter 2, satellite imagery data have revealed that the forest cover in the district has declined within a short span of five years from 7865km² in 1995 to 7808km² in 2001. What is more disturbing is that the dense forest cover as a proportion of total forest cover, including scrub area, declined during the same period from 94 per cent to 83.3 per cent, while open forest cover rose sharply from 5.4 per cent to 16.7 per cent. If this trend is not reversed it will spell the doom of the rich forests and biodiversity of the region.

Dandeli wildlife sanctuary

Dandeli Wildlife Sanctuary, which falls within the Western Ghats region, was notified as a wildlife sanctuary in 1956 covering an area of 204.33km². This was subsequently extended to 5725.07km² in 1978 making it the largest wildlife sanctuary in Karnataka state. Subsequently, however, due to the logistics and problems of managing such a big sanctuary and pressures from the larger economy for diverting forests to non-forest uses – for example forest-based industries, mining and hydro-electric projects – the size of the wildlife sanctuary was reduced to 834.16km^2 in 1988 and still further to 475.02km^2 in 1994. Approximately 250km^2 of the erstwhile Dandeli Wildlife Sanctuary was notified as Anshi National Park. Of the sanctuary's total area, roughly 274.6km^2 constitutes the core zone, and 200.4km^2 the buffer zone. The tourism zone runs across both the core and buffer zones, although most of the area lies in the buffer zone. The Dandeli Wildlife Sanctuary, which is also bounded by the Mahaveer Wildlife Sanctuary in the neighbouring state of Goa, is located at 14°52′ to 15°12′ North latitude and 74°16′ to 74°44′ East longitude. The sanctuary is characterized by undulating hills with steep slopes, deep river valleys and rich hilly forest terrain. The altitudes range from 100–970m while temperatures in the area range from 16° to 36°C; annual rainfall varies from 1250–5000mm with an average of 2500mm (www.junglelodges.com).

The sanctuary is mostly covered by moist deciduous and semi-evergreen forests. Common natural forest tree species found here include *Dalbergia latifolia*, *Terminalia paniculata*, *T. tomentosa* and *T. bellerica*. Teak plantations also cover part of the sanctuary. The area is noteworthy for its bamboo resources, herbs and climbers of medicinal value (www.junglelodges.com). The sanctuary also has several notable streams, especially River Kali and its tributaries, Kaneri and Nagajhari.

The sanctuary is home to a range of flora and fauna including many on the endangered list such as the Asiatic elephant, royal Bengal tiger, leopards, sloth bear, Indian bison, wild boar, deer of various types, wild dogs and Malabar giant squirrel. Crocodiles and other reptiles also abound in the sanctuary and there is an impressive population of avian species. Approximately 196 bird species are listed here such as the Malabar and great pied hornbills, blue throated barbet, different species of parakeets and bulbuls. The sanctuary was recently included under Project Tiger. Notwithstanding its high biodiversity value, the sanctuary is under pressure due to anthropogenic and other factors.

Sample selection

After discussions with local forest and village officials and field visits, two villages, Kegdal and a hamlet of Badaganasirada from Haliyal taluk in Uttar Kannada district, were purposively selected for the case study. While Kegdal falls within the Dandeli Wildlife Sanctuary, Badaganasirada is located on the periphery. Kegdal is situated about 25km from Haliyal, the taluk headquarters and 18km from the nearest town, Dandeli, whereas Badaganasirada is 10km from Haliyal and 3–4km from Dandeli. Kegdal village extends to an area of about 727.5ha, while Badaganasirada reports an area of 1510.8ha. According to the 2001 Population

Table 5.1 *Distribution of the sample households within and outside Dandeli Wildlife Sanctuary, Uttar Kannada district, India*

Land holding class in acres	Sample villages		Total	
	Kegdal (Inside sanctuary)	Badaganasirada (Outside sanctuary)	Number	%
Below 2.5	15	23	38	47.5
2.5–5	9	13	22	27.5
5–10	5	9	14	17.5
10 and above	4	2	6	7.5
All	33 (40)	47 (60)	80 (100)	100

Note: Figures in parentheses are percentages of the total number of sample households.

Census, Kegdal village has a population of 292 persons and 60 households, while for Badaganasirada these figures are 2114 persons and 438 households respectively. The work participation rate in Kegdal (over 53 per cent) is conspicuously higher than in Badaganasirada (over 34 per cent). Cultivators and agricultural labourers account for over 86 per cent of workers in Kegdal, compared with around 26 per cent in Badaganasirada. About a tenth of the population in Kegdal belong to scheduled tribes; in Badaganasirada this proportion is much lower at less than 2 per cent. While there are no scheduled castes in Kegdal, in Badaganasirada they constitute about 5 per cent of the village population. Both the villages are predominantly agricultural cum pastoral villages. The two major crops grown in the area are rice and cotton. Other crops such as banana, coconut and vegetables are also grown.

To select the sample households for the in-depth study, cluster sampling was used. All the households in Kegdal and the hamlet of Badaganasirada available and present at the time of the survey were surveyed and interviewed. In total 80 sample households from the two villages were surveyed. Around 60 per cent of the total households surveyed belonged to Badaganasirada and the remaining 40 per cent came from Kegdal (Table 5.1). While the sample households of Kegdal belong to *Nayak* (scheduled tribe), *Siddi* (Negroid origin) and *Maratha* communities, those from Badaganasirada (except one) are from *Maratha* community.

Profile of the sample households

Socio-economic characteristics

The socio-economic characteristics of the sample households are analysed here. Table 5.2 presents information on the average household size and sex ratio of the sample households by land holding classes in Kegdal and Badaganasirada villages

Table 5.2 *Average household size and sex ratio of the sample households by land holding classes and villages in Uttar Kannada district, India*

Land holding class in acres and villages	Average household size (persons per household)	Sex ratio
Kegdal (inside sanctuary)		
Below 2.5	5.1	714.6
2.5–5	5.0	788.1
5–10	7.8	637.5
10 and above	7.8	547.6
All	5.7	699.7
Badaganasirada (outside sanctuary)		
Below 2.5	4.3	844.2
2.5–5	5.5	548.7
5–10	6.4	747.0
10 and above	8.0	616.7
All	5.2	742.6
Both villages		
Below 2.5	4.6	791.0
2.5–5	5.3	641.8
5–10	6.7	717.8
10 and above	7.8	570.6
All	5.4	725.5

Note: Sex ratio is the number of females per 1000 males.

and the two villages taken together. The data indicate that, for the sample as a whole, the average size of households is 5.4; this is higher in Kegdal at 5.7 persons per household than in Badaganasirada where the average is 5.2 persons per household. Average household size varies positively with farm size, ranging from 4.6 persons per household among small holdings of below 2.5 acres to around 7.8 persons per household on very large holdings of 10 acres and above. For the sample as a whole the sex ratio, that is the number of females per 1000 males is above 725, which is well below the average for Uttar Kannada district (970), Karnataka state (964) and all India (933) according to the Population Census for 2001. The sex ratio for the sample households is relatively higher in Badaganasirada (742.6) than in Kegdal (699.7). Interestingly the sex ratio is higher among small holdings when compared to other land holding groups in both the villages.

Both of the villages have very low literacy levels. As Table 5.3 shows, in both villages around two-thirds of the sample household population excluding children below 7 years are illiterate. Even among the educated, it can be seen that the proportion of those who have completed only lower primary education is very high. The sample household population of the two villages is also lagging behind in

Table 5.3 *Literacy status of the sample household population (excluding children below 7 years) by land holding classes and villages in Uttar Kannada district (percentages to total sample household population)*

Land holding class in acres and villages	Illiterate	Completed lower primary education	Completed upper primary	Completed high school
Kegdal (inside sanctuary)				
Below 2.5	71.4	19.2	9.4	0.0
2.5–5	72.0	25.8	2.2	0.0
5–10	33.3	55.9	10.8	0.0
10 and above	67.0	19.8	13.2	0.0
All	66.6	25.0	8.4	0.0
Badaganasirada (outside sanctuary)				
Below 2.5	62.0	32.3	5.7	0.0
2.5–5	68.6	28.1	3.3	0.0
5–10	72.4	8.0	15.6	4.0
10 and above	48.1	45.9	6.0	0.0
All	65.3	26.1	7.6	1.0
Both villages				
Below 2.5	66.4	26.2	7.4	0.0
2.5–5	70.5	26.8	2.7	0.0
5–10	55.2	29.0	13.5	2.3
10 and above	57.6	32.8	9.6	0.0
All	66.0	25.6	7.9	0.5

terms of literacy status and levels in comparison with the sample households of Maldari, the coffee growing village analysed in Chapter 3.

Workers constituted roughly 61.2 per cent of the sample household population. The rest were either unemployed or not in the labour force. Information on the occupational structure of the sample households of Kegdal and Badaganasirada villages presented in Table 5.4 indicates that agriculture and agricultural labour are the main occupations of the people in the two villages. Overall, 54.8 per cent of the sample household population are cultivators or agricultural labourers or both. The proportion of cultivators to total household population varies positively with farm size. Those whose main occupation is agricultural labour are concentrated among holdings of up to 5 acres. About 38.8 per cent of the sample household population are either not in the labour force or reported as unemployed. The remaining 6 per cent of the sample household population reported as general labourers or engaged in business or salaried employment. Interestingly, while over 33 per cent of the household population in Badaganasirada are cultivators, in Kegdal, which is located inside the sanctuary, this proportion was only about 16 per cent. The proportion of those either unemployed or reported as

THE CONTEXT OF AGRICULTURAL CUM PASTORAL VILLAGES   173

Table 5.4 Occupational structure of the sample household population by land holding classes and villages in Uttar Kannada district (percentages of total workers)

Land holding class in acres and villages	Cultivators	Agricultural labourers	Cultivation and agricultural labourers	General labourers	Business	Salaried	Not in labour force or unemployed
Kegdal (inside sanctuary)							
Below 2.5	3.3	3.2	29.8	3.1	2.3	7.3	51.0
2.5–5	21.3	10.4	25.8	0.0	5.0	0.0	37.5
5–10	34.0	0.0	6.3	4.2	8.2	0.0	47.3
10 and above	43.9	0.0	6.3	2.0	0.0	0.0	47.8
All	16.7	4.2	22.7	2.3	3.4	3.6	47.0
Badaganasirada (outside sanctuary)							
Below 2.5	25.4	16.8	21.2	3.0	1.1	1.3	31.2
2.5–5	33.5	0.0	22.1	0.0	2.3	1.8	40.3
5–10	51.9	0.0	14.9	1.5	0.0	0.0	31.7
10 and above	25.0	0.0	36.7	8.3	0.0	0.0	30.0
All	33.3	8.4	20.6	2.2	1.1	1.1	33.3
Both villages							
Below 2.5	16.5	11.4	24.5	3.1	1.6	3.7	39.2
2.5–5	28.3	4.5	23.7	0.0	3.4	1.0	39.1
5–10	47.1	0.0	12.7	2.2	2.2	0.0	35.8
10 and above	37.6	0.0	16.4	4.1	0.0	0.0	41.9
All	26.7	6.7	21.4	2.3	2.0	2.1	38.8

not in the labour force is higher in Kegdal (47 per cent) than in Badaganasirada (33.3 per cent). There are higher numbers of respondents in Kegdal with salaried employment or engaged in business. In both villages, a high proportion of people are engaged in cultivation as well as working as agricultural labourers. Thus, it is clear that agriculture is the main source of occupation of the sample households in the two selected villages of Uttar Kannada district.

Land characteristics

The average land holding size of the sample households in the two villages taken together is 3.5 acres per household (Table 5.5). The average land holding size is higher in Kegdal (3.9 acres per household) than in Badaganasirada (3.1 acres per household). Table 5.5 reveals that land is unevenly distributed in the two villages. Holdings below 5 acres, which account for three-quarters of the total sample households, operated only about 40.5 per cent of the total operated area, whereas 25 per cent of the sample households, who operated holdings of 5 acres and above, accounted for almost 60 per cent of the total operated area. Distribution of land holdings appears to be more unequal in Kegdal village, located within the Dandeli wildlife sanctuary, than in Badaganasirada located on the periphery of the sanctuary. For instance, holdings of below 5 acres, which accounted for 72.7 per cent of total sample households in Kegdal, accounted for only 33.2 per cent of the total operated area, whereas bigger holdings of 5 acres and above, which account for 27.3 per cent of the sample households, claimed over two-thirds of the total operated area. In Badaganasirada holdings of below 5 acres, which accounted for 76.6 per cent of the sample households, claimed 46.8 per cent of the total operated area, while holdings of 5 acres and above accounted for over 53 per cent of the total operated area.

Another aspect of the land characteristic of the sample households which merits attention is the legal status and mode of acquisition of their operational holdings. As Table 5.6 shows, for the sample as a whole, over 21 per cent of the total operated area is without secure title. Interestingly, this proportion is conspicuously higher in Badaganasirada village which is located outside on the periphery of the Dandeli Wildlife Sanctuary. Overall, about 35 per cent of the operated area of the sample households of Badaganasirada is without secure title. This proportion is very high among the small and large holdings at over 65 and 45.5 per cent respectively. In contrast, in Kegdal only about 5.8 per cent of the operated area is without secure title. This is partly due to the fact that the households residing in Kegdal obtained titles to their land holdings prior to the formation of the wildlife sanctuary. Although in proportionate terms small holdings have a higher proportion of land without secure title for the sample as a whole, the average size of land holdings without secure title varies positively with farm size ranging from 0.5 acres per household among holdings of below 2.5 acres to around 1.7 acres per household among very large holdings of 10 acres and above.

Table 5.5 *Particulars of land holdings of the sample households by land holding classes and villages in Uttar Kannada district*

Land holding class in acres and villages	Average size of operated area in acres per household	Total operated area	
		Acres	%
Kegdal (inside sanctuary)			
Below 2.5	1.1	15.9	12.3
2.5–5	3.0	27.0	20.9
5–10	6.6	33.0	25.6
10 and above	13.3	53.0	41.2
All	3.9	128.9	100.0
Badaganasirada (outside sanctuary)			
Below 2.5	1.1	24.6	16.6
2.5–5	3.4	44.7	30.2
5–10	6.3	56.7	38.3
10 and above	11.0	22.0	14.9
All	3.1	148.0	100.0
Both villages			
Below 2.5	1.1	40.5	14.6
2.5–5	3.3	71.7	25.9
5–10	6.4	89.7	32.4
10 and above	12.5	75.0	27.1
All	3.5	276.9	100.0

Most of the lands without secure title appear to be encroachments on forest and common lands.

In this context, it would be interesting to examine the mode of land acquisition by the sample households of the two villages. Table 5.7 indicates that for the sample as a whole, around 18.7 and 7.8 per cent of the sample households reported that they have acquired land by converting from forest and common lands respectively. About 6.7 per cent of the households reported their land to be revenue lands. The proportion of households who reported their land holdings as having been converted from forest and common lands is higher in Kegdal than that in Badaganasirada. It is significant to note that about a quarter of the sample households in Kegdal village located within the Dandeli Wildlife Sanctuary reported their lands to have been converted from forest lands. Over a tenth of the sample households in Badaganasirada reported that their holdings were revenue lands. Over two-thirds of the sample households reported their land holdings to have been acquired through purchase, or from the landlord, or as ancestral property.

A look at the land utilization pattern shows that most of the land operated by the sample households in the two villages is under cultivation (Table 5.8). Between

Table 5.6 *Legal status of land holdings of the sample households by land holding classes and villages in Uttar Kannada district*

Land holding class in acres and villages	With title	Without title	With title	Without title
	(acres per household)		(as % total operated area)	
Kegdal (inside sanctuary)				
Below 2.5	0.9	0.2	84.3	15.7
2.5–5	3.0	0.0	100.0	0.0
5–10	5.6	1.0	84.9	15.1
10 and above	13.3	0.0	100.0	0.0
All	3.7	0.2	94.2	5.8
Badaganasirada (outside sanctuary)				
Below 2.5	0.4	0.7	34.9	65.1
2.5–5	2.4	1.0	70.9	29.1
5–10	4.9	1.4	77.5	22.5
10 and above	6.0	5.0	54.5	45.5
All	2.0	1.1	65.0	35.0
Both villages				
Below 2.5	0.6	0.5	54.3	45.7
2.5–5	2.7	0.6	81.9	18.1
5–10	5.1	1.3	80.2	19.8
10 and above	10.8	1.7	86.7	13.3
All	2.7	0.8	78.6	21.4

Table 5.7 *Sources of acquisition of land holdings of the sample households by land holding classes and villages in Uttar Kannada district*

Land holding class in acres and villages	Converted from forest	Converted from common land	Revenue land	Purchased	From landlord	Ancestral property	Total
Kegdal (inside sanctuary)							
Below 2.5	25.0	6.2	6.2	25.0	12.6	25.0	100
2.5–5	12.4	0.0	0.0	12.4	0.0	75.2	100
5–10	24.8	0.0	0.0	0.0	0.0	75.2	100
10 and above	50.0	0.0	0.0	50.0	0.0	0.0	100
All	25.0	3.1	3.1	21.9	6.3	40.6	100
Badaganasirada (outside sanctuary)							
Below 2.5	12.4	25.0	4.2	4.2	4.2	50.0	100
2.5–5	18.3	0.0	9.1	9.1	45.2	18.3	100
5–10	9.1	0.0	27.5	0.0	54.3	9.1	100

10 and above	0.0	0.0	0.0	50.0	0.0	50.0	100
All	12.5	12.5	10.4	6.3	25.0	33.4	100
Both villages							
Below 2.5	18.8	15.6	5.2	14.6	8.4	37.4	100
2.5–5	15.1	0.0	4.2	10.9	21.8	48.0	100
5–10	14.8	0.0	17.6	0.0	35.2	32.4	100
10 and above	37.4	0.0	0.0	50.6	0.0	12.0	100
All	18.7	7.8	6.7	14.1	15.6	37.0	100

Table 5.8 *Land use pattern of the sample households in Uttar Kannada district*

Land holding class in acres and villages	Land use pattern				Total
	Under cultivation	Under buildings	Other uses	%	Operated area in acres
	(as % to total operated area)				
Kegdal (inside sanctuary)					
Below 2.5	88.5	3.3	8.2	100	15.9
2.5–5	99.5	0.5	—	100	27.0
5–10	93.7	0.2	6.1	100	33.0
10 and above	99.0	0.1	0.9	100	53.0
All	96.5	0.6	2.9	100	128.9
Badaganasirada (outside sanctuary)					
Below 2.5	99.1	0.9	—	100	24.6
2.5–5	99.4	0.6	—	100	44.7
5–10	97.8	0.4	1.8	100	56.7
10 and above	99.4	0.6	—	100	22.0
All	98.8	0.6	0.6	100	148.0
Both villages					
Below 2.5	94.9	1.9	3.2	100	40.5
2.5–5	99.5	0.5	—	100	71.7
5–10	96.4	0.3	3.3	100	89.7
10 and above	99.1	0.3	0.6	100	75.0
All	97.7	0.6	1.7	100	276.9

Note: Other uses = land not cultivated or under other non-agricultural uses.

88 and 99 per cent of the land operated by the sample households across different land holding classes is under cultivation. The remaining area is under buildings such as farm houses and cattle sheds, under other uses or not cultivated.

Rice is the predominant crop cultivated in both the villages, followed by cotton (Table 5.9). Around three-quarters of the cropped area is under rice cultivation and the rest is mostly cotton. Overall the proportion of the cropped area

Table 5.9 *Cropping pattern of the sample households by land holding classes and villages in Uttar Kannada district (in percentages of total cropped area in each size class)*

Land holding class in acres and villages	Rice	Cotton	Other crops	Total %	Cropped area in acres
Kegdal (inside sanctuary)					
Below 2.5	62.7	35.2	2.1	100	14.1
2.5–5	76.2	23.8	—	100	26.9
5–10	71.0	29.0	—	100	31.0
10 and above	74.3	25.7	—	100	52.5
All	72.6	27.2	0.2	100	124.5
Badaganasirada (outside sanctuary)					
Below 2.5	79.7	20.3	—	100	24.3
2.5–5	76.7	23.3	—	100	44.5
5–10	80.0	20.0	—	100	55.5
10 and above	54.9	45.1	—	100	21.9
All	75.2	24.8	—	100	146.2
Both villages					
Below 2.5	73.4	25.8	0.8	100	38.4
2.5–5	76.5	23.5	—	100	71.4
5–10	76.8	23.2	—	100	86.5
10 and above	68.6	31.4	—	100	74.4
All	74.0	25.9	0.1	100	270.7

under rice is slightly higher in Badaganasirada village than in Kegdal village. For the sample as a whole, the proportion of the cropped area under rice increases with farm size up to 10 acres and then declines. In the case of cotton, however, this proportion varies inversely with farm size up to holdings of 10 acres and then rises again. Areas under other crops such as banana, coconut in the two villages are negligible.

The opportunity costs of biodiversity conservation

Agricultural benefits

Rice cultivation

To assess the opportunity costs of biodiversity conservation, we need to estimate the net benefits from agriculture and other sources obtained by the sample households of the two villages in Uttar Kannada district. As noted earlier, rice and cotton are the two important crops grown by the sample households. Hence, the net benefits derived from rice and cotton need to be estimated. Before estimating these benefits, the salient features of rice and cotton cultivation among the sample households is discussed here. Table 5.10 furnishes information on the area, production and disposals of rice by the sample households by land holding classes for the two villages under review. The average area under rice cultivation for the sample as a whole is 2.5 acres per household. The average area under rice cultivation is higher in Kegdal, located within the Dandeli Wildlife Sanctuary, than in Badaganasirada which is located outside the sanctuary. The average area under rice cultivation also varies positively with farm size. Overall for the sample the average production of rice is above 2100kg per household. This average is higher in Badaganasirada than in Kegdal. Over 63 per cent of the rice produced is retained for self consumption and the rest is marketed. Interestingly, taking all farms together, over 50 per cent of the rice production in Kegdal is marketed, whereas this proportion is just over 30 per cent in Badaganasirada. The proportion of rice production that is marketed also varies positively with farm size.

Table 5.10 *Details of rice area, production and disposals reported by the sample households by land holding classes and villages in Uttar Kannada district*

Land holding class in acres and villages	Average area under rice in acres per household	Rice production in kg per household	Proportion of rice production	
			Retained for household consumption %	Sold in the market %
Kegdal (inside sanctuary)				
Below 2.5	0.6	320	87.5	12.5
2.5–5	2.3	1540	55.2	44.8
5–10	4.4	2870	59.9	40.1
10 and above	9.8	6720	34.5	65.5
All	2.7	1740	49.4	50.6
Badaganasirada (outside sanctuary)				
Below 2.5	0.8	1000	89.0	11.0
2.5–5	2.6	2530	63.6	36.4
5–10	4.9	4700	60.5	39.5
10 and above	6.0	5600	100.0	0.0
All	2.3	2390	69.6	30.4
Both villages				
Below 2.5	0.7	730	89.9	11.0
2.5–5	2.5	2110	60.6	39.4
5–10	4.7	4210	60.3	39.7
10 and above	8.5	6350	53.7	46.3
All	2.5	2130	63.4	36.6

Table 5.11 *Cost of rice cultivation reported by the sample households of Kegdal and Badaganasirada, Uttar Kannada (in rupees per acre per annum)*

Cost items	Kegdal (inside sanctuary)		Badaganasirada (outside sanctuary)		Both villages	
	Rupees per acre	%	Rupees per acre	%	Rupees per acre	%
Labour	488.0	33.3	598.0	32.7	549.8	32.8
Animal labour	157.4	10.7	72.7	4.0	109.7	6.5
Seeds	50.4	3.4	57.0	3.1	53.7	3.2
Chemical fertilizer	197.5	13.4	202.9	11.1	200.2	12.0
Farmyard manure	179.1	12.2	249.2	13.6	214.1	12.8
Pesticide	27.0	1.8	32.2	1.8	29.6	1.8
Maintenance and repair of capital equipment	370.9	25.2	616.7	33.7	518.4	30.9
Total costs	1470.3	100.0	1828.7	100.0	1675.5	100.0

The important costs incurred for rice cultivation are the cost of seeds, and other material inputs such as chemical fertilizers, farmyard manure, pesticides, labour, animal labour, and the cost incurred for the repair and maintenance of agricultural implements, etc. The sample households on average incurred a cost of about Rs1676/acre per annum for rice cultivation (Table 5.12). The costs incurred for rice cultivation are comparatively higher in Badaganasirada (over Rs1828/acre) than in Kegdal (over Rs1470/acre). Labour costs constitute the major item of expenditure (32.8 per cent), followed by the maintenance and repair of agricultural implements (30.9 per cent) and the cost of material inputs (29.8 per cent). The study area falls within a high rainfall region, and rice is, therefore, mostly rainfed.

Besides these costs, the sample households incur additional costs by way of damage caused by wildlife to their crops and property, and defensive expenditure required to protect against wildlife attacks. According to farmers, it is the paddy crop (rice) which mostly bears the brunt of attacks from marauding wild animals, especially wild elephants and boar. Bananas are also a favourite target of wild animals. These are the external costs borne by the sample households due to wildlife conservation. Since this aspect is covered in detail in a later section, we may avoid repetition here, except to state that overall these external costs incurred by the sample households were about Rs449/acre per year for the sample as a whole (Table 5.12).

The bulk of these costs is accounted for by wildlife damage and the rest is defensive expenditures against wildlife attacks. It is not surprising to note that these external costs are the highest (over Rs659/acre) for the sample households residing within the wildlife sanctuary (Kegdal) where the frequency and intensity of wildlife

Table 5.12 *External cost of agriculture in rupees per acre per year*

Items	Kegdal (inside sanctuary)	Badganasirada (outside sanctuary)	Both villages
Wildlife damage cost	649.6	256.2	437.1
Wildlife defensive expenditure	9.7	13.7	11.8
Total	659.3	269.9	448.9

attacks is greater, and lower (Rs269.9/acre) for the households of Badaganasirada situated outside on the periphery of the sanctuary. When estimating the net benefits from paddy cultivation, these external costs also need to be accounted for. The farmers were unable to break down these costs by crop. However, since paddy crop (rice) is most affected by attacks from wild animals, the entire costs arising on this account have been deducted from the gross rice benefits to estimate the net benefits from rice. To avoid double counting, these costs are not included when estimating the net benefits obtained by the sample households from cotton.

The annual receipts from rice obtained by the sample households of the two villages in kgs and rupees per acre are presented in Table 5.13. For the sample as a whole, the average yields obtained from rice are roughly 832kg/acre. Rice yields in Badaganasirada are conspicuously higher (over 995kg/acre) than in Kegdal (over 621kg/acre). Overall, the gross receipts obtained from rice are above Rs6015/acre. While these gross receipts from rice average around Rs7207/acre in Badaganasirada, in Kegdal they are above Rs4854/acre. The net receipts from rice after deducting costs, excluding external costs, are above Rs4340/acre for the sample as a whole, and over Rs3891/acre after the external costs have also been deducted. These values are used to estimate the opportunity costs of biodiversity conservation in terms of forgone rice benefits borne by the sample households of the two villages in Uttar Kannada district.

Table 5.13 *Annual receipts from rice obtained by the sample households of Kegdal and Badaganasirada villages in Uttar Kannada district*

Rice yields/ benefits	Unit	Kegdal (inside sanctuary)	Badaganasirada (outside sanctuary)	Both villages
Rice yields	Kg per acre	621.4	995.8	832.0
Gross receipts	Rupees per acre	4854.8	7207.3	6015.9
Net receipts excluding external costs	Rupees per acre	3384.5	5378.6	4340.4
Net receipts including external costs	Rupees per acre	2725.2	5108.7	3891.5

Note: External costs = Wildlife damage costs and defensive expenditures to protect against wildlife attacks.

Table 5.14 *Net present value of benefits from rice excluding and including external costs obtained by the sample households of Kegdal and Badaganasirada villages, Uttar Kannada district (for cash flow summed up over 25 years at 1999–2000 prices)*

Land holding class in acres and villages	Net present value of paddy (rice) in rupees per acre					
	Excluding external costs (Discount rates)			Including external costs (Discount rates)		
	8%	10%	12%	8%	10%	12%
Below 2.5	31,618.6	26,858.6	23,183.3	22,571.8	19,165.8	16,536.2
2.5–5	38,065.8	32,340.8	27,920.2	32,147.8	27,308.6	23,572.1
5–10	49,474.6	42,050.5	36,317.6	41,667.6	35,412.0	30,581.5
10 and above	50,214.3	42,688.2	36,876.2	45,079.8	38,322.2	33,103.7
All	46,332.8	39,398.0	34,042.4	41,540.9	35,323.3	30,521.6

Net benefits from rice

Table 5.14 indicates the net present value (NPV) of the benefits from rice obtained by the sample households at 8, 10 and 12 per cent discount rates for cash flows summed over 25 years. Excluding external costs, that is wildlife damage costs and defensive expenditure to protect against wildlife attacks, these NPVs range from over Rs34,042 to Rs46,332 per acre. Including external costs, the NPVs range from over Rs30,521 to over Rs41,540 per acre. Thus, even after accounting for the external costs, the farmers in the villages surveyed report positive and high benefits from rice cultivation. This is true of all size classes of farms.

Cotton cultivation

The second most important crop grown by the sample households of both villages is cotton. The salient features of cotton cultivation and cost structure and receipts obtained from cotton are discussed below. The area under cotton cultivation for the sample as a whole is roughly 0.9 acre per household (Table 5.15). The average area under cotton increases with farm size. The average cotton production is around 275kg per household for the sample as a whole. Average cotton yields are around 314kg/acre and these are higher in Badaganasirada than in Kegdal. For the sample as a whole, the per acre yields of cotton increase with farm size up to 5 acres and then decline. The costs incurred for cotton cultivation are labour; seed and other material inputs such as chemical fertilizers, farmyard manure, pesticides; maintenance and repair of agricultural implements; transport charges, etc. On average, the sample households incurred a cost of about Rs2249/acre for cotton cultivation (Table 5.16). The average cost of cultivation of cotton was higher in Kegdal than in Badaganasirada. Material inputs account for the bulk of the costs (over 58 per cent) for cotton cultivation, followed by the maintenance and repair of agricultural implements, and then labour.

Table 5.15 *Area and production of cotton reported by the sample households by land holding classes and villages in Uttar Kannada district*

Land holding class in acres and villages	Average area under cotton in acres per household	Cotton production in kg	
		Per household	Per acre
Kegdal (inside sanctuary)			
Below 2.5	0.3	67.2	203.6
2.5–5	0.7	256.0	360.0
5–10	1.8	340.0	189.5
10 and above	3.4	875.0	259.8
All	1.0	257.9	251.9
Badaganasirada (outside sanctuary)			
Below 2.5	0.2	86.6	402.4
2.5–5	0.8	385.0	482.6
5–10	1.2	410.7	333.6
10 and above	4.9	1400.0	284.0
All	0.8	287.1	372.1
Both villages			
Below 2.5	0.3	79.0	303.0
2.5–5	0.8	332.2	435.8
5–10	1.4	385.4	269.1
10 and above	3.9	1050.0	270.0
All	0.9	275.1	314.1

Table 5.16 *Cost of cotton cultivation reported by the sample households of Kegdal and Badaganasirada villages, Uttar Kannada district*

Cost items	Kegdal (inside sanctuary)		Badaganasirada (outside sanctuary)		Both villages	
	Rupees per acre	%	Rupees per acre	%	Rupees per acre	%
Labour	454.8	18.3	337.8	16.0	384.6	17.1
Seeds	520.2	21.0	248.9	11.8	357.6	15.9
Chemical fertilizer	608.6	24.5	370.9	17.5	466.0	20.7
Farmyard manure	116.0	4.7	239.0	11.3	177.5	7.9
Pesticide	375.2	15.1	264.0	12.5	308.5	13.7
Transport	34.0	1.4	38.2	1.8	36.1	1.6
Maintenance and repair	370.9	15.0	616.7	29.1	518.4	23.1
Total costs	2479.7	100.0	2115.5	100.0	2248.7	100.0

Table 5.17 *Gross and net receipts from cotton obtained by the sample households of Kegdal and Badaganasirada villages in Uttar Kannada district (rupees per acre)*

Cotton receipts	Kegdal (inside sanctuary)	Badaganasirada (outside sanctuary)	Both villages
Gross receipts from cotton	5808.8	9749.0	7761.4
Net receipts from cotton	3329.1	7633.5	5512.7

The average gross and net receipts from cotton in value terms for the sample as a whole was above Rs7761 and Rs5512 per acre respectively (Table 5.17). Owing to higher productivity and lower costs of cultivation, the net receipts from cotton was conspicuously higher in Badaganasirada, than in Kegdal.

Net benefits from cotton

The net benefits from cotton in present value terms are presented in Table 5.18, which illustrates that the NPVs range from Rs43236/acre to over Rs58846/acre for the sample as a whole. These NPVs are relatively low among small farmers as compared to other size classes of farmers. As stated earlier, the external costs due to damage caused by wildlife and defensive expenditure to protect against wildlife attacks have been accounted for while estimating the net benefits from rice. Hence, to avoid double counting, these are not included here while estimating the net benefits from cotton. Moreover, as stated earlier, it is mostly rice which bears the brunt of marauding wild animals, although the cotton crop may also get damaged in the process.

Table 5.18 *Net present value of benefits from cotton obtained by the sample households of Kegdal and Badaganasirada villages, Uttar Kannada district (for cash flows summed up over 25 years at 1999–2000 prices)*

Land holding class in acres	Net present value of cotton in rupees per acre		
	Excluding external costs (discount rates)		
	8%	10%	12%
Below 2.5	3414.7	2876.2	2460.9
2.5–5	71,062.6	60,938.9	52,164.2
5–10	69,155.2	58,785.5	50,777.7
10 and above	26,6997.1	22,7024.2	19,6154.2
All	58,846.8	50,039.0	43,236.9

Benefits from forest resources

Grazing benefits

Grazing pressure is an important factor contributing to biodiversity loss in many developing countries, including India. This is because forests are treated as open access resources with the result that they are subject to overgrazing and other unsustainable uses leading to forest degradation, the kind of phenomenon elaborated by Hardin (1968) in 'The Tragedy of the Commons'. Examples of once pristine forests turning into scrub and degraded woodland due to overgrazing and other factors are not uncommon. Grazing in protected areas not only deprives wild herbivores of their food sources but also puts them at risk of contracting communicable diseases such as rinderpest (foot and mouth disease) from domestic cattle. In fact, forest officials in Karnataka State point to an instance in the early 1970s when almost the entire Indian bison population in the Bandipur National Park (bordering Nagarhole National Park, analysed in Chapter 4) was wiped out due to rinderpest disease contracted from domestic cattle that grazed in the national park. The National Commission on Agriculture (1976) estimated that almost 88 per cent of India's forests are open to grazing, and only about 12 per cent remain closed to grazing (Chopra et al, 1999).

The sample households depend on the Dandeli Wildlife Sanctuary and surrounding forests for grazing their cattle, for fuelwood and other non-timber forest products (NTFPs). Table 5.19 indicates that three-quarters of the sample households maintain livestock. This proportion is higher for the sample households residing in Badaganasirada, on the periphery of the wildlife sanctuary than that for the households residing in Kegdal within the sanctuary. The livestock is largely cattle. Households of Badaganasirada, also maintain buffaloes in addition to cattle. None of the sample households maintain small ruminants such as sheep and goats. The proportion of households maintaining livestock varies positively with farm size.

In order to assess the grazing values appropriated by the sample households from the Dandeli forests the total number of livestock or grazing animals owned by the sample households needs to be converted into standardized animal units using the standard cattle equivalent units (Mishra and Sharma, 1990). Then the quantity of green fodder and natural herbage grazed by these animals must be estimated. This, however, is not an easy task since the quantity of green fodder/natural herbage that the grazing livestock consume varies depending on the age, sex and composition of the livestock, such as whether they are breeding, draught or milch animals, and also whether they are in milk or dry. The National Wastelands Development Board (NWDB), Government of India in its Report on Fodder and Grasses (1987) indicates the norms of feed of green and dry fodder for different categories of livestock based on scientific methods of estimation (see Chopra et al, 1999). According to this report, an adult cattle or buffalo (i.e. above three years) requires 10–16kg of green fodder and 5–8kg of dry fodder per

Table 5.19 *Details of livestock maintained by the sample households by land holding classes and villages in Uttar Kannada district*

Land holding class in acres and villages	Per cent of sample households maintaining livestock	Number of livestock				
		Bullocks	Cows	Buffaloes	Calves	Sheep/goats
Kegdal (inside sanctuary)						
Below 2.5	40.0	10	1	—	2	—
2.5–5	77.8	10	5	—	2	—
5–10	100.0	14	11	—	2	—
10 and above	100.0	16	13	—	–	—
All	66.7	50	30	—	6	—
Badaganasirada (outside sanctuary)						
Below 2.5	60.9	25	5	2	4	—
2.5–5	100.0	23	14	6	6	—
5–10	100.0	31	18	3	7	—
10 and above	100.0	10	12	1	—	—
All	80.9	89	49	12	17	—
Both villages						
Below 2.5	52.6	35	6	2	6	—
2.5–5	90.9	33	19	6	8	—
5–10	100.0	45	29	3	9	—
10 and above	100.0	26	25	1	—	—
All	75.0	139	79	12	23	—

day. On average the green fodder needs of adult cattle are about 13kg per day. For calves below 3 years, these green and dry fodder needs are 1–3kg per day. An alternative estimate by Shah et al (1980, see Chopra et al, 1999) suggests that the per head green fodder and natural herbage needs for adult cattle and buffaloes (i.e. above 3 years) are 4.9–13kg per day, for dry fodder 3.4–6kg per day, and for concentrates 0.2–1kg per day. For cross-breed cattle and improved buffaloes these per day feeding rates are still higher: 10–19.5kg in respect of green fodder and natural herbage, 3.1–4.9kg of dry fodder, and 0.7–2kg of concentrates (Shah et al, 1980). The National Commission on Agriculture (1976) estimated the green fodder needs of different types of cattle and buffaloes including cross-breed varieties to be 3.5–20kg per head per day (see Chopra et al, 1999). The body weight of animals, aside from morphological and physiological factors, is considered to be the single most important factor determining the dietary choices and feeding habits of grazing animals (Rook et al, 2004). For instance, small herbivores generally require more energy relative to their gut capacity than large ones, and they have to select high quantity foods. In contrast, large animals with relatively large gut capacity in relation to their metabolic requirements can retain digesta in the gastro-intestinal tract for a longer time and then digest it more thoroughly (Illius and Gordon, 1993, see Rook et al, 2004). Consequently small herbivores are more selective than large ones. According to another study, as per animal nutritionists, grazing animals consume biomass equivalent to 3 per cent of their body weight per day (cited in Nadkarni et al, 1994). Furthermore, it is assumed that 50 per cent of this requirement is met by free grazing during half the year including the rainy season, and only 25 per cent of it during the rest of the year (Nadkarni et al, 1994).

The biodiversity outcomes of grazing by domestic cattle in forests differ depending on the type of animals involved. As stated earlier, grazing by livestock in protected areas puts wild animals at risk of contracting diseases from domestic cattle and also encourages the growth of unpalatable weeds (Jyothis, 2002). According to the Chief Wildlife Warden of Karnataka State, grazing by a single cattle head destroys habitat requisites of two chital (spotted deer). In addition to the deer facing a crisis of survival, the grazing cattle also pose a hazard to endangered species such as tigers when the foodchain ecosystem of herbivores and carnivores is taken into account. The survival of tigers critically depends on the availability of an adequate prey population (News Item, *The New Indian Express*, 15 September, 2003, p3). A study of livestock grazing pressure in the Mudumalai Wildlife sanctuary in the Western Ghats region of India notes that livestock grazing coupled with the removal of cattle dung from the forest floor (which is being sold to the tea and coffee estates surrounding the sanctuary) adversely affected forest regeneration and also encouraged the proliferation of weeds (Silori and Mishra, 2001).

Studies on grazing patterns in eastern and southern Africa rangelands suggest two major changes in the diversity of rangeland vegetation. The first is the loss of perennial grasses and their replacement by annuals, which vary far more in response to fluctuations in rainfall. The second is a reduction in the phenological diversity of the grass sward, an ecological mechanism to counteract interannual variation in production (Perrings, 2000). Rising grazing pressures frequently have the effect of lowering the resilience of rangelands (Perrings and Walker, 1995; 1997, see Perrings, 2000). Another study of cattle grazing in the Victoria Alpine National Park in Australia cites evidence to show that cattle-grazing has a substantial and lasting impact, altering the structure and composition of sub-alpine grassland, heath and vegetation, as well as significantly influencing the natural regeneration of the ecosystems (Fraser and Chisholm, 2000). The study notes further that cattle grazing reduces the structural and floristic diversity of the vegetation, impacting upon the summer display and luxuriance of the wild flowers, such a notable feature of ungrazed high alpine plains. As regards the claim that grazing reduces the likelihood of upland bush fires, the study notes that cattle mostly eat snowgrass and other herbs and that shrub cover has increased as a result which does not reduce fire risk, but instead is more likely to enhance it. Fire prevention is, therefore, held as a spurious claim to justify the continuation of grazing, which also has been partly responsible for spreading exotic weeds (Wahren et al, 1994, see Fraser and Chisholm 2000). Another study pertaining to Lake Mburo National Park in Uganda noted that although decreased grazing pressure helped bush regeneration and wildlife population to increase, it also resulted in the spread of tsetse fly which was detrimental to pastoral activities in the park and surrounding areas (Emerton, 1999b). A study of plant and insect diversity to variations in grazing intensity in North Germany noted that vegetation complexity was significantly higher on ungrazed grasslands compared to pastures, but did not differ between intensively and extensively grazed pastures. The study also noted that insect species richness was higher on extensively than on intensively grazed pastures (Kruess and Tscharntke, 2002). Loss of resilience of tropical forest ecosystems due to overgrazing and other factors are likely to have more serious short- and long-term consequences, especially considering their importance from the viewpoint of global biodiversity.

Keeping in view the above, in order to estimate the grazing values derived by the sample households from the Dandeli forests, it is assumed that a grazing adult animal, while free grazing, consumes an average quantity of 13kg of green fodder/natural herbage per head per day. Furthermore, as stated above, it is assumed that 50 per cent of this is met by free grazing during six months (including the rainy season) and 25 per cent during the remaining six months. On this basis, an average adult cow while free grazing consumes about 1779.38kg of green fodder or natural herbage per annum from the forests. Crop residues such as paddy straw produced on the farms and purchased feeds are assumed to supplement and meet the rest of the daily feeding needs of the livestock maintained by the sample households. In order to value the green fodder/natural herbage grazed by the livestock, the price of a close substitute, paddy straw, which is about Rs0.90/kg (at 1999–2000 prices) has been used.

Using the above norms, estimates of the animal units owned by the sample households, and the quantity and value of grazing benefits appropriated by them are presented in Table 5.20. The number of livestock owned by the sample households in standardized animal units is around 3.1 animal units per household for the sample as a whole. The number of animal units owned per household is higher in Badaganasirada village (3.5), located on the periphery of the Dandeli Wildlife Sanctuary, compared to that in Kegdal village (2.5), located within the sanctuary. The number of livestock in animal units varies positively with farm size in both the sample villages. Taking the two villages together, the number of livestock in animal units owned by the sample households ranges from 1.2 animal units per household among small holdings of below 2.5 acres to 8.7 animal units per household among very large holdings of 10 acres and above. On a per acre basis, it appears that the number of livestock in animal units maintained by small farmers is higher in comparison with other categories of farmers. It is also higher among Badaganasirada farmers compared to their counterparts in Kegdal village. For the sample as a whole, it is estimated that the quantity of green fodder or natural

Table 5.20 *Average number of livestock in standardized animal units owned by the sample households and the quantity and value of green fodder or natural herbage grazed by them from the Dandeli forests per year by land holding classes and villages in Uttar Kannada district*

Land holding class in acres and villages	Number of livestock in animal units owned		Quantity of green fodder or natural herbage grazed by livestock in kg per household per annum	Value of green fodder or natural herbage grazed by livestock in rupees per household per annum
	Per household	Per acre		
Kegdal (inside sanctuary)				
Below 2.5	0.8	0.8	1423.5	1281.2
2.5–5	1.8	0.6	3202.9	2882.6
5–10	5.2	0.8	9252.8	8327.5
10 and above	7.3	0.6	12,989.5	11,690.6
All	2.5	0.7	4448.5	4003.7
Badaganasirada (outside sanctuary)				
Below 2.5	1.5	1.4	2669.1	2402.2
2.5–5	3.7	1.1	6583.7	5925.3
5–10	6.3	1.0	11,210.1	10,089.1
10 and above	11.7	1.1	20,818.7	18,736.8
All	3.5	1.1	6227.8	5605.0
Both villages				
Below 2.5	1.2	1.2	2135.3	1921.8
2.5–5	2.9	0.9	5160.2	4644.2
5–10	5.9	0.9	10,498.3	9448.5
10 and above	8.7	0.7	15,480.6	13,932.5
All	3.1	0.9	5516.1	4964.5

herbage grazed by the livestock while free grazing in the forests averages over 5516kg per household per annum valued at over Rs4964. The grazing value derived by the sample households is higher in Badaganasirada village than in Kegdal village. Since the number of livestock in animal units owned by the sample households varies positively with farm size, the grazing values appropriated by the households from the forests also varies positively with farm size ranging from over Rs1921 per household among small holdings to over Rs13,932 among very large holdings.

Fuelwood benefits

Forest and rural communities in many low income countries depend on forests and other wooded lands to meet their household energy needs. Fuelwood is a major item collected by those communities from forests and other wooded lands. FAO (2000, SCBD, 2001a) statistics suggest that some 1.86 billion m^3 of wood is extracted from forests for fuelwood and conversion to charcoal. Of this total, roughly 50 per cent comes from Asia, 28 per cent from Africa, 10 per cent from South America, 8 per cent from North and Central America and 4 per cent from Europe (SCBD, 2001a). The World Energy Council, in its Survey of Energy Resources, 2001 notes that in 1999 about 1.4 billion tonnes of fuelwood were produced worldwide, which is about 470 Mtoe (Million tonnes of oil equivalent) or about 5 per cent of the world's total energy requirement. Total world fuelwood production in 1999 averaged about 472.3 Mtoe. Of this Asia's share was 45.8 per cent, followed by Africa (29.9 per cent), North and South America (each around 8 per cent), Europe (7.4 per cent) and the remaining by other regions. Annual per capita consumption of woodfuels (i.e. fuelwood, charcoal and black liquor) averaged around 0.3–0.4m^3 for the world as a whole. Per capita annual woodfuel consumption is highest in Africa (0.77m^3); for Asia the overall per capita consumption is low but shows wide variations across countries with some South and Southeast Asian countries consuming around or more than 0.5m^3 per capita annually. For India, fuelwood is estimated to provide almost 60 per cent of energy in rural areas and around 35 per cent in urban areas. Annual consumption of fuelwood in India in 1998 was estimated at around 217 million tonnes, of which only about 18 million tonnes constitutes sustainable availability from forests; approximately half of fuelwood supplies is from sources outside forests such as farms, village woodlots, etc., and the rest from unsustainable removal from forests. For sub-Saharan Africa, it is estimated that woodfuels account for between 90–98 per cent of household energy consumption (www.worldenergy.org). The International Energy Agency (1998) estimates that 11 per cent of world energy consumption comes from biomass, mainly fuelwood. The IEA (1998) estimates that about 42 per cent of India's primary energy consumption comes from biomass, the figure for developing countries is about 35 per cent (SCBD, 2001a).

In terms of the biodiversity outcomes of fuelwood collection, the general perception is that fuelwood collection is a major factor behind forest degradation and biodiversity loss. Whether fuelwood collection or timber felling is to be blamed is debatable, and possibly the factors behind forest degradation and biodiversity loss will differ across countries, regions and forest sites. Typically forest degradation will impact on fuelwood collection with fuelwood collectors having to travel greater distances and spend more time on fuelwood collection. The distances travelled and time spent will depend on the terrain of a forest site and other factors, and will obviously differ in tropical forest ecosystems as compared to rangelands and savannas. Regarding the adverse environmental consequences of fuelwood collection, one study from Malawi cites evidence of destructive harvesting techniques such as trees being felled for firewood and collectors destroying coppices from stumps and saplings which are required for natural regeneration (Knact Consultants, 1999, see Fisher, 2004). This study, however, acknowledged that from an environmental standpoint, the most worrisome commercial forest activities in the study area are charcoal production and timber extraction resulting in the felling of indigenous and protected trees, soil erosion and loss of habitat for plant and animal species (Fisher, 2004).

Details regarding the fuelwood collected by the sample households from the Dandeli forests, such as the number of household members involved in collecting fuelwood, time spent and distance travelled for fuelwood collection as well as the quantity and value of fuelwood appropriated from the Dandeli forests is presented in Table 5.21. Overall about two persons per household are involved in fuelwood collection per trip. This rate is slightly higher for the households residing outside on the periphery of the Dandeli Wildlife Sanctuary in comparison with the households residing within the sanctuary. Overall the sample households spent about 10 hours per week collecting fuelwood from the Dandeli forests. Obviously those households residing in the village located on the periphery of the wildlife sanctuary spent more time (12.3 hours per week) compared to the households

Table 5.21 *Details of fuelwood collection by the sample households from the Dandeli forests by land holding classes and villages in Uttar Kannada district*

Land holding class in acres and villages	Number of household members collecting firewood (persons per trip per household)	Time spent and distance travelled for fuelwood collection per household		Quantity and value of fuelwood collection per annum	
		Hours per week	km per trip	kg per household	Rupees per household
Kegdal (inside sanctuary)					
Below 2.5	1.9	4.5	1.9	2140.0	1712.0
2.5–5	2.0	7.4	2.5	1955.6	1564.5
5–10	2.0	5.0	2.6	2540.0	2032.0
10 and above	2.0	13.0	3.4	2400.0	1920.0
All	1.9	6.4	2.4	2181.8	1745.4
Badaganasirada (outside sanctuary)					
Below 2.5	1.9	12.3	2.9	1826.1	1460.9
2.5–5	2.2	12.0	2.7	2446.2	1957.0
5–10	2.2	11.8	2.8	2288.9	1831.1
10 and above	2.5	16.5	5.5	2600.0	2080.0
All	2.1	12.3	2.9	2119.1	1695.3
Both villages					
Below 2.5	1.9	9.2	2.5	1950.0	1560.0
2.5–5	2.1	10.2	2.6	2245.5	1796.4
5–10	2.1	9.4	2.7	2378.6	1902.8
10 and above	2.2	14.2	4.1	2466.7	1973.4
All	2.0	10.1	2.7	2145.0	1716.0

(6.4 hours per week) residing within the sanctuary. It is significant that contrary to the popular notion that it is the poor and small farmers who primarily depend on the forests for meeting their fuelwood and biomass needs, our data show that large holdings spend more time collecting fuelwood compared to smaller holdings. Thus, for the sample as a whole, while households with holdings of below 10 acres spent 9–10 hours per week per household on fuelwood collection, the corresponding figure for very large holdings with 10 acres and above was 14 hours. Overall the sample households travelled a distance of about 2.7km per trip for fuelwood collection. The average distance travelled is obviously higher for the households of Badaganasirada village compared to that for Kegdal village. Larger holdings travelled a greater distance per trip for fuelwood collection compared to other holdings. Overall the sample households collected about 2145kg of firewood per household per annum, valued at around Rs1716. The quantity of fuelwood collected and the values appropriated are higher for the sample households of Kegdal located within the wildlife sanctuary than those for the households residing outside the sanctuary.

NTFP (bamboo) benefits

Uttar Kannada has been famed for its rich forest and wildlife resources from colonial days, as noted earlier. In fact in the 17th century both the British and the Dutch established trade stations on its coast for trading in forest resources such as wild pepper, cardamom, sandalwood and teakwood (Gadgil, 1992). Forest policy during the colonial period was geared to exploiting forests for the export market, constructing infrastructure such as railways, and building forest-based industries, especially plywood and paper industries. This process of forest exploitation accelerated after independence when forest-based industries were encouraged through a supply of cheap raw materials such as bamboo, which was found in abundance in the rich evergreen forests of the district (Nadkarni et al, 1989; Ninan, 1996). This not only put further pressure on the forest wealth of Uttar Kannada but also aggravated conflicts between the local and larger economies over the appropriation and use of forest resources.

The sample households also depend on the Dandeli forests for other NTFPs, especially bamboo for construction purposes such as to make huts, cattle sheds, fencing, etc. Bamboo is collected only once each year. The data presented in Table 5.22 show that almost 39 per cent of the sample households collected bamboo poles from the forests. Interestingly the proportion of sample households collecting bamboo from the forests varies positively with farm size. This proportion is relatively higher (over 42 per cent) for the sample households residing within the Dandeli Wildlife Sanctuary compared to that (over 36 per cent) for the households residing outside the sanctuary. The sample households on average spent about 5.8 hours per reporting household per annum to collect bamboo from the Dandeli forests. The time spent on bamboo collection is not only higher for the

Table 5.22 *Details of bamboo resources collected by the sample households from the Dandeli forests by land holding classes and villages in Uttar Kannada district*

Land holding class in acres and villages	Proportion of sample households collecting bamboo	Time spent on bamboo collection in hours per reporting household per annum	Average quantity of bamboo collected, i.e. number of poles per reporting household per annum	Value of bamboo collected in rupees per reporting household per annum
Kegdal (inside sanctuary)				
Below 2.5	46.7	2.6	19.3	772.0
2.5–5	33.3	4.0	13.3	532.0
5–10	40.0	3.5	37.5	1500.0
10 and above	50.0	4.5	7.5	300.0
All	42.4	3.3	18.9	756.0
Badaganasirada (outside sanctuary)				
Below 2.5	26.1	6.7	25.8	1032.0
2.5–5	46.2	8.0	20.7	828.0
5–10	44.4	7.3	20.3	812.0
10 and above	50.0	16.0	30.0	1200.0
All	36.2	7.8	22.9	916.0
Both villages				
Below 2.5	34.2	4.5	22.3	892.0
2.5–5	40.9	6.7	18.2	728.0
5–10	42.9	6.0	26.0	1040.0
10 and above	50.0	8.3	15.0	600.0
All	38.8	5.8	21.1 (8.2)	844.0 (327.5)

Note: Figures in parentheses are on a per sample household basis.

households residing outside the sanctuary but also varies positively with farm size. On average the sample households collected over 21.1 bamboo poles per reporting household per annum (or 8.2 poles per sample household) valued at about Rs844 (or Rs327.5 per sample household). Only very few households reported the collection of other NTFPs such as honey and wild mushrooms.

Present value of benefits from forest resources

The economic incentive to extract forest resources depends on the net benefits that the households are able to obtain. For this the cost of collecting and related costs need to be accounted for. While the households were able to furnish details of the time spent on fuelwood and bamboo collection in the forests, making it relatively easy to estimate these costs, estimating the grazing costs was not so straightforward. In the study area there was no controlled grazing. Usually the livestock are taken to the forests for free grazing by household members when they go for fuelwood collection. In the context of joint costs one method is to apportion such costs in terms of the share of the value of each product. This is commonly applied in agricultural economics to apportion joint costs in order to estimate net returns from crop and livestock production. However, in this case this method is not suitable since, even though the fuelwood collection requires considerable labour and time, in value terms the value of fuelwood collected is much lower than the grazing values appropriated by the households. For the households, the only grazing cost incurred was to take the livestock along with them when they go to the forest for fuelwood collection and allow them free grazing. Using our value judgement, about 20 per cent of the cost of time spent on fuelwood collection has been apportioned and considered as the grazing costs. The cost of time spent on fuelwood and bamboo collection (including taking the livestock along for free grazing) has been valued at the cost of the minimum wages forgone which was about Rs35 per human day during the reference period. Using these cost estimates and the gross benefit (undiscounted) values presented earlier, the gross and net benefits from total forest resources, that is grazing, fuelwood and bamboo benefits, obtained by the sample households in present value terms at 8, 10 and 12 per cent discount rates for cash flows summed up over 25 years at 1999–2000 prices is presented in Table 5.23.

As Table 5.23 shows, the sample households appropriated forest resources from the Dandeli forests to the tune of over Rs54,964 per household in gross terms and over Rs39,996 per household in net terms at a 12 per cent discount rate. Grazing values account for the dominant share of the total value of forest resources extracted by the households, followed by fuelwood and bamboo. The sample households are estimated to extract forest resources valued at Rs4.4 million in gross terms and Rs3.2 million in net terms at a 12 per cent discount rate for cash flows summed up over 25 years at 1999–2000 prices.

An attempt is also made to estimate the net forest resources appropriated by the sample households from the Dandeli Wildlife Sanctuary on a per hectare basis, both excluding and including external costs. Following the procedure outlined in Chapter 4, it is assumed that 1, 2.5 and 5 per cent of the sanctuary area serves as the catchment area for the sample households to extract forest resources, that is fuelwood, bamboo and grazing by their livestock. Table 5.24 shows that, excluding external costs, the sample households appropriate forest resources valued at Rs172–Rs860.7/ha per year or US$4–19.9/ha per year. Including external costs, the net values appropriated by them are Rs157–784 or US$3.6–18.1 per ha per year.

Table 5.23 *Present value of gross and net benefits of forest resources appropriated by the sample households of Kegdal and Badaganasirada villages, Uttar Kannada district from the Dandeli forests (for cash flows summed over 25 years at 1999–2000 prices)*

Forest resources	Discount rates %	Gross benefits (Present values)		Net benefits (Net present values)	
		Rupees per household	Total sample households in million Rs	Rupees per household	Total sample households in million Rs
Grazing	8	52,994.9	4.2	48,941.5	3.9
	10	45,063.0	3.6	41,616.2	3.3
	12	38,937.3	3.1	35,959.1	2.9
Fuelwood	8	18,317.9	1.5	2104.2	0.2
	10	15,576.2	1.2	1789.3	0.1
	12	13,458.8	1.1	1546.0	0.1
Bamboo	8	3496.0	0.3	3391.5	0.3
	10	2972.7	0.2	2883.9	0.2
	12	2568.6	0.2	2491.8	0.2
Total forest resources	8	74,808.8	6.0	54,437.2	4.4
	10	63,611.9	5.1	46,289.4	3.7
	12	54,964.7	4.4	39,996.9	3.2

Notes: Total forest resources is the sum of grazing, fuelwood and bamboo values.
To estimate the gross or net benefits from forest resources appropriated by the sample households the per household values were multiplied by the total number of sample households, i.e. 80 households.

Table 5.24 *Estimated net forest resource benefits appropriated by the sample households of Kegdal and Badaganasirada villages, Uttar Kannada district from the Dandeli Wildlife Sanctuary in rupees and US$/ha per year*

Assumed sanctuary catchment area as % of total wildlife sanctuary area	Net forest resource benefits	
	Excluding external costs	Including external costs incurred by the sample households
	Rupees per ha per year	
1	860.7	784.9
2.5	344.3	314.0
5	172.1	157.0
	US$ per ha per year	
1	19.9	18.1
2.5	7.9	7.2
5	4.0	3.6

Notes: Sanctuary catchment area refers to that proportion of the wildlife sanctuary area that is assumed to be accessible and used by the sample households to extract forest resources.
External costs refers to wildlife damage costs and defensive expenditure to protect against wildlife.
The figures in Indian rupees have been converted to US dollars by using the exchange rate of US$1 = Rs43.33 during 1999–2000.

Forest resources and household income

Information on the source of the annual gross income of the sample households is presented in Table 5.25. It is clear that in both villages agriculture contributed the major share, that is around 60 per cent of the annual gross income of the sample households. Interestingly, the share of forest resources in the annual gross income of the sample households is conspicuously higher in Kegdal village (over 34 per cent), located within the Dandeli sanctuary, compared to in Badaganasirada village (over 27 per cent) located outside on the periphery of the sanctuary. However, in absolute terms, the sample households of Badaganasirada appropriated more forest resources (over Rs7632 per household) than the sample households of Kegdal (over Rs6070 per household). In addition, the annual gross income of the sample households of Badaganasirada is much higher than that of the households of Kegdal. The share of agriculture in gross annual household income generally increases with farm size. Although in proportionate terms the share of forest resources in gross annual household income varies inversely with farm size, what is most interesting to note is that in absolute terms the value of forests resources appropriated by the sample households varies directly with farm size, ranging from

Table 5.25 *Annual gross income by source of sample households of Kegdal and Badaganasirada villages, Uttar Kannada district in rupees per household*

Villages and land holding class in acres	Source of gross household income			
	Agriculture	Forest resources	Other sources	Total gross household income
Kegdal (inside sanctuary)	10,663.6 (60.0)	6070.3 (34.2)	1041.2 (5.8)	17,775.1 (100)
Badaganasirada (outside sanctuary)	16,956.3 (60.9)	7632.2 (27.5)	3239.0 (11.6)	27,827.5 (100)
Both villages				
Below 2.5	4287.2 (36.3)	3787.1 (32.1)	3741.2 (31.6)	11,815.5 (100)
2.5–5	15,321.6 (66.6)	6738.8 (29.3)	939.2 (4.1)	22,999.6 (100)
5–10	22,744.3 (63.8)	11,797.0 (33.1)	1118.3 (3.1)	35,659.6 (100)
10 and above	47,527.5 (73.7)	16,205.9 (25.1)	753.3 (1.2)	64,486.7 (100)
All	13,777.3 (59.5)	7009.0 (30.3)	2359.9 (10.2)	23,146.2 (100)

Notes: Figures in parentheses are the percentage distribution by source of gross income to total gross household income.
Forest resources include fuelwood, grazing and bamboo benefits.
Other sources of income refer to income from non-agricultural sources.

over Rs3787 per household among small holdings, to over Rs16,205 per household among very large holdings. Since larger holdings own more livestock, the grazing benefits derived by them from the Dandeli forests are also higher which largely explains this trend.

Wildlife damage costs and defensive expenditure

The costs of conservation borne by the local communities, apart from the forgone benefits, include the cost of damages caused by wildlife to their crops and property and the defensive expenditure necessary to protect against wildlife attacks. These are the negative externalities of wildlife conservation that are borne by the local communities living within and on the fringes of protected areas and forests. Table 5.26 illustrates these external costs as borne by the sample households. For the sample as a whole, 40 per cent of the sample households reported incurring wildlife damage costs. If the preceding 5 years are considered, the proportion of households reporting wildlife damage rose to 70 per cent. Quite understandably a higher proportion of households residing within the sanctuary (i.e. Kegdal) reported wildlife damage compared to those living on the periphery of the sanctuary (i.e. Badaganasirada). Overall, the sample households incurred an average cost of Rs3695 per reporting household (and Rs4183 in the last five years) owing to wildlife damage. Interestingly, although the proportion of households reporting damage by wildlife is greater among those residing within the sanctuary compared to those living on the periphery of the sanctuary, in value terms the damage borne by the households living outside the sanctuary is higher. Thus, while the wildlife damage costs incurred by the Kegdal households averaged around Rs3673 per reporting household during 1999, these costs were conspicuously higher (Rs5025) for Badaganasirada households. This can be explained by the fact that the Badaganasirada households report more area under cultivation and hence incurred comparatively higher costs. Rice, followed by banana, is the crop most affected by the depredations of wildlife, especially wild elephants and boar. In fact the households in the surveyed villages observed that due to a reduction in the population of predators, especially tigers and leopards, the population of wild boar in the area has increased, resulting in greater frequency of attacks by wild boar and other wild animals on their crops and property. For the sample as a whole the average wildlife damage costs increase with farm size up to holdings of 10 acres, and then declines. The sample households also bear additional costs by way of defensive expenditure to protect against wildlife attacks – for example bursting firecrackers or beating drums to scare away the wild animals that threaten their farms, life and property. These defensive expenditures average around Rs356 per reporting household per year and are higher in Badaganasirada than in Kegdal. On a per acre basis, these external costs are over Rs448 for the sample as a whole. These per acre costs are comparatively higher among households residing within

Table 5.26 Particulars of external costs (wildlife damage costs and defensive expenditure to protect against wildlife) incurred by sample households of Kegdal and Badaganasirada villages, Uttar Kannada

Land holding class and sample villages	Per cent of sample households reporting wildlife damages		Wildlife damage costs in rupees per reporting household		Wildlife defensive expenditure during 1999 rupees per reporting household	Total external costs rupees per acre
	Last 5 years	During 1999	Last 5 years	During 1999		
Kegdal (inside sanctuary)						
Below 2.5	53.3	46.7	4538	5114	200	2560.4
2.5–5	100.0	88.9	2611	2188	200	673.1
5–10	100.0	100.0	4200	4200	200	691.0
10 and above	100.0	50.0	3875	3250	Nil	123.9
All	78.8	66.7	3704	3673	200	659.3
Badaganasirada (outside sanctuary)						
Below 2.5	69.6	17.4	1931	2042	1000	304.2
2.5–5	61.5	30.8	4756	4750	500	451.1
5–10	66.7	44.4	11,500	14,250	Nil	216.1
10 and above	Nil	Nil	Nil	Nil	Nil	Nil
All	63.8	42.6	4598	5025	667	269.9
Both villages						
Below 2.5	63.2	28.9	2800	3836	600	1130.5
2.5–5	77.3	54.5	3621	3046	320	534.7
5–10	78.6	50.0	8182	4714	200	386.2
10 and above	66.7	33.3	3875	3250	Nil	87.5
All	70.0	40.0	4183	3695	356	448.9

Note: Total external costs include wildlife damage costs plus wildlife defensive expenditures.

the sanctuary as compared to those living on the periphery of the sanctuary. These per acre costs also vary inversely with farm size.

As stated in Chapter 3, in order to give an incentive to local communities to support conservation efforts, the State Forest departments give compensation to eligible households affected by wildlife damage. Table 5.27 shows that about a quarter of the sample households filed claims for compensation during 1999. This proportion varies from 13.2 per cent among small holdings to about 43 per cent among medium holdings of 5 to 10 acres and then declines again to 16.7 per cent among very large holdings. Thus, although almost two-thirds of the sample households reported damage caused by wildlife to their crop and property, only a quarter of the households filed claims for compensation. As indicated in Chapter 3, the high transaction costs of obtaining compensation acts as a disincentive to claim compensation. Also according to the Forest Department regulations for claiming compensation, only those with secure titles to their land are eligible for compensation, which is another reason for lower claims. The average amount claimed by the sample households was over Rs2204 and the amount actually received at the time of the survey was Rs259.4, that is just 11.8 per cent of the amount claimed. Interestingly, the proportion of the amount received to the amount claimed as compensation towards wildlife damages varies positively with farm size. Whether this illustrates the fact that large farmers are able to use their superior bargaining power to extract better compensation from the local forest officials or whether the claims by the small farmers are inflated (given the general tendency to overstate compensation claims in the hope of getting higher compensation) is difficult to state and merits being investigated further.

Table 5.27 also sheds light on the transaction cost incurred by the sample households to claim compensation. For the sample as a whole, the households made an average of 2.6 trips per reporting household to the local forest office to pursue their compensation claim. These trips also vary positively with farm size (although not smoothly). The average expenditure incurred to pursue the compensation claims including the opportunity cost of time in terms of forgone income is over Rs439 per reporting household. This also varies positively with farm size. The average expenditure incurred per rupee of compensation realized is about Rs1.7 for the sample as a whole and varies positively (although not smoothly) with farm size. In other words, as seen in previous chapters, the transaction costs of claiming compensation are high. This is a disincentive to the local communities to support conservation efforts. Interestingly, the expenditure incurred by the sample households of Dandeli per rupee of compensation received is comparatively lower (Rs1.7) than that reported by the sample households of Maldari, the coffee growing village (Rs3.6) analysed in Chapter 3. Per capita incomes of the growers in Maldari are comparatively higher, which may partly explain this differential.

Table 5.27 *Particulars of compensation claimed and received for wildlife damage and transaction costs incurred to claim compensation by sample households of Kegdal and Badaganasirada villages, Uttar Kannada during 1999–2000*

Land holding class in acres	Per cent of sample households who filed claims for compensation during 1999	Amount of compensation		Amount received as % to amount claimed
		Claimed	Received	
		(Rupees per reporting household)		
Below 2.5	13.2	1818.2	190.9	10.5
2.5–5	36.4	2504.2	233.3	9.3
5–10	42.9	2285.7	342.9	15.0
10 and above	16.7	2250.0	500.0	22.2
All	25.0	2204.7	259.4	11.8

Land holding class in acres	Transaction cost for claiming compensation			Total expenditure per rupee of compensation realized
	No. of trips made per reporting household	Cost of time in terms of income forgone rupees per reporting household	Total expenditure rupees per reporting household	
Below 2.5	1.7	97.1	216.6	1.1
2.5–5	3.2	302.8	544.5	2.3
5–10	2.4	334.4	524.4	1.5
10 and above	4.0	850.0	1000.0	2.0
All	2.6	256.5	439.2	1.7

Notes: Assuming that one trip to the local forest office requires one human day's work.
Total expenditure includes total expenses actually incurred plus cost of time in terms of the income forgone for trips made to pursue the compensation claims. To estimate the income forgone the monthly income reported by the sample households in the survey has been used.

The local community's perception and attitudes towards the environment and biodiversity conservation

As in the case of Maldari and Nagarhole, in the sample villages of Uttar Kannada we also elicited the preferences of the people towards the environment and bio-diversity conservation. The sequence of the questions asked was similar to that of Maldari and Nagarhole.

Table 5.28 furnishes information on the attitudes of the villagers towards the environment and biodiversity issues in general. It is interesting to note that all the households agreed on the importance of environmental issues and on the issue of the conservation of biodiversity. However, when it came to biodiversity as an important environmental issue and the need to avoid biodiversity loss at any cost,

Table 5.28 *Local community's attitude towards environmental and biodiversity issues (in percentages of total sample respondents)*

Issues	Important	Not important	Total respondents (in nos)
Environmental issues as important	100.0	0.0	80
Biodiversity loss as an important environmental issue	82.5	17.5	80
Biodiversity must be conserved	100.0	0.0	80
Biodiversity loss must be avoided at any cost	85.0	15.0	80

the opinion of the people differed. More than 15 per cent of the households considered protecting biodiversity as not very important to them. For these households, biodiversity loss is not the most important environmental issue, although they agreed on the need to conserve biodiversity. None of the households showed any indifferent attitudes towards these questions.

Since all the households expressed positive attitudes towards biodiversity conservation, we further explored the reasons cited by them for biodiversity conservation. In this case we also presented the respondents with six reasons for biodiversity conservation and asked them to state whether they consider these reasons to be important or not.

It is significant to note that almost 99 per cent of the sample households of the two villages in Uttar Kannada considered biodiversity conservation to be important for its ecological value and as a source of livelihood. Ninety-five per cent of the sample households considered its importance for future generations and also for its aesthetic and recreational values. Other reasons such as its cultural, ritual and spiritual values and its option value (the possibility of finding new uses for biodiversity in future, say, developing a new drug) were assigned less importance.

The respondents were also asked to rank the reasons for biodiversity conservation in order of importance in their opinion. It is interesting to see that, just like the tribals of Nagarhole analysed in the previous chapter, a majority of the

Table 5.29 *Local community's responses towards the various reasons for biodiversity conservation (in percentages of total sample respondents)*

Reasons	Important	Not important
The ecological importance of biodiversity	98.8	1.3
Its ritual and cultural value	80.0	20.0
Its aesthetical and recreational benefits	95.0	5.0
For the future generation	95.0	5.0
The present generation may find new uses in the future	73.8	26.3
It provides a livelihood for many people	98.8	1.3

respondents here, that is 60 per cent of the 80 sample households, assigned first rank to the importance of biodiversity conservation as a source of livelihood. This, of course, stands in contrast to the views expressed by the sample households of Maldari, the coffee-growing village of Kodagu district for whom its value for future generations was assigned first rank, followed by its livelihood and eco-system functions. The top ranking assigned to the livelihood function to justify biodiversity conservation stated by the sample households of the two villages in Uttar Kannada district is, of course, not surprising considering the substantial direct benefits appropriated by them from the Dandeli forests, such as grazing, fuelwood and other NTFP (bamboo) benefits, as noted earlier. The importance of biodiversity conservation for its ecosystem function was assigned second rank by the sample respondents. Almost 79 households responded positively towards this question and among these, while 26.6 per cent assigned first rank, 43 per cent placed it second and 21 per cent third. The importance of conserving biodiversity for future generations – its bequest value – and its recreational and aesthetic values were the reasons placed next in order of importance. Other reasons, such as its ritual and cultural value and its option value, were assigned lesser importance by the respondents.

After eliciting the attitudes of the villagers towards biodiversity conserva-tion, we concentrated on the specific issue of elephant conservation. The Dandeli Wildlife Sanctuary is also an important elephant habitat. Like their counterparts in Maldari village in Kodagu district, the sample households of the two villages in Uttar Kannada have also reported attacks on their crops and property by wild elephants and other wild animals. Fragmentation of the habitat has resulted in the wild elephants and other wild animals raiding human habitations and villages in

Table 5.30 *Ranking of reasons stated by the sample respondents of Kegdal and Badaganasirada villages in Uttar Kannada district for biodiversity conservation*

Reasons	Rank 1	Rank 2	Rank 3	Rank 4	Rank 5	Rank 6	Total
Keeps ecosystem stable and functioning	21 (26.6)	34 (43.0)	17 (21.0)	6 (7.6)	1 (1.3)	0 (0.0)	79 (100)
Ritual and cultural value	1 (1.6)	9 (14.1)	11 (17.2)	19 (29.7)	11 (17.2)	13 (20.4)	64 (100)
Aesthetic and recreational value	4 (5.3)	7 (9.2)	22 (28.9)	25 (32.9)	16 (21.1)	2 (2.6)	76 (100)
Importance for future generations	6 (7.9)	15 (19.7)	20 (26.3)	12 (15.8)	20 (26.3)	3 (3.9)	76 (100)
Importance for developing a new product in the future	1 (1.7)	2 (3.4)	6 (10.2)	18 (30.5)	31 (52.5)	1 (1.7)	59 (100)
Important as a source of livelihood	48 (60)	13 (16.3)	8 (10)	8 (10)	3 (3.8)	0 (0)	80 (100)

Note: Figures in parentheses are percentages of row totals.

search of food and water. The frequency of these attacks is on the increase according to the sample farmers. Given this situation, it is important to find out whether the villagers have a positive attitude or not towards elephant conservation. As stated earlier, wild Asian elephants, a keystone and threatened species, were the focus of our CVM survey. Just as in Maldari and Nagarhole, we imparted adequate information to the respondents about the status of the wild elephants in Asia and South India in particular. The respondents were then asked to respond and state whether they considered it important to conserve elephants in this situation.

- *According to the IUCN's Species Survival Commission's Asian Elephant Specialist Group, there are only 20,000 to 24,000 elephants surviving in India. In the Southern states of India (Karnataka, Tamil Nadu and Kerala) there are about 6000 elephants only. According to the Zoological Survey of India this animals is vulnerable in its status. Due to illicit killing for tusks the proportion of male elephants are declining. In this situation do you think it is important to conserve our wild elephants?*

The respondents were asked to indicate their 'Yes' or 'No' answer to the above question. Interestingly the survey revealed that around 98 per cent of the sample households agreed that it is important to conserve wild elephants.

We probed further to find out the reasons for the responses stated by the respondents. From those who answered 'yes', the reasons for elephant conservation as perceived by the respondent was elicited. We presented the respondents with a further set of six reasons why elephants need to be conserved and asked them to respond and state whether the reasons are important or not. The respondents were also asked to rank the reasons for elephant conservation in order of importance in their opinion (Table 5.31). The three most important reasons for elephant conservation in terms of being ranked first and second by the villagers are: the right of elephants to exist; the fact that elephants are beautiful animals; and their usefulness for domestic work such as transporting logs and use in temple rituals. Over 69 per cent assigned first rank to the right of elephants to exist followed by 62.8 per cent who assigned second rank to the reason that elephants are beautiful animals. Other reasons for elephant conservation, such as its educational and option values were relatively less important to the villagers. Out of 70 households, 70 per cent assigned third or fourth rank to the spiritual value of elephants justifying their conservation.

Table 5.31 *Ranking of reasons assigned by the sample respondents of Kegdal and Badaganasirada villages in Uttar Kannada district for elephant conservation*

Reasons	Rank 1	Rank 2	Rank 3	Rank 4	Rank 5	Rank 6	Total
Elephants are beautiful animals	16 (20.5)	49 (62.8)	13 (16.7)	0 (0.0)	0 (0.0)	0 (0.0)	78 (100)
Elephants have their own right to exist	54 (69.2)	18 (23.1)	3 (3.8)	3 (3.8)	0 (0.0)	0 (0.0)	78 (100)
Elephants have educational value	0 (0.0)	0 (0.0)	0 (0.0)	0 (0.0)	1 (14.3)	6 (85.7)	7 (100)
Elephants are useful for domestic work	3 (6.0)	22 (44.0)	21 (42.0)	4 (8.0)	0 (0.0)	0 (0.0)	50 (100)
We may find new uses of elephants in the future	3 (9.4)	14 (43.8)	13 (40.6)	2 (6.3)	0 (0.0)	0 (0.0)	32 (100)
The elephant has spiritual value in our life	8 (11.4)	8 (11.4)	31 (44.3)	18 (25.7)	5 (7.1)	0 (0.0)	70 (100)

Note: Figures in parentheses are percentages of the row total.

Valuing the local community's preferences for biodiversity conservation

As stated earlier, of the two sample villages selected for this case study, one is located within the Dandeli Wildlife Sanctuary, and the other is situated outside on the periphery of the sanctuary. As a result, the villagers incur additional costs for agriculture due to attacks from wild animals such as wild elephants, wild boar, etc. In such a situation, we tried to discover what role the respondents would play in the conservation of biodiversity using the contingent valuation method (CVM). We presented the respondents with the following hypothetical situation of elephant conservation and asked them to respond and state the role that they would like to play in it.

- *The elephants require a certain kind of habitat for their survival. In recent years this habitat has been increasingly threatened due to different forms of human activities in the periphery of our forest. In order to arrest many of these activities, we have to educate ourselves. Moreover, there is a need for promoting participatory forest protection in the fringe area of our forest. To ensure the existence of elephants in the Western Ghats for the future generation (say your kith and kin), what role do you think you have to play.*

We defined the 'major role' that the respondents can play for participatory elephant conservation separately for those living in Badaganasirada village outside the sanctuary and Kegdal village within the sanctuary. For respondents residing in Badaganasirada, the major role defined was their willingness to follow the existing wildlife protection rules and spend time voluntarily with the forest officials for the better management and conservation of the elephants' habitat. For respondents residing in Kegdal, the major role defined was their willingness to accept compensation and other facilities from the government and leave the forest in order to provide a better habitat for the wildlife.

It is interesting to note that almost 98 per cent of the sample households in Badaganasirada indicated their willingness to participate in participatory biodiversity conservation. The households were asked how much time they are willing to spend on participatory elephant conservation – for example participating in elephant proof trenching, fire protection measures, etc. It is interesting to note that, on average, the Badaganasirada villagers were ready to spend 25 human days per household in a year for activities related to elephant conservation (Table 5.32). The opportunity cost of time that they are willing to spend on participatory elephant conservation is calculated at over Rs2590 per household per annum in terms of their forgone income. The opportunity cost of time in terms of forgone income varies positively with farm size, since household incomes vary positively with farm size.

In Kegdal, the villagers were asked to play a major role by indicating their willingness to leave the forest by accepting compensation from the government. The respondents were asked an open ended question about the minimum amount they would be willing to accept to relocate outside the wildlife sanctuary. A summary of their willingness to accept (WTA) is presented in Table 5.33, which shows that the minimum amount they were willing to accept ranged from Rs25,000 to Rs1,800,000 per household. The mean amount for the sample as a whole was Rs457,424 per household. However, they emphasized the need to get certain assurances from the government, such as providing fertile land, a house, agricultural

Table 5.32 *Willingness to pay in terms of spending time for participatory elephant conservation by sample respondents of Badaganasirada, Uttar Kannada*

Land holding class in acres	Willingness to pay in terms of spending time for participatory elephant conservation		Opportunity cost of time in terms of the income forgone (Rs/household/annum)
	Hours per week per household	Human days per household per annum	
Below 2.5	3.8	24.9	2017.3
2.5–5	3.8	24.5	2330.6
5–10	4.0	26.0	3514.8
10 and above	4.0	26.0	7150.0
All	3.9	25.0	2590.7

Note: To estimate the opportunity cost of time in terms of the income forgone, we have used the stated monthly income of the sample households indicated during the survey.

Table 5.33 *Average willingness to accept compensation to relocate outside the Dandeli Wildlife Sanctuary as stated by the sample households of Kegdal village, Uttar Kannada (in rupees per household)*

Land holding class in acres	Minimum amount	Maximum amount	Mean amount
Below 2.5	25,000	600,000	215,666.7
2.5–5	280,000	500,000	353,333.3
5–10	500,000	1,000,000	616,000.0
10 and above	1,000,000	1,800,000	1,400,000
All	25,000	1,800,000	457,424.2

implements and employment. If the government were to provide these without fail, the sample households of Kegdal expressed their readiness to relocate outside the sanctuary, even though they hold legal titles to their land.

However, about 12 per cent of the sample households also opined that they were not ready to accept compensation or facilities, if any, offered by the government. For them the major reasons were the fear of not being able to cope with the new surroundings, a fear of losing accessibility to the forests and the fear that their livelihood would be affected if they went out of the forest.

To evaluate the variables influencing the Kegdal respondents' willingness to accept compensation and relocate outside the Dandeli Wildlife Sanctuary, a tobit model (also known as a censored regression model) has been used. The definition and summary statistics of the variables used in the tobit function are indicated in Table 5.34.

Table 5.34 *Definition and summary statistics of variables used in tobit function*

Variables	Minimum	Maximum	Mean	Standard deviation
Willingness to accept (WTA) (amount in rupees)	0	1,800,000	457,424.24	442,101.02
Age of respondent	17	75	39.45	16.56
Sex of respondent (dummy variable where Male = 1; Female = 0)	0	1	0.91	0.29
Literacy status of respondent (dummy variable where Literate = 1; Otherwise = 0)	0	1	0.82	0.39
Household size	2	12	5.73	2.34
Land holding size	0.01	18	4.00	4.19
Wildlife damage costs (amount in rupees for last 5 years)	0	13,000	2736.6	3063.2

Table 5.35 *Maximum likelihood estimates using tobit model of willingness to accept compensation by sample households of Kegdal village, Uttar Kannada district and relocate outside the Dandeli Wildlife Sanctuary*

Variables	Coefficient	Standard error	t ratio
Constant	−3138.50	134,500.0	−0.023
Age of respondent	1985.10	2233.0	0.889
Sex of respondent	108,880.00	122,000.0	0.892
Household size	−26,792.00***	15,980.00	−1.677
Land holding size	100,780.00*	8731.00	11.542
Wildlife damage cost	8.20	11.35	0.723
'a' Sigma	185,000.00*	25,110.00	7.368
Log-likelihood value:	−397.3308		
Number of observations:	33		

Note: *, *** indicate statistically significant at 1 and 10 per cent levels of significance.

Table 5.35, which presents the maximum likelihood estimates of the parameters in the tobit function, indicates that land holding size and household size are the significant variables influencing the amount the Kegdal respondents are willing to accept as compensation to relocate outside the Dandeli Wildlife Sanctuary. The land holding size variable is positive and significantly related with the dependent variable. This, of course, is not surprising and indicates that the minimum amount that the Kegdal respondents are willing to accept as compensation to move out of the sanctuary is positively associated with the size of the land holdings they operate. Household size is negatively related with the dependent variable, implying that bigger households are less inclined to accept compensation and move out of the sanctuary. It was also hypothesized that the respondents' willingness to accept compensation is positively correlated with the cost of wildlife damage borne by them. Although the wildlife damage cost variable is found to positively influence the WTA variable, it was not statistically significant. This could be because even after accounting for wildlife damage costs, the sample households, as noted earlier, obtain significant and high benefits from the sanctuary. The age and sex variables were also not statistically significant. The significance of sigma, which is the inverse of Mill's ratio, indicates that omission of responses with zero willingness to accept compensation would bias the results. The estimated equation is highly significant with a log likelihood value of −397.33.

Summary

The forgoing analysis shows that the opportunity costs of biodiversity conservation in terms of forgone agricultural benefits and forest resources, that is grazing, fuelwood and bamboo, are quite high and significant. Excluding external costs (wildlife damage costs and defensive expenditures to protect against wildlife attacks), the NPVs from agriculture were over Rs77,279/acre (at a 12 per cent discount rate for cash flows summed up over 25 years at 1999–2000 prices) and over Rs73,758/acre when these external costs were also accounted for. The net benefits obtained from grazing, fuelwood and bamboo were also positive and significant. The NPVs from forest resources were over Rs39,996 per household at a 12 per cent discount rate for cash flows summed up over 25 years at 1999–2000 prices. Interestingly, contrary to the popular perception that the poor and those with small holdings depend more on forests for their livelihoods as compared to the better off and those with larger holdings, the evidence presented here shows that in absolute terms the large holdings appropriate more forest resources compared to small holdings. It is estimated that the sample households of Kegdal and Badaganasirada in Uttar Kannada district extract forest resources to the tune of Rs4.4 million (at 12 per cent discount rate) in gross terms and Rs3.2 million in net terms for cash flows summed up over 25 years at 1999–2000 prices. On a per ha basis, it is estimated that the sample households extract forest resources from the Dandeli Wildlife Sanctuary to the value of from Rs157 to over Rs784/ha per year or US$3.6–18.1/ha per year after including external costs.

It is redeeming to note that a majority of the sample households had a positive attitude towards environmental issues in general and biodiversity conservation in particular. The local community emphasized livelihood and ecosystem functions, and also bequest values to justify biodiversity conservation. Asked to justify and rank the reasons for conserving wild Asian elephants, a keystone and threatened species in the region, the sample households emphasized their existence rights and aesthetic value. Interestingly a significant number also emphasized the spiritual value of elephants as worshipped by Hindus as a God, to justify their conservation. Households living on the periphery of the sanctuary indicated that they were willing to spend an average of about 25 human days per year on participatory elephant conservation, which can be calculated to over Rs2590 per household per year in terms of their forgone income. A CVM survey of households residing within the Dandeli Wildlife Sanctuary revealed that landholding size and household size were the two significant variables influencing their willingness to accept compensation to move out of the sanctuary. The amount that the households were willing to accept as compensation was also positively related (although not statistically significant) to the wildlife damage costs incurred by them. However, their willingness to accept compensation is subject to obtaining suitable agricultural land with irrigation facilities, houses, agricultural implements, etc.

6

Summary, Conclusions and Policy Recommendations

Introduction

The Convention on Biological Diversity (CBD) to which 188 countries including India are signatories is the key instrument through which the international community seeks to address its concern and commitment to biodiversity conservation. The CBD has set three major goals: to conserve biodiversity; promote sustainable use of its components; and ensure a fair and equitable sharing of the benefits arising out of the utilization of genetic resources. The convention sets out broad commitments by governments to take action at the national level for the conservation and sustainable use of biodiversity. The strategic plan of the convention adopted by the sixth meeting of the Conference of Parties (COP) to the CBD has set a target of achieving a significant reduction in the current rate of biodiversity loss by the year 2010. This was endorsed by the World Summit on Sustainable Development (WSSD) held in Johannesburg in 2002, which reaffirmed that biodiversity plays a critical role in overall sustainable development and poverty eradication. The prospects for achieving the 2010 target of reducing the current rate of biodiversity loss, however, appear to be bleak. The Millennium Ecosystem Assessment Report (2005) notes that the current species extinction rates are up to 1000 times higher than the fossil record of less than one species per 1000 mammal species becoming extinct every millennium (WRI, 2005). The projected future extinction rate is more than ten times higher than the current rate. It is also reported that 12 per cent of bird species, 25 per cent of mammals, and 32 per cent of amphibians are threatened with extinction over the next century (WRI, 2005). Given this not too optimistic scenario, how best can biodiversity be protected? Establishing an institutional environment and incentives conducive to biodiversity conservation and balancing development goals with conservation, therefore, poses a major challenge to governments, nations and societies.

India happens to be one of the twelve megadiversity countries in the world. Of 25 biodiversity hotspots listed in the world, two – the Western Ghats and the Eastern Himalayas (part of the Indo-Burmese biodiversity hotspot) – are located within the Indian subcontinent (Myers, 1990; Myers et al, 2000). The Western Ghats also figures as one of the eight hottest biodiversity hotpots in the world in terms of five factors: number of endemic plants; number of endemic vertebrates; endemic plants/area ratio; endemic vertebrates/area ratio; and remaining prima- ry vegetation as percentage of original extent (Myers et al, 2000). The Western Ghats region runs parallel to the south-western Coast of India and is spread over six states of southern and western India. About one-third of the geographical area of the Western Ghats is under forests of different types – evergreen to semi- evergreen forests, moist to deciduous forests, etc. The region is rich in forest and hydel resources and biodiversity. Most of the rivers in peninsular India, such as the Godavari, Krishna, Cauvery, Kali Nadi and Periyar, have their origin in the Western Ghats, and the health of these water courses is intimately bound up with the health of the forest catchments in the Western Ghats. The region is a treasure house of several known and unknown flora and fauna, including several mamma- lian species on the endangered list, such as the lion-tailed macaque, four-horned antelope, fishing cat and mouse deer. Some of the best wildlife areas and sanctuar- ies of the Indian subcontinent, with the last remnant populations of such major animals as the tiger, leopard, elephant and Indian bison, are found in the Western Ghats. Other groups, such as birds and amphibians are equally rich in species. Of the 13,000 species of flowering plants found in India, some 3500 are found in the Western Ghats alone and some 1500 are endemic to this region. These include wild relatives of many economically valuable plants such as pepper, cardamom, ginger, mango, jackfruit, and varieties of millets and rice. Some of the most valu- able commercial timbers in the world are found in the Western Ghats. The biodi- versity of the region is under great stress and various stages of degradation due to demographic and economic pressures, market failures and inappropriate policies.

There is a host of legislation and policy pronouncements in India concerned with species and habitat protection. The Madras Wild Elephants Preservation Act of 1873 enacted in the Madras Presidency was the first piece of wildlife legisla- tion in India (Bist, 2002). Subsequently, the Government of India enacted the Elephants Preservation Act of 1879 which along with the Indian Forest Act of 1927 and some other state Acts remained a major legal tool for protecting ele- phants in most parts of the country until 1972 (Bist, 2002). The first codified leg- islation for species and habitat protection in India was the Wild Birds Protection Act of 1887 (World Bank, 1996). However, the most comprehensive Act passed by the Government of India for the protection of wildlife in the country since independence has been the Indian Wildlife (Protection) Act of 1972, which was subsequently amended several times. The Act affords varying degrees of protec- tion to the range of species and habitats under different schedules and enables the setting up of protected areas for the protection of wildlife in the country. The network of protected areas constitutes nearly 4.8 per cent of the total geographical area of India. Another important piece of legislation recently passed by the Indian Parliament was the Biodiversity Conservation Bill in December 2002, which seeks to provide for the conservation of biodiversity, sustainable use of its components and equitable sharing of the benefits arising out of the use of biological resources. In addition, India is a signatory to the CBD and CITES.

In view of its economic and social significance, biodiversity conservation is receiving considerable attention from policy makers and international donor agencies and organizations. This study, which focuses on the tropical forests of the Western Ghats biodiversity hotspot, has tried to assess the status of the biodiversity of the Western Ghats region in terms of the status and changes in the vegetative cover of the forests, and the population of endangered species, as well as assess the comparative economics of biodiversity conservation vis-à-vis the benefits forgone or realizable from alternative land use options for forests, such as for utilizing and sustaining agriculture, plantation crops, animal husbandry, tourism and recreation and other activities. Apart from estimating some of the use and non-use values of tropical forests, the study has also tried to assess the extent of dependence on forests for various products and services by different socio-economic groups and regions as well as analyse the socio-economic and institutional factors inhibiting or promoting biodiversity conservation. The study has tried to analyse the perceptions and attitudes of the local communities towards biodiversity conservation in general and wildlife protection in particular, taking wild Asian elephants, a keystone and threatened species in our study region, as a case study. An attempt was also made to assess the willingness to pay (WTP) or willingness to accept (WTA) compensation for biodiversity conservation and wildlife protection.

To analyse the above issues, the study made an in depth survey of households located in three villages or cluster of villages representing different situations – a plantation dominant village in Kodagu district of Karnataka state where growing plantation crops such as coffee constituted a land use option of forests, a cluster of tribal villages/hamlets within and on the fringes of the Nagarhole National Park in Mysore and Kodagu districts, and two farming villages with a close interaction between agriculture, livestock and forests within/near the Dandeli Wildlife Sanctuary in Uttar Kannada district of Karnataka. In total, 305 households were surveyed from these villages and regions. Apart from a detailed socio-economic survey, a contingent valuation survey was also conducted. As a background to the in-depth survey based on primary investigation, the study analysed the land use and crop pattern changes, population and livestock pressure on natural resources in the study region during 1960–1961 to 1999–2000 as well as the status and changes in the biodiversity of the Western Ghats biodiversity hotspot.

Major findings

Historically, habitat and land use change have had the biggest impact on biodiversity across biomes (WRI, 2005). For terrestrial ecosystems such as tropical forests the most important driver of biodiversity loss in the past 50 years has been land cover changes (WRI, 2005). An analysis of the land use and crop pattern changes in the selected regions from 1960–1961 to 1999–2000 reveals that the net area sown and total cropped area as a proportion of the reporting area has risen for all India, Karnataka and selected districts and taluks in Kodagu, Mysore and Uttar Kannada districts. This increase in net area sown has largely come through reductions in area of other land use categories such as permanent pastures and grazing lands, land under miscellaneous tree crops, cultivable wastes, etc. The forest cover in the country and Karnataka seems to have increased slightly over the time period under review. Across districts it is seen that while Kodagu and Uttar Kannada report a marginal decline in their forest cover in recent decades, Mysore district interestingly records a marginal rise in the forest cover. This, however, does not tell us anything about the state of the forests and biodiversity in these three districts which is degraded in many parts due to encroachments and other human interventions. An analysis of the crop pattern and changes over the same time period reveals that the relative share of crops such as rice and banana which are highly prone to attacks from wildlife – such as elephants, wild boar – have declined in the selected areas which, apart from other factors, may also be a preventive measure undertaken by farmers to reduce losses arising from damage to these crops by wildlife. The decline in the area under permanent pasture, grazing land, and under fodder crops (for example in Uttar Kannada district), as well as the decline in the availability of paddy straw following the reduction in rice area, implies that there will be greater pressure on forest resources to meet the biomass needs of livestock, which will further accelerate biodiversity loss. The area under coffee has increased rapidly in Kodagu district and Virajpet Taluk in particular during the period under review, aided by favourable coffee prices. Higher coffee prices, apart from other factors, also encourage farmers and others to deforest and encroach on forest lands and cultivate coffee and other crops, which is detrimental to biodiversity conservation. Population and livestock pressure on forests and other natural resources are increasing over time and this trend is more conspicuous in Karnataka and the three districts under review.

The status of biodiversity in the Western Ghats biodiversity hotspot was assessed by examining the status and changes over time of the extent and quality of forests in terms of the dense and open forest cover, and scrub, as well as the population of endangered species such as royal Bengal tigers, Asiatic elephants, leopards and other wild species. Although data for India as a whole and the six Western Ghat states indicate that the forest cover has increased between the forest assessment years 1995 and 2001, a disturbing feature to note is that satellite imagery data indicate that the dense forest cover (i.e. those forests with canopy cover of >40 per cent) in Karnataka and the three districts especially, Kodagu and Uttar Kannada, have registered a significant decline, whereas open forest cover (i.e. those forests with canopy cover of 10 to <40 per cent) has increased substantially, which indicates the extent of degradation of forests in the state and districts under review. However, the latest Forest Survey of India (FSI) report for 2003 paints a gloomier picture and shows that the dense forest cover in the country as a whole and four out of the six states in the Western Ghats region – Karnataka, Kerala, Gujarat and Maharashtra – declined between the forest assessment years 2001 and 2003. The FSI 2003 report reveals that each of these states recorded a loss of more than 2000km² of dense forest. This indicates the extent of degradation of forest and biological resources in the Western Ghats biodiversity hotspot.

India is perhaps one of the few countries in the world which recognized the importance of systematic collection of wildlife census data on a periodic basis for tigers, an endangered species from 1972 onwards, and for other major species such as elephant, leopard, and large prey populations subsequently. Assuming that these data are reliable, they can shed light on the health of the ecosystem since species such as tiger and elephant are considered as umbrella, keystone or flagship species and a decline in their population may signify a deterioration in the health of the ecosystem. An analysis of wildlife census data revealed that over the wildlife census years between 1972 and 2001–2002, although the population of tigers increased in India as a whole, and in states like Karnataka, Kerala, Andhra Pradesh, Maharashtra and Tamil Nadu up to the 1980s and early 1990s, thereafter their numbers have declined or remained stagnant, except in Karnataka where their population has shown a consistent increase. Thus, although trends up to the 1980s and early 1990s seemed to offer a ray of hope that conservation efforts initiated in India under Project Tiger in 1972 had helped to reverse the alarming decline of the tiger population in India from around 40,000 at the beginning of the last century to less than 2000 by 1972, recent trends are disturbing. Some wildlife experts even opine that the tiger population of India is just half of that indicated by the wildlife census. In the case of elephants and leopards, wildlife census data suggest that overall there is an improvement in their numbers at all-India level, although 2001–2002 wildlife census data suggest that the population of elephants has declined in comparison to 1997 wildlife census figures. Among the Western Ghat states Karnataka, Kerala and Tamil Nadu reported an increase in the elephant population between the wildlife census years 1993 and 1997, but thereafter their numbers have dwindled or remained stagnant. While the population of leopards increased in Gujarat and Karnataka between 1984 and 1997, other states reported their population to be declining or remaining stagnant. Apart from tigers and leopards, wildlife census data suggest that the population of other species such as wild boar and Indian bison increased in Karnataka between the wildlife census years 1977 and 1997–1998. However, while the elephant population in Karnataka increased between 1977 and 1997–1998, thereafter as per 2001–2002 wildlife census data their numbers decreased, as noted earlier. Of more concern is the sex ratio of elephants. Usually it is the adult male elephants that are the target of poachers who seek the tusks which command a premium in the illegal international wildlife trade. The sustainability of elephants also hinges upon a favourable male to female ratio. The male to female elephant ratio in Karnataka appears to have declined over the wildlife census years 1993 to 2001–2002 from 1:2.6 to

1:3.5. The recent trends indicating a decline in the dense forest cover and in endangered species such as tigers and elephants are a matter of concern. As they are considered as an umbrella or flagship species, their decline indicates a deterioration in the health of the ecosystem, despite conservation efforts. This, along with continued poaching and the flourishing illegal trade in wildlife products such as tiger and leopard skins, ivory, etc., indicates the extent of threats faced by wildlife in India, and the need for sustained measures to conserve India's rich and varied wildlife.

Our analysis covering a cross-section of local communities in the Western Ghats region of India revealed that the opportunity costs of biodiversity conservation in terms of the forgone coffee, agricultural, NTFP and other forest resource benefits are quite high. Even after including external costs – wildlife damage costs and defensive expenditure to protect against wildlife – the sample households of Maldari, the coffee-growing village, reported the net benefits from coffee to be quite high for all land holding groups, with the NPVs in the range Rs17,000–106,100 per acre (at 12 per cent discount rate for cash flows summed over 50 years at 1999 prices) and the IRRs ranging between 16.6–23 per cent. Sensitivity analysis revealed that even if the expected benefits were to decrease by 20 per cent and costs rise by 20 per cent, the net benefits from coffee were still reasonably high and significant with NPVs of Rs53,000–116,300 per acre (using alternate discount rates), and IRRs of around 19.5 per cent. The tribal households living within or near the Nagarhole National Park who depend on the park for NTFPs reported the net benefits from NTFPs to be quite high. Even after including external costs, the NPVs from NTFPs were Rs30,378–41,346 per household using alternate discount rates (8, 10 and 12 per cent) for cash flows summed up over 25 years at 1999 prices. Sensitivity analysis revealed that even if the NTFP benefits were to reduce by 50 per cent, and costs of NTFP extraction to rise by 50 per cent, the NPVs from NTFPs were still positive, being over Rs9967 per household at a 12 per cent discount rate. Most interesting, however, is that if the external costs imposed on third parties such as the coffee growers of Maldari (close to the Nagarhole National Park) are also taken into account, the net benefits from NTFPs became negative: Rs –510.7 per household per year (undiscounted value) or Rs –3212 at a 12 per cent discount rate for cash flows summed up over 25 years at 1999 prices. In other words, although from the viewpoint of the tribals, that is the NTFP extractors, NTFP extraction is a viable activity, from the society's viewpoint it is not. The forgone agricultural benefits reported by the farmers in the two farming villages within/near the Dandeli wildlife sanctuary in Uttar Kannada district exceeded Rs73,700 per acre even after the external costs were accounted for. The net benefits from forest resources (i.e. grazing, fuelwood and bamboo) extracted by the sample households of Dandeli were over Rs39,900 per household per annum. Considering that the local opportunity costs of biodiversity conservation reported by the sample households in the three sets of villages surveyed by us are quite high, it appears that from an economic perspective it is primarily the unpriced and non-market benefits that justify biodiversity conservation.

The tribals living within and on the periphery of the Nagarhole National Park depend on the park for NTFPs. While NTFPs such as fuelwood, wild edible tubers and green leaves, wild fruits and nuts, and bush meat, etc., are collected solely for meeting their subsistence needs, other NTFPs such as honey, honey wax, tree seeds, gooseberry, gum, bamboo and fibre are also being marketed. Overall about 15 per cent of the total value of NTFPs is marketed. In value terms, it is the tribals residing within the national park who realized the higher value of Rs908 per household per year from marketing of NTFPs as compared to Rs466–581 per household per year for tribals living on the periphery of the park. Overall for the sample tribal households, the share of NTFPs in their gross annual household income was over 28 per cent. This proportion was higher – around 47 per cent – for tribals residing within the national park, and 12.5–35.7 per cent for tribals residing on the periphery of the park. Employment on coffee estates, forest employment and NTFPs contributed to around three-quarters of the gross annual household income of the tribals. Using alternative assumptions regarding the Park's catchment area (i.e. 10, 25 and 50 per cent) that is accessed by the tribals and others living within and on the periphery of the Nagarhole National Park, it was estimated that the net NTFP benefits extracted from the Nagarhole National Park (after including external costs) were Rs1442.5–7212.4/ha per year or US$33.5–167.5/ha per year. Interestingly, these estimates fall within the range of US$1–188/ha per year of NTFP values estimated by other studies covering a cross-section of countries (SCBD, 2001a).

The farm households in the two villages, one within and the other on the fringe of the Dandeli Wildlife Sanctuary in Uttar Kannada district depend on the Dandeli forests to meet their grazing, fuelwood and NTFP (bamboo) needs. Excluding external costs, the NPV of forest resource benefits derived by the farm households were Rs39,996–54,437 per household using alternate discount rates (i.e., 8, 10 and 12 per cent) for cash flows summed up over 25 years at 1999–2000 prices. Using alternative assumptions regarding the sanctuary's catchment area (i.e. 1, 2.5 and 5 per cent) that is accessed by farm households living within and on the fringe of the sanctuary, it is estimated that the net forest resource benefits derived by the farm households from the Dandeli Wildlife Sanctuary (excluding external costs) were Rs157–784/ha per year or US$3.6–18.1/ha per year. Forest resource benefits accounted for around 30.3 per cent of gross annual household income of the farm households in Dandeli. The value of total forest resource benefits per household varied positively with farm size, implying that, contrary to popular perception, it is the better off farmers who extract more forest resources than the small and marginal farmers. Since the bigger holdings own a greater number of livestock, the grazing benefits appropriated by them is higher, which largely accounts for this trend.

The external costs of wildlife conservation borne by the local communities residing within or near reserve forests or protected areas include wildlife damage costs and defensive expenditure to protect against wildlife attacks. In order to give an incentive to the local communities to support biodiversity conservation efforts, the State Forest Department has a mechanism to compensate farmers and others who suffer wildlife damages. Our analysis shows that there is no perfect correspondence between the proportion of households reporting wildlife damage and those filing claims for compensation. For instance, in Maldari, the coffee-growing village, while 38.4 per cent of the sample households reported wildlife damage during 1999–2000, only 22.4 per cent of the sample households had filed claims for compensation. In the two villages in Uttar Kannada, 40 per cent of the sample households reported wildlife damage during 1999, but only 25 per cent filed claims for compensation. This is partly due to the fact that the transaction costs to receive this compensation are so high that it acts as a disincentive for conservation. For instance, the sample households of Maldari reported the total expenditure (i.e. actual expenditure plus the cost of time in terms of the income forgone for trips to the local forest office to pursue the compensation claims) per rupee of compensation realized to be Rs3.6. Interestingly while very large holdings with 10 acres and above spent Rs3.2 per rupee of compensation realized, among holdings of below 10 acres these expenditures are considerably higher: Rs3.4–21.7 per rupee of compensation realized, which suggests that the costs of conservation borne by small holdings in this respect is much higher than that borne by large holdings. However, it may be noted that small farmers in particular get tangible benefits such as NTFPs, which is an incentive for conservation. In the case of the two villages in Uttar Kannada, while the average amount of compensation claimed by the sample households was Rs2204 per reporting household, the amount received at the time of the survey was Rs259.4 per reporting household; that is, just 11.8 per cent of the amount claimed. It is worth noting that the proportion of the amount received to the amount claimed as compensation towards wildlife damages varied positively with farm size. Whether this illustrates that large farmers are able to use their superior bargaining power to extract better compensation from the local forest officials, or whether the claims by the small farmers are inflated (given the general tendency to overstate compensation claims in the hope of getting higher compensation) is difficult to state and merits detailed probing.

In devising biodiversity conservation strategies, it is important to know about the perceptions and attitudes of the local communities towards biodiversity conservation in general and wildlife protection in particular, as well as the local values of biodiversity. In this context, it is interesting to see the similarities and contrasts in the perceptions and attitudes of the local communities surveyed by us. Asked to justify and rank the reasons for biodiversity conservation, the sample households of the coffee-growing village emphasized its bequest value, ecosystem and livelihood functions (in that order), whereas the tribals of Nagarhole who depend on the Nagarhole National Park for NTFPs and forest employment emphasized its livelihood function, bequest value, ecosystem function, ritual and cultural values. The sample households of the two farming villages, who depend on the Dandeli Wildlife Sanctuary for grazing, fuelwood and NTFPs, apart from agricultural benefits, also assigned importance to its livelihood function, followed by its eco-system function, bequest value, recreation and aesthetic value. Asked to justify and rank the reasons why wild Asian elephants need to be conserved, the three local communities surveyed by us emphasized its right to existence, its aesthetic value, its usefulness for work and its option value (for future developments). The spiritual value of elephants worshipped by Hindus as a god was also cited as a reason to justify elephant conservation by the sample households of the two farming villages in Uttar Kannada district.

In order to study the value preferences of the local communities towards biodiversity conservation, wild Asian elephants were the focus of our CVM survey. The contingent valuation method (CVM) has been widely used to value biodiversity and endangered species (cf. Jakobsson and Dragun, 1996; Moran, 1994; Pearce and Moran, 1994). It is also the only known method to value non-use values. From the conservationists' perspective this focus (on elephants) is rationalized by the frequently inseparable nature of the subject good from its biosphere and supporting species links. In other words, the purchase of a good offered in a CV exercise often implies the purchase of a complimentary bundle of biodiversity (Moran, 1994). The sample households of Maldari, the coffee growing village, were asked about their willingness to pay in terms of cash or to spend time on participatory elephant conservation (participating in environmental awareness campaigns, constructing elephant proof trenching, forest fire protection measures, etc.). The respondents were also asked to choose between three institutional alternatives while stating their willingness to pay for participatory elephant conservation. These options were a decentralized government organization, a non-governmental organization, and willingness of households to participate irrespective of the institution. It is interesting to note that a majority of the respondents expressed their willingness to pay in terms of spending time on participatory elephant conservation, and they also preferred a decentralized government organization for this purpose. On average the sample households of Maldari were willing to spend 25.8 human days per household annually on participatory elephant conservation. In terms of their forgone income, this costs over Rs6000 per household per annum. This figure varied positively with farm size due to income differentials across different land holding groups.

To evaluate the variables influencing the 'Yes' or 'No' responses of the respondents in Maldari a logit model was used. The analysis showed that landholding size and respondent's educational level were negatively and significantly related with the dependent variable. The external costs of wildlife conservation and the transaction costs to obtain compensation for wildlife damages incurred by small holdings were higher than for large holdings, which partly explains why they are more likely to say 'Yes' to the WTP bid. Of course, some of the large holdings who expressed their inability to spend time on participatory elephant conservation, indicated their willingness to pay in terms of cash. Interestingly the settler variable was positive and significant, which indicates that settlers unlike migrants have a high probability of saying 'Yes' to spending time on participatory elephant conservation. The results also showed that the respondents had a clear preference for a decentralized government organization structure for participatory biodiversity conservation as against other institutional alternatives, possibly because they feel that transparency, accountability and a sense of participation are better under a decentralized government set up for participatory biodiversity conservation.

The tribal households residing within the Nagarhole National Park were asked whether they are ready to play a major role in biodiversity conservation by expressing their willingness to accept the rehabilitation package offered by the government and relocate outside the park in order to provide a better habitat for wildlife. A logit model was used to estimate the valuation function. The results indicated that those tribals residing within the core zone of the national park, and having more income from employment on coffee estates located in the periphery of the park and forest employment were less likely to say 'Yes' to the WTA question. This suggests that they are not fully confident about the economic activities that they can take up in case they are relocated outside the park. Although the tribals derive considerable NTFP benefits from the national park, it was perplexing to note that the coefficient of the NTFP variable had a positive sign, although not statistically significant. This may also be due to the fact that extraction of NTFPs from protected areas is illegal under the Indian Wildlife (Protection) Act of 1972, and hence the tribal respondents are more concerned about losing the income from employment in coffee estates and the forest in case they have to relocate outside the national park. Those tribals who gave protest answers cited reasons such as difficulty and uncertainty about coping with new surroundings, fears about their livelihood, protests from community leaders and losing accessibility to forests, to justify their protest responses.

The sample in Uttar Kannada includes farm households residing in a village (Badaganasirada) located on the periphery of the Dandeli Wildlife Sanctuary and those residing in a village (Kegdal) within the sanctuary. The major role that the respondents can play for participatory elephant conservation was defined separately for those residing within the sanctuary and those residing outside on the periphery of the sanctuary. For the respondents residing on the periphery of the sanctuary the major role defined was their willingness to follow the existing wildlife protection rules and spend time voluntarily with forest officials for the better management and conservation of this elephant habitat. The respondents in Badaganasirada were asked to indicate the time they were willing to spend on participatory elephant conservation such as participating in environmental awareness campaigns, elephant proof trenching, forest fire protection works, etc. It is interesting to note that on average the Badaganasirada villagers were willing to spend 25 human days per household in a year for participatory elephant conservation. The opportunity cost of time that they are willing to spend on participatory elephant conservation works to over Rs2590 per household per annum in terms of their forgone income. The opportunity cost of time in terms of their forgone income also varies positively with farm size since household incomes vary positively with farm size.

The respondents in Kegdal village located within the sanctuary were asked to play a major role by indicating their willingness to accept compensation from the government and leave the forest. They were asked an open ended question about the minimum amount that they would be willing to accept as compensation. The minimum WTA indicated by the respondents was Rs25,000–1,800,000 per household with a mean of Rs457,000 per household. The respondents emphasized the need to get certain assurances from the government such as providing fertile land, a house, agricultural implements, and employment. To evaluate the Kegdal respondents' willingness to accept compensation and relocate outside the Dandeli Wildlife Sanctuary a tobit (censored regression) model was used. The results showed that landholding size and household size were the significant variables influencing the minimum amount that the Kegdal respondents would be willing to accept as compensation to relocate outside the sanctuary. The landholding size variable was positively and significantly related with the dependent variable, implying that the Kegdal respondents' minimum WTA was positively associated with landholding size. The household size variable was negatively and significantly related with the dependent variable, implying that bigger households are less inclined to accept compensation and move out of the sanctuary. Although it was hypothesized that the Kegdal respondents' WTA is positively correlated with the cost of wildlife damage borne by them, the results showed that although the coefficient of the wildlife damage variable was positive, it was not statistically significant. This could be due to the fact that even after accounting for wildlife damage costs, the sample households obtained high and significant benefits from the Dandeli forests, as noted earlier.

Table 6.1 summarizes the economic values and various benefits derived by the local villagers living near/within the tropical forests of the Western Ghats region of Karnataka in terms of US dollars.

Policy implications

The study has important implications for biodiversity conservation and policy. While policies for biodiversity conservation need to be addressed at different scales – global, regional and local levels, understanding the local values of biodiversity conservation and the incentives and disincentives for biodiversity conservation, especially those operating at the local level, is critical to devising appropriate strategies for biodiversity conservation. The study clearly shows that the local opportunity costs of biodiversity conservation are quite high. Hence, the local communities within or near forests and protected areas need to be compensated by the global community at large and others who benefit from biodiversity conservation in order to given an incentive to them to forgo the development option.

Table 6.1 *Summary of economic values and benefits appropriated by the local communities living within or near the tropical forests in the Western Ghats region of Karnataka, India (in US$)*

Economic values/benefits from the ecosystem	Valuation method	Currency/unit	Value			
					(discount rates)	
			–	8%	10%	12%
			(Time span assumed: 50 years; cash flows at 1999 prices)			
NPV of coffee benefits (Maldari)	Opportunity cost approach	US$/ha[a]	–	11,185.6	7948.7	5785.1
		[b]	–	10,818.3	7650.3	5532.5
Willingness to pay for participatory elephant conservation (Maldari)	Non-market valuation – contingent valuation method	Human days/hh/year	25.8	–	–	–
	Opportunity cost of time valued in terms of forgone income	US$/hh/year	139.4	–	–	–
			(Time span assumed: 25 years; cash flows at 1999 prices)			
NPV of NTFP benefits (Nagarhole)	Market-based valuation – local market price of the good or that of a close substitute used	US$/hh[a]	–	985.4	837.9	724.0
		b*	–	960.3	816.6	705.6
		b**	–	-101.5	-86.3	-74.6
			(Assumed park catchment area)			
			–	10%	25%	50%
Estimated net NTFP benefits from Nagarhole National Park	Market-based valuation	US$/ha/year[b]	–	167.5	67.0	33.5
			(Time span assumed: 25 years; cash flows at 1999–2000 prices)			
NPV of agricultural benefits – paddy and cotton (Uttar Kannada)	Opportunity cost approach	US$/ha[a]	–	5998.1	5100.4	4407.0
		b	–	5724.9	4868.0	4206.3

	Valuation method	Unit	Value	(Assumed park catchment area)		
				1%	**2.5%**	**5%**
NPV of net forest resource benefits, i.e. grazing, fuelwood and NTFPs (Uttar Kannada)	Market-based approach	US$/hh[a]	—	1256.3	1068.3	923.1
Estimated net forest resource benefits from Dandeli Wildlife Sanctuary	Market-based approach	US$/ha/year[b]	—	18.1	7.2	3.6
Willingness to accept compensation and relocate outside Dandeli Wildlife Sanctuary (Kegdal villagers, Uttar Kannada)	Non-market valuation – contingent valuation method	US$/hh	10,556.8	—		
Willingness to pay for participatory elephant conservation (Badaganasirada villagers, Uttar Kannada)	Non-market valuation – contingent valuation method	Human-days/hh/year	25.0	—		
	Opportunity cost of time valued in terms of forgone income	US$/hh/year	59.8	—		

Notes:
a – excluding external costs, i.e., wildlife damage costs and defensive expenditure to protect against wildlife attacks
b – including external costs
b* – including external costs incurred by NTFP extractors
b** – including external costs incurred by NTFP extractors and third parties (i.e. coffee growers of Maldari)
NPV – net present value; hh – household; ha – hectare.

Source: Primary Survey

For instance, the water from the river Cauvery, which has its origin in the forest catchment of the Western Ghats region in Kodagu district, is used to provide drinking water to the cities of Bangalore, Mysore and other towns, as well as to irrigate agricultural and farm lands in the Cauvery delta region in Karnataka and Tamil Nadu states. It would be worth considering instituting and levying a biodiversity conservation cess on the citizens of those cities/towns and farmers who benefit from the river Cauvery, and the fund so collected could be used for conservation and development activities in Kodagu district, and other similarly placed districts. This is similar to a watershed protection charge where those, especially downstream users, pay for the benefits received by them from watershed protection (Perrings and Lovett, 2000). Although it is suggested that the watershed value of forests may be captured through water and hydro-power pricing (which also includes a watershed protection charge), given the prevalent hostile environment towards raising water and energy prices, especially in developing countries, it is desirable that the biodiversity conservation cess or watershed protection charge is levied separately. Given the pro-environmental attitude of the general public, such a cess or charge has a better chance of being accepted instead of it being part of the water and energy prices. Furthermore, there is also a strong case for international aid for biodiversity conservation programmes. In this context, it is gratifying to note that the Global Environment Facility (GEF) of the World Bank along with Conservation International (CI) have created a US$150 million fund to protect the Western Ghats' biodiversity hotspot together with other biodiversity hotspots in developing countries. The fund aims to better safeguard the world's vulnerable biodiversity hotspots where about 60 per cent of all terrestrial species are found on only 1.4 per cent of the planet's land surface.

The CVM analysis revealed that the factors influencing the local communities' willingness to pay (in terms of spending time) for participatory elephant conservation or willingness to accept compensation to relocate outside protected areas differ from locale to locale. In the coffee-growing village, the probability to say 'Yes' to the WTP question was higher among small holdings and settlers. Among the Nagarhole tribals the probability to say 'Yes' to the WTA question and relocate outside the Nagarhole National Park was lower among those tribals living in the core zone of the park and also those having income from employment on coffee estates or forest employment. Among the farm households residing within the Dandeli Wildlife Sanctuary, landholding size and household size were the significant variables influencing the probability of their saying 'Yes' to the WTA question. The wildlife damage costs were also a factor positively influencing their WTA, although the coefficient was not statistically significant. While the respondents in the coffee-growing village assigned prime importance to bequest value, followed by ecosystem and livelihood functions to justify biodiversity conservation, these rankings were reversed among the tribals of Nagarhole and farm households of Dandeli who assigned first rank to the livelihood function, followed by bequest value, ecosystem function, and ritual and cultural value, to justify biodiversity conservation. In view of the above it is clear that biodiversity conservation strategies ought to take into account regional and local level conditions in case they are to be more effective. In accordance with the requirements of the CBD, India has also formulated a National Biodiversity Strategy and Action Plan (NBSAP) with regional and sub-regional action plans. While this is laudable, it is important that the biodiversity conservation strategy needs to be flexible enough to accommodate local level factors and conditions in order to be more effective. Moreover, in areas where livelihood issues are dominant, biodiversity conservation policies ought to give a stake in conservation or provide sustainable alternative livelihoods to local and indigenous communities who are affected by the policy for establishing protected areas to conserve biodiversity. This will help to reduce the social costs of conservation.

The study also clearly shows that the present system of giving compensation to farmers affected by wildlife damage is highly inefficient and that the transaction costs to obtain the compensation are quite high. Rather than being an incentive to the local community to conserve biodiversity conservation, it is turning out to be a disincentive, and needs to be thoroughly revamped. Further, the eligibility norms for compensation need to be relaxed so as to cover others affected by wildlife attacks, in order to improve the incentive structure for biodiversity conservation. For instance, settlements within protected areas are deemed to be illegal under the Indian Wildlife (Protection) Act of 1972 and hence tribals and others who were living in protected areas even before such forests were declared protected areas become ineligible to receive compensation for wildlife damage, except in those cases where they have legal titles to the land or property they occupy. For example, most of the farm households in Kegdal village located within the Dandeli Wildlife Sanctuary analysed in Chapter 5 have legal titles to the lands they occupy and hence they are eligible to receive compensation for wildlife damage. The above situation is another disincentive to the local communities to support biodiversity conservation. The case of tribals and others settled in forests prior to the declaration of such forests as protected areas should be treated differently from actual encroachers in forest lands, who do not merit such compensation. Furthermore, in order to improve the incentive structure for biodiversity conservation, subsidies and concessional loans may be given to coffee planters, farmers and other households to install solar-powered electric fencing around their coffee estates and farms to reduce the hazards of wildlife attacks. The state for its part also needs to undertake elephant proof trenching works, solar-powered electric fencing and other preventive measures wherever feasible to reduce the hazards of wildlife attacks on coffee estates, agricultural lands and farms surrounding protected areas and forests.

Notwithstanding the fact that the local communities in the three study sites suffer frequent losses due to wildlife attacks on their crops and property, it is redeeming to note that they have a positive attitude towards biodiversity conservation in general, and wildlife protection in particular, and this needs to be tapped for organizing environmental awareness campaigns at the local level in order to create a better environment for biodiversity conservation. The study also suggests that a decentralized and participatory-based strategy for biodiversity conservation promises to be more effective than other institutional alternatives.

For proper conservation planning and monitoring, availability of reliable data is important, especially on wild flora and fauna. In this connection, it is worth noting that the COP have emphasized to the CBD the need to formulate appropriate indicators to monitor the progress towards the 2010 target of bringing about a significant reduction in the current rates of biodiversity loss envisaged under the CBD. To this end, COP has identified indicators such as trends in the extent of selected biomes, ecosystems and habitats, trends in abundance and distribution of selected species, and change in the status of threatened species, etc. It is, therefore, redeeming to note that India has been conducting a wildlife census every four years since 1972 to collect data on the population of royal Bengal tigers, an endangered species, and other endangered species such as Asian elephants, leopards and their prey population subsequently. However, as stated earlier, there are serious doubts about the reliability of the wildlife census data and suspicions that forest officials are fudging census data in order to present a rosy picture of the wildlife situation in India in an attempt to ward off inconvenient questions and alarm in Parliament, state assemblies and the public domain, especially since considerable funds including from international donor agencies have been channelled to conservation projects in India. The recent public outcry following a news report in a prominent English-language daily regarding the disappearance of tigers from the Sariska Tiger Reserve (one of the tiger reserves covered under Project Tiger in India where special efforts are being made to conserve tigers) led the Prime Minister of India to order an enquiry by the CBI which confirmed that tigers had indeed disappeared from the reserve, although wildlife census data indicated the contrary. This led to the setting up of the Tiger Task Force by the Government of India to recommend measures to improve tiger conservation in India. The wildlife census operations in India need to be thoroughly revamped and streamlined. In order to improve the reliability and credibility of wildlife census data, it is important that experts and representatives of the civil society, such as NGOs and environmentalists, are also involved in the design and collection of wildlife census data to prevent and minimize the scope for fudging by forest officials who have a vested interest in presenting a rosy picture of the wildlife situation in the country. Also, in the case of endangered species such as tigers, elephants and leopards, it may be worth considering having the census conducted on an annual basis, at least until such time that the population of these endangered species is confirmed to have improved to levels that may be considered as a safe minimum standard. It is also desirable that data on the sex composition of tiger and elephant populations are also collected. Such information can give clues regarding the sustainability of these animals. If this information is being collected, it is not being published, except in the case of elephants in states like Karnataka. It is also necessary that data on prey populations are collected in the censuses since the survival of tigers, leopards and other carnivores depends upon the availability of an adequate prey population. Presently this is being done on a piecemeal basis. In addition the techniques used for recording the presence of wild animals in the wildlife census operations needs a rethink, for instance, the pugmark technique that has traditionally been used to record the presence of tigers and other big cats. Doubts have been expressed about the reliability of this method as well as its vulnerability to data fudging. Camera trapping, although expensive is thought to be a more reliable technique and was used by wildlife experts such as Ulhas Karanth to record the presence of tigers in the Nagarhole National Park and other parks/sanctuaries in the country. Estimates of tiger populations for the Nagarhole National Park based on camera trappings were presented in Chapter 4. In the tiger census for the year 2005–2006, it is reported that a GIS technique is to be used to estimate the tiger population. DNA sampling of tiger droppings has also been suggested as a way to estimate the tiger population. Along with these scientific techniques, it is also worth considering conducting surveys of those local communities residing within or near protected areas and finding out about their encounters with wild animals, especially endangered species such as tigers, leopards and elephants. While this may not be helpful in estimating the population of wild animals, it will at least give some clues regarding their presence. For instance, in our study, the local communities were asked about the number of times, places and years that they encountered tigers, elephants, etc., in or near the Nagarhole National Park and Dandeli Wildlife Sanctuary. Although we have not presented these results here, they suggested that the local community's encounters with tigers, for instance, were relatively more frequent in the Nagarhole National Park than in the Dandeli Wildlife Sanctuary where such encounters were rare. Sightings of elephants, bison and deer were more frequent than of other wild animals, such as tigers, leopards, etc., according to the responses of the local communities.

The Wildlife Laws in India lack teeth and need to be sharpened. Forest offenders, especially poachers and those dealing in the illegal trade of wildlife products are often able to escape with light penalties and obtain bail from courts and continue with their activities. The best example is the recent case of a tiger poacher thought to be the kingpin behind many tiger poaching cases in India. Despite having several poaching cases filed against him in a number of Indian states, it emerged that he was always able to obtain bail from the courts and continue with his activity. Penalties for forest offences, especially poaching, should be enhanced and also categorized as non-bailable offences. Long-term imprisonment and in the case of habitual offenders, especially poachers, even the death penalty may be prescribed so as to act as a deterrent to those intending to commit such offences. It is worth recalling that during the Tokugawa period in Japan, 1603–1867, known as the Feudal Period of Japan, the Feudal governments prescribed stiff penalties for those offenders violating forest regulations (Ninan, 1996). While in some fiefs habitual forest offenders (even for stealing protected trees or species) were liable to be beheaded, in other fiefs even first time offenders were liable to be beheaded. Mountain villages that were entrusted with the task of guarding forests in return for some privileges such as rights to gather firewood, nuts and leaves prior to other villages were fined in cases where they failed to identify the offender/s. Penalties for forest offences ranged from fines to imprisonment, banishment, compulsory labour, stripping of user rights and privileges to village community forests or lord's forests and beheading (Ninan, 1996). If the offender was the village leader or forest guard, the punishment was extremely severe, more than normally prescribed for others (Ninan, 1996). Even in ancient India, there is evidence of stiff penalties for forest offenders. Kautilya's Arthasastra, an ancient Indian political treatise which gives valuable insights into the management of forests during the reign of an ancient Indian King, Chandragupta Maurya in 300BC notes that those who indulged in the unauthorized killing of elephants, considered as royal animals, faced the death penalty (Lal, 1989, see Ninan, 1996; Chaturvedi, 1992, see Ninan, 1996). Some of these penalties – especially beheading or long-term imprisonment for habitual offenders and double the normal penalties if the offenders were forest officials and guards or if they connive with forest offenders, timber smugglers and poachers – are worth considering and incorporating into the Indian Wildlife (Protection) Act of 1972. If endangered species such as tigers, leopards and elephants, are to be saved from extinction, then such tough measures need to be taken. Furthermore, despite CITES, there is a flourishing illegal market for wildlife products and parts such as tiger or leopard skins, ivory, etc., especially in Southeast Asian countries such as China, Thailand, etc. This calls for close international cooperation and effort to stop this illegal trade.

The question of which institutional set-up or management regime (or governance type) is most appropriate for protected areas cannot be easily resolved. While some argue that state or government managed protected areas are most suitable for biodiversity conservation and wildlife protection, others argue the case for community managed protected areas, especially in areas where indigenous or local communities depend heavily on these forests for their livelihoods. Still others favour co-management, where different stakeholders are represented, or privately managed wildlife reserves. The experience of South Africa, where privately managed game reserves exist along with state run protected areas, and there is also commercial utilization of wildlife resources, has been cited to justify the case for similar initiatives in other countries. How far South Africa's experience can be replicated elsewhere is worth debating. It is difficult to generalize and state whether publicly or privately managed protected areas are ideal for biodiversity conservation and wildlife protection. For instance, one can cite the example of poorly managed private forests in Japan against well-managed public forests in Canada to illustrate the above (Ninan, 1996). One can also give examples of well managed state or community managed protected areas as well as poorly managed state or community managed protected areas. Keeping these contrasting experiences in view, it appears that for most countries it is more appropriate to have a mix of state and community managed or co-managed protected areas, as well as privately managed wildlife reserves where this is feasible, in order to promote biodiversity conservation as well as minimize the social costs of conservation.

Glossary

Bequest value   A non-use value that refers to individuals placing a high value on the conservation of forests or species for the benefit of future generations.

Biodiversity   The term biological diversity, or biodiversity for short, is an umbrella term used to describe the number, variety and variability of living organisms in an assemblage – biodiversity may be described in terms of genes, species and ecosystems.

Biodiversity hotspot   An area characterized by exceptional concentrations of species with high levels of endemism and high degree of fragmentation. Myers et al, 2000 have identified 25 biodiversity hotspots in the world based on indicators such as the concentration of species and endemic species, degree of fragmentation of forests, etc.

Biological resources   Genetic resources, organisms or parts thereof, population or any other biotic components of ecosystems with actual or potential use or value for humanity constitute biological resources. Biological resources are strictly speaking not the same as biodiversity or biological diversity. While diversity refers to the variety of biological entities, biological resources refers to the quantity of biological entities.

Biomass   A measure of the amount of organic matter in the system. If biomass is increasing, the system has positive net productivity, i.e. organic matter is being added to the system. If biomass is decreasing the system must be 'running down', i.e. it has negative net productivity. Biomass is thus a stock concept and productivity is a flow concept, like income (flow) and wealth (stock).

Biomes   Biomes represent broad habitat and vegetation types across biogeographic realms, and are useful units for assessing global biodiversity and ecosystem services because they stratify the globe into ecologically meaningful and contrasting classes. The World Wildlife Fund (WWF) identified 14 terrestrial biomes based on WWF terrestrial ecoregions.

Biopiracy	Biopiracy refers to the appropriation of genetic resources (wild or agricultural) without payment or recognition of peasant or indigenous ownership.
Bioprospecting	The search for new chemicals in living organisms that will have some medicinal or commercial use, bioprospecting must adhere to international treaties and national laws. It should respect informed consent, i.e. the source country must know what will be done with the resource and which benefits will be shared and must give permission for collecting; and there must be fair agreement on benefit sharing between the bio-rich country and the prospecting firm and entity. Benefits may include support for conservation, research, equipment, technologies, knowledge transfer, development, royalties, etc.
Biosafety	The safe transfer, handling and use of living modified organism resulting from modern biotechnology that may have adverse effects on the conservation and sustainable use of biodiversity, taking into account risks to human health, and specifically focusing on transboundary movements. The Cartagena Protocol on Biosafety agreed in 2000 under the CBD seeks to protect biological diversity from the potential risks posed by living modified organisms resulting from modern biotechnology. The Protocol establishes a Biosafety Clearing House to facilitate the exchange of information on living modified organisms and to assist countries in the implementation of the protocol.
Biosphere reserve	These are sites considered by the IUCN or UNESCO to be of international importance for conservation, study and sustainable development. By 1999 there were 357 such sites around the world.
Benefits transfer	An exercise whereby estimates of economic benefits derived by revealed or stated preference method are 'transferred' from a site where a study has already been done to a site of policy interest. How representative the site of policy interest is to the site for which estimates are made is an issue to be considered.
Charismatic species	Species such as pandas, tigers, etc., that have a lot of charisma centred around them, and which are the symbol of biodiversity conservation efforts or campaigns.
CITES	The Convention on International Trade in Endangered Species (CITES) of Wild Flora and Fauna is an international agreement put together at a meeting of representatives of 80 countries in Washington DC, US on 3 March, 1973, and which came into force on 1 July, 1975. CITES regulates the international trade of wild animals and plants; and seeks to ensure international

cooperation to safeguard certain species from over-exploitation. It is among the conservation agreements with the largest membership, with 169 parties at the time of writing. About 5000 species of animals and 28,000 species of plants are protected by CITES against over-exploitation through international trade. While CITES Appendix I lists species that are the most endangered among CITES-listed animals and plants, Appendix II lists species that are not necessarily threatened with extinction but that may become so unless trade is closely controlled, and Appendix III lists species at the request of a party that already regulates the exploitation/trade in the species and that needs the cooperation of other countries to prevent unsustainable or illegal exploitation.

Closed forests	Dense forests in which grass cover is small or non-existent due to low light penetration through the forest canopy.
Consumptive use values	Refers to the timber, non-timber, recreation, plant genetics, and medicinal benefits provided by forests.
Contingent valuation method	A non-market valuation technique widely used in environmental economics to value environmental goods and services, biodiversity and endangered species. Actually it values people's preference for the environment and biodiversity. It is so called because it tries to get people to say how they would act if they were placed in contingent situations. CVM is the only known method to date used to value non-use values of biodiversity. It is also referred to as a stated preference method. Usually the people or respondents being interviewed are asked to state the maximum amount that they are willing to pay (WTP) or the minimum amount that they are willing to accept (WTA) as compensation to protect the environment, biodiversity or endangered species.
Convention on Biological Diversity (CBD)	An international agreement signed by over 100 countries (188 countries at the time of writing) after the Rio Summit of the UNCED held in 1992 and concerned with biodiversity conservation. The CBD has set three major goals: to conserve biodiversity; promote sustainable use of its components; and ensure a fair and equitable sharing of genetic resources. The Secretariat of the Convention on Biological Diversity (SCBD) based at Montreal under the aegis of the United Nations Environment Programme (UNEP) oversees the implementation of the CBD.
Dense forest	A forest with crown canopy cover of over 40 per cent.
Direct use values	The goods and services provided by forests such as timber and non-timber products, recreation, medicines, plant genetics, etc.

Ecological measures of biodiversity	Ecological measures of biodiversity are rooted in ecology and weigh different species according to their relative abundance in the system. This is based on the premise that the functional role of the species varies in proportion to the abundance of that species in the system. Species richness, Simpson's diversity index, and the Shannon-Weiner diversity index are examples of ecological measures of biodiversity (Baumgartner, 2004).
Economic measures of biodiversity	Economic measures of biodiversity stress that different species should be given different weights in the diversity measures due to the attributes they possess. Unlike the ecological measures that use the number of different species in a system as well as their relative abundance, economic measures use the number of species as well as their characteristics. The economic measures are based on the premise that diversity of species to an important extent stems from dissimilarity between species. The economic measures use two different approaches. One uses the concept of a distance function to measure the pairwise dissimilarity between species. The diversity of a set of species in this approach is taken to be an aggregate measure of the dissimilarity between species. The Weitzman index, which is based on this approach, defines a diversity measure based on the fundamental idea that the diversity of a set of species is a function of the pairwise dissimilarity between species. The dissimilarity between two species is measured by a distance function. The other approach pioneered by Nehring and Puppe generalizes the Weitzman approach by taking into account multiple attributes and does not rely on any metric assumption about the attribute space. Like Weitzman, they base a measure of species diversity on the characteristic features of species. But in contrast to Weitzman, the elementary data are not the pairwise dissimilarities between species, but the characteristic features themselves (Baumgartner, 2004).
Economic value of biodiversity	This consists of the direct and indirect use values, option value and non-use values of biodiversity. Direct use values, for example, refer to the goods and services provided by forests such as timber and non-timber forest products, recreation, medicines, plant genetics, etc. Indirect use value refers to the ecological services and functions of the forests in terms of facilitating nutrient cycling, watershed protection, carbon fixing, etc. Option value is concerned with the future use of the above two, such as the future value of drugs. Non-use values refer to existence values (i.e. viewing forests or species as objects of inherent value which need to be conserved) and bequest value (i.e. individuals

placing a high value on the conservation of forests/species for future generations to use.

Ecosystem	A system of living things or biota in relationship with their environment. Ecosystems are not static communities and change with exogenous factors such as climate and endogenous factors whereby the occupying species alter their habitat.
Ecosystem diversity	The variety of habitats, biotic communities and ecological processes in the biosphere as well as the diversity within ecosystems.
Ecosystem value of biodiversity	The ecosystem value of biodiversity refers to the positive role that biodiversity plays in maintaining the health of ecosystems, such as maintaining the resilience of ecosystems to environmental shocks, the preservation of evolutionary potential, etc.
Endemic species	A species that is found only in or is restricted to the area of concern.
Existence value	A non-use value unrelated to current or future use and concerned with viewing forests or species as objects of inherent value which need to be conserved in their own right. For instance, one may not have seen the blue whale but would like to see it conserved in its own right.
Ex situ conservation	Conserving wild plants and animals outside their original habits and natural surroundings. Conserving wild varieties of plants in germ plasm banks, and wild animals in zoos are examples of *ex situ* conservation.
External cost	The difference between private and social costs.
External costs of wildlife conservation	Wildlife damage costs and defensive expenditure to protect against wildlife attacks incurred by local communities living within or near forests and protected areas are examples of the external costs of wildlife conservation borne by the local communities.
Extinct species	A species is considered to be extinct when there is no reasonable doubt that the last individual has died or no living representative exists. Dinosaurs are the best example of an extinct species.
Flagship species	A flagship species, normally a charismatic large vertebrate, is one that can be used to anchor a conservation campaign because it arouses public interest and sympathy.
Functional biodiversity	How an ecosystem functions and the relative abundance of functionally different kinds of organisms.
Genetic diversity	The sum of genetic information contained in the genes of individuals of plants, animals and micro-organisms.

Global value of biodiversity	The value or benefits of biodiversity accruing to the global or international community. While the benefits accruing to the global community are believed to be large, the costs are most often borne by the local communities.
Habitat	The locality or area used by a population of organisms and the place where they live.
Incremental cost of biodiversity	The difference between global biodiversity benefit and forgone (local) development benefit is the incremental cost of biodiversity. This concept was used by the Global Environmental Facility (GEF). The GEF meets this cost as aid. This is not the same as marginal cost. The concept of incremental cost is important since it appears to determine the flow of resources from North to South to secure global environmental benefits.
Indicator species	A species whose presence and fluctuations are believed to reflect those of other species in the community, and hence indicate the health of the ecosystem. Amphibians and birds, for instance, are considered to be indicator species. However, the indicator species is problematic because there is no consensus on what the indicator is supposed to indicate and because it is difficult to know which is the best indicator species even when one agrees on what it should indicate. For instance, while some consider species richness to be indicative of ecosystem health, others emphasizes structural diversity and aspects of functions such as nutrient cycling, independent of species richness or composition.
Indirect use value	The ecological services and functions of the forests in terms of facilitating nutrient cycling, watershed protection, carbon fixing, etc.
In situ conservation	Conserving wild plants and animals in their original habitats or natural surroundings is referred to as *in situ* conservation. Conserving wild plants and animals in forests, national parks or sanctuaries are examples of *in situ* conservation.
Intrinsic value	The value that intrinsically resides in biodiversity or environmental assets, and is unrelated to human use or preferences for or against environmental goods and services which involves assessing the economic value. In other words, the value of an asset, for example, an ecosystem or a species which is separate from its role as an instrument in providing well-being to humans. Intrinsic value refers to the value of the object in and of itself and has been used to justify the conservation of, for example, biodiversity.

Invasive species	A species imported from an ecosystem or area and introduced into another ecosystem or area. The introduction of non-native species into a new ecosystem is known to have caused serious decline in native species.
Keystone species	Species whose activities in an ecosystem govern the well-being of many other species, often far beyond what might have been expected from a consideration of their biomass or abundance. Elephants, for instance, are considered as a keystone species, since their presence not only influences the well-being of other species but also has a significant impact on the environment through their impact on plant composition, ecosystem diversification, seed dispersal, etc.
Local value of biodiversity	The value or benefits of biodiversity accruing to local communities. The local opportunity costs of biodiversity conservation in developing countries are quite high (Perrings, 2000). Local communities in developing countries often find the incentives for land conversion to be high, and hence unless appropriate incentives are given to capture and internalize the benefits of conservation to local communities, they will always favour land conversion over conservation.
Market value of biodiversity	The value of biodiversity in the context of market exchange. Numerous studies show that biodiversity can have a substantial market value.
Marginal value of biodiversity	The marginal impact of an extra unit of biodiversity (e.g. species or population). This will generally be sensitive to the type of species being added to the existing mix of species. If one thinks about biodiversity as the natural capital equivalent of a portfolio of assets, this is the impact on the value of the portfolio of adding an extra unit of biodiversity and depends on the effect of the covariance in 'yields' between the marginal and existing species. It is generally much higher in species-poor systems than in species-rich systems (Charles Perrings, personal communication).
Marginal value of biodiversity conservation	The opportunity cost of development; the benefit (in terms of the goal of conservation) yielded by an extra dollar committed to conservation. It is often much higher in species-poor, heavily impacted areas than it is in areas of high species richness and endemism (Charles Perrings, personal communication,).
Megadiversity state	An area identified as being of high species endemism. Twelve countries in the world, including India, are identified as megadiversity countries in terms of this parameter.

Multi-criteria analysis	Multi-criteria analysis (MCA) is based on a neo-classical paradigm and is an alternative approach to the cost–benefit analysis (CBA) technique, which is based on monocriterian analysis (e.g. NPV or IRR). MCA uses multiple criteria in decision making. It is based on non-monetary valuation methods and unlike CBA includes both quantitative and qualitative indicators. The values attached to different aspects of biodiversity by stakeholders can be analysed using MCA to arrive at scores on different aspects of value. This gives a relative ranking to alternative notions of value such as use, bequest, option and existence values and provides a crucial input into stakeholders perceptions with respect to biodiversity. A disadvantage of MCA is that when conflicting evaluation criteria are taken into account, an MCA problem may be mathematically ill-defined, making a complete axiomization and hence a simple decision criteria difficult to arrive at.
Non-consumptive use values	For example: tourism benefits, or the viewing value of elephants and other species, etc.
Non-timber forest benefits	Includes tangibles as well as non-tangibles, extractive values such as NTFPs, watershed and carbon sequestration services, etc., and preservation values such as option and existence values (Bishop, 1998; Lampietti and Dixon, 1995).
Non-timber forest products	Includes any product or service other than timber that is produced in forests: fruits and nuts, vegetables, fish and game, medicinal plants, resins, essences, barks and fibres, etc. While some exclude fuelwood from NTFPs, international bodies like CIFOR and SCBD include fuelwood among NTFPs.
Non-wood forest products	Includes all forest products of plant and animal origin other than wood (industrial woods, fuelwood, charcoal, and small woods), as well as services derived from forests and allied land uses.
Open forest	A forest with crown canopy cover of 10–40 per cent.
Opportunity cost approach	An approach or method for evaluating projects in terms of forgone opportunities or the next best alternative available.
Opportunity cost of biodiversity conservation	The opportunity cost of biodiversity conservation is the forgone benefits or forgone development benefits or the next best alternative. In the context of tropical forests this refers to the forgone agricultural benefits, forgone animal husbandry benefits, benefits derived by converting forests to plantation crops, etc. Studies show that the opportunity costs of biodiversity conservation are high. This is because unpriced and non-market benefits of biodiversity conservation are often not taken into

account, and hence the total economic value of forests are grossly underestimated.

Option value — Concerned with the option of future use, such as the future value of a drug.

Passive use values — The value that individuals place on the non-consumptive use of a natural resource. It is a direct use value. Examples of passive use values of natural resources include bird watching, whale watching, wildlife viewing, etc.

Primary value — The underlying functions of ecological systems which are prior to the ecological functions like watershed protection which are secondary values. Essentially they are system characteristics upon which all ecological functions are contingent. There cannot be a watershed protection but for the underlying value of the system as a whole. If this is true there is a total value to an ecosystem or ecological process which exceeds the sum of the values of the individual species.

Private value of biodiversity — The value of biodiversity accruing to private individuals or economic agents and revealed in the market, and not accounting for social costs and benefits. When markets are perfect, private and social values coincide whereas when markets fail or there are missing markets, as is often the case in a public good like biodiversity, private and social values of biodiversity diverge.

Productive use values — The plant breeding benefits.

Protected area — The IUCN defines a protected area 'as an area of land and/or sea especially dedicated to the protection of and maintenance of biological diversity and of natural and associated cultural resources, managed through legal or other effective means'. The IUCN has defined a series of six protected area management categories based on the primary management objective such as: strict nature reserve – a protected area managed mainly for science; wilderness – an area mainly for wilderness protection; national park – for ecosystem protection and recreation; national monument – for conservation of specific natural features; habitat/species management area; protected landscape/seascape for landscape/seascape conservation and recreation; and managed reserve for the sustainable use of natural ecosystem. Since 1981, the UNEP/WCMC has been identifying and compiling information on the protected areas of the world to produce comprehensive datasets and maps.

Quasi-option value	The expected value derived from delaying the conversion of forests today.
Rainforest demand price	The amount that the rest of the world will pay for rainforest conservation (i.e. it affects the rainforest demand price).
Rainforest supply price	The implicit minimum requirement for an international transfer (the so-called rainforest supply price) to compensate and fund rainforest conservation in order to give an incentive to the rainforested country not to exploit the rainforest, and therefore forgo the development option.
Ramsar site	Wetlands of international importance defined under the Wetlands Convention signed in Ramsar, Iran, in 1971. In order to qualify as a Ramsar site an area must have international significance in terms of ecology, botany, zoology, limnology or hydrology. The convention on wetlands is an intergovernmental treaty that provides the framework for national action and international cooperation for the conservation and wise use of wetlands and their resources. There are at present 133 contracting parties to the convention, with 1179 wetland sites, totalling 102.1 million ha designated for inclusion in the Ramsar list of wetlands of international importance (www.wri.org, see under biodiversity and protected areas – 2003, technical notes).
Rare species	A rare species is not necessarily a threatened species, nor is a threatened species a rare species. Charles Darwin in the *On the Origin of Species* (1859) states: 'Rarity is the attribute of a vast number of species in all classes, in all countries. For most biotas studies show that many if not most species are rare. A species may be rare according to distributional patterns, a highly restricted geographic range, high habitat specificity, small local population size or combinations of these characteristics. Rarity is a characteristic of a large number of tropical forest species. Rarity may be defined in biological or human terms, but this is not easy' (Myers, 1997).
Red List	A list compiled by the World Conservation Union (IUCN) and the World Conservation Monitoring Centre (WCMC) that classifies species at high risk of global extinction. Based on their status and risk factors the Red List identifies the following broad categories: extinct; extinct in the wild; threatened species which includes critically endangered, endangered and vulnerable species; near threatened; and species of least concern.
Resilience	The capacity of a system to retain productivity following disturbance.

Secondary value	The value of ecological functions or services such as watershed protection, nutrient cycling, etc. Secondary values depend on system characteristics or primary values upon which all ecological functions are contingent.
Shannon–Weiner Index of Diversity	A measure or index of diversity. This index is based on information theory and deals with predicting correctly, the species of the next individual collected in a sample. It is given by:

$$H^* = \sum_{i=1}^{s} (P_i)(\log P_i)$$

where H^* is the index of species diversity, s is the number of species, and P_i is the proportion of the total sample belonging to the ith species. The larger the value of H^*, the greater the diversity. Unlike the Simpson diversity index which is more sensitive to change in the more abundant species, the Shannon–Weiner index is more sensitive to changes in the rare species.

Simpson's Diversity Index	A species diversity index that reflects both the number of species (or species richness) and their relative abundance. The Simpson Index is based on the fact that diversity is inversely related to the probability that two individuals picked at random belong to the same species. For a population of infinite size, this is given by D $= \sum P^2_i$, where D is the Simpson index and P_i is the proportion of species i in the community. The Simpson's diversity index ranges from zero for low diversity to almost 1.
Social discount rate	The rate at which society weighs future consumption vis-à-vis present consumption. It is also referred to as the social time preference rate.
Social value of biodiversity	The value of biodiversity that accrues to the society where social costs and benefits are taken into account. When markets are perfect, private and social values coincide, whereas when markets fail or there are missing markets – as is often the case for a public good like biodiversity – private and social values of biodiversity diverge. The social value of biodiversity takes into account the aggregate impact on the welfare of all individuals in society, both now and in the future.
Species–area relationship	The positive relationship between the area of land which an ecosystem occupies and the number and types of species which can exist on it. Thus, it is a relationship between an area of land and a measure of biodiversity and reflects the fact that habitat loss – as land is converted from natural ecosystem to alternative uses –

is a major factor in biodiversity loss. The species–area relationship is complex and depends on many environmental, climatic and other factors.

Species diversity	The variety and variability of species in a given region or area.
Species evenness	Species evenness explains the abundance of each species in the community.
Species richness or abundance	The simplest measure of diversity and widely used in ecology as a measure of species diversity. It is the total number of different species found in an ecosystem or community.
Stewardship value	A value not necessarily related to human use of the environment but rather to maintaining the health of the environment for the continued use of all.
Threatened species	Species that are genetically impoverished, dependent on patchy or unpredictable resources, extremely variable in population density, persecuted or imperiled by extinction due to other interferences. The Red List compiled by the IUCN includes under threatened species those that are categorized as critically endangered, endangered and vulnerable species.
Total economic value (TEV)	The direct and indirect use values plus option and non-use values such as existence value and bequest value.
Transaction costs	The cost of collecting rents relative to the value of the resource in question.
Travel cost method	A valuation technique widely used in environmental economics to estimate the consumer demand for recreation, and based on revealed preference method. This technique is used to estimate the recreational demand for a site/park when market prices are not available. It uses the cost of travel to a site/park as a proxy for the entrance price to a site. Econometric or regression analysis is used to relate visitation rates to travel cost and socio-economic variables such as income. The demand curve for the site/park can be derived by applying the assumption that visitors would respond to an increase in price in the same way as to an increase in travel cost. This method works when the site in question is not congested as congestion reduces demand artificially. Hence the result would underestimate the true demand if this method were used in the derivation of demand for a congested site.
Umbrella species	Those species whose conservation results in the protection of many other species, just as an umbrella protects those under it from rain or sunlight. Tigers, for instance, are considered as an 'umbrella species'. Because of the tiger's large habitat needs,

saving wild tigers will require protecting large areas of forests which will indirectly protect many other wild species.

Value of biodiversity
The value of biodiversity consists of economic and non-economic values. While economic values refer to the direct and indirect use values, option and existence values of biodiversity, non-economic values include ethical, cultural and other non-economic values.

Willingness to accept (WTA)
CVM is a non-market valuation technique widely used in environmental economics to value people's preferences for environmental goods and services. There are two formats that are used in CVM: willingness to pay (WTP) and willingness to accept (WTA). Under WTA the respondents or people surveyed are asked to state the minimum amount that they would be willing to accept as compensation for suffering a loss in environmental quality or for not receiving a benefit.

Willingness to pay (WTP)
WTP is used to measure the benefit to a consumer due to a change in the price, quantity or quality of a good. Under WTP the respondents or people surveyed are asked to state the maximum amount that they would be willing to pay to obtain a benefit (say an improvement in environmental quality or better environment) or avoid a loss (say, a loss in environmental quality).

References

Adgers, W. N., Brown, K, Cervigni, R. and Moran, D. (1995) 'Total economic value of forests in Mexico', *Ambio*, vol 24, no 5, pp286–296

Agarwal, A. (ed) (1992) 'The prices of forests', Proceedings of a Seminar on the Economics of the Sustainable Use of Forest Resources, Centre for Science and Environment, New Delhi

Appayya, M. K. (2001) 'Management plan for Rajiv Gandhi (Nagarhole) National Park (2000–2010)', Karnataka Forest Department, Bangalore, 30 June

Arnold, J. E. M. and Perez, M. R. (2001) 'Can non-timber forest products match tropical forest conservation and development objectives?', *Ecological Economics*, vol 39, pp437–447

Bandara, R. and Tisdell, C (2002) 'Asian elephants as agricultural pests: Economics of control and compensation in Sri Lanka', *Natural Resources Journal*, Summer, vol 42, no 3, pp491–519

Bandara, R. and Tisdell, C. (2003) 'Use and non-use values of wild Asian elephants – A total economic valuation approach', Working Paper No. 8, Economics, Ecology and the Environment, The University of Queensland, Brisbane

Bandara, R. and Tisdell, C. (2004) 'The net benefit of saving the Asian elephant: A policy and contingent valuation study', *Ecological Economics*, vol 48, pp93–107

Barbier, E. B., Burgess, J. C., Swanson, T. M. and Pearce, D. W. (1990) *Elephants, Economics and Ivory*, Earthscan, London

Barnes, J. I. (1996) 'Changes in the economic use value of elephant in Botswana: The effect of international trade prohibition', *Ecological Economics*, vol 18, no 3, pp215–230

Baumgartner, S (2004) *Measuring the Diversity of What? and for What Purpose? A conceptual comparison of ecological and economic measures of biodiversity*, Interdisciplinary Institute for Environmental Economics, University of Heidelberg, Germany

Bennet, E. L. and Robinson, J. G. (2001) 'Hunting of wildlife in tropical forests – implications for biodiversity and forest peoples', Biodiversity Series Impact Studies, Environment Department, Paper No. 76, March, World Bank, Washington DC

Beukering, Pieter, J. H. van, Cesar, H. S. J. and Janssen, M. A. (2003) 'Economic valuation of the Leuser National Park in Sumatra, Indonesia', *Ecological Economics*, vol 44, pp43–62

Bishop, R. C. and Welsh, M. P. (1992) 'Existence values in benefit–cost analysis and damage assessments', *Land Economics*, vol 69, pp405–417

Bishop, J. T (1998) *The Economic Benefits of Non-timber Forest Benefits: An overview*, Gatekeeper 98-01, International Institute of Environment and Development, London, December

Bist, S. S. (2002) 'An overview of elephant conservation in India', *The Indian Forester*, Vol 128, no 2, February, Focus on Elephant Management and Conservation in India, Dehra Dun

Bowker, J. M. and Stoll, J. R. (1988) 'Use of dichotomous choice non-market methods to value the whooping crane resource', *American Journal of Agricultural Economics*, vol 70, no 2, pp372–381

Brock, W. A. and Xepapadeas, A (2003) 'Valuing biodiversity from an economic perspective: A unified economic, ecological and genetic approach', *American Economic Review*, vol 93, no 5, pp1597–1614

Brookshire, D. S., Eubanks, L. S. and Randall, A (1983) 'Estimating option prices and existence values for wildlife resource', *Land Economics*, vol 59, no 1, pp1–15

Brown, G. and Goldstain, J. H. (1984) 'A model for valuing endangered species', *Journal of Environmental Economics and Management*, vol 11, pp303–309

Brown, G. and Henry, W. (1993) 'The viewing value of elephants', in Barbier, E. B. (ed) *Economics and Ecology – New Frontiers and Sustainable Development*, Chapman and Hall, London, pp146–155

Brown, K. and Moran, D. (1993) 'Valuing biodiversity: the scope and limitations of economic analysis', CSERGE GEC Working Paper No. 93-09, Centre for Social and Economic Research on the Global Environment, University of East Anglia and University College London, UK

Bulte, E. and van Kooten, G. C. (2002) 'Downward sloping demand for environmental amenities and international compensation: Elephant conservation and strategic culling', *Agricultural Economics*, vol 27, pp15–22

Byron, A. M. (1999) 'What future for the people of the tropical forests?' *World Development*, vol 27, no 5, pp798–805

Campbell, B. M. and Luckert, M. K. (eds) (2002) *Uncovering The Hidden Harvest – Valuation Methods for Woodland and Forest Resources*, People and Plants Conservation Series, Earthscan, London

Carson, R. T. (1998) 'Valuation of tropical rainforests: philosophical and practical issues in the use of contingent valuation', *Ecological Economics*, vol 24, no 1, pp15–29

Carson, R. T., Wilks, L. and Imber, D. (1994) 'Valuing the preservation of Australia's Kakadu conservation zone', *Oxford Economic Papers*, vol 46, pp727–749

Chandlok, H. L. and Policy Group (1990) *India Data base – The Economy, Annual Time Series Data*, vol 1, The Policy Group, New Delhi

Chopra, K., Chauhan, M., Sharma, S. and Sangeeta, N. (1997) 'Economic valuation of biodiversity – A case study of Keoladeo national park, Bharatpur', Institute of Economic Growth, Delhi

Chopra, K., Kadekodi, G. K., Gilbert, A., Groot, A. M., Opshoor, J. B. and Verbruggen, H. (1999) *Operationalising Sustainable Development – Economic-Ecological Modelling for Developing Countries*, Indo-Dutch Studies on Development Alternatives 22, Sage, New Delhi

Coffee Board (2002) *Data Base on Coffee*, Coffee Board, Government of India, Bangalore

Costanza, R., Farber, S. C. and Maxwell, J. (1989) 'The valuation and management of wetland ecosystems', *Ecological Economics*, vol 1, pp335–362

Diamond, P. A. and Hausman, J. A. (1999) 'Contingent valuation: Is some number better than no number?', *Journal of Economic Perspectives*, vol 8, no 4, pp46–64

Dixon, J. and Sherman, P. B. (1990) *Economics of Protected Areas: A New Look at Costs and Benefits*, Island Press, Washington

Dixon, J. and Sherman, P. B. (1991) 'Economics of protected areas', *Ambio*, vol 20, no 2, pp68–74

Dyavaiah, C. C. (2000) *India Eco-Development Project – Rajiv Gandhi National Park Nagarhole*, Special Report for 4–5 February 2000 Meeting at Gir, Gujarat, Conservator of Forests, Mysore

Echeverria, J., Hanrahan, M. and Solorzano, R. (1995) 'Valuation of non-priced amenities provided by the biological resources within the Monteverde Cloud Forest Preserve, Costa Rica', *Ecological Economics*, vol 13, pp43–52

Ehrlich, P. R. and Ehrlich, A. H. (1992) 'The value of biodiversity', *Ambio*, vol 20, no 3, May, pp219–226

Emerton, L. (1999a) 'Mount Kenya: The economics of community conservation', Evaluating Eden Discussion Paper 4, September, International Institute for Environment and Development, London, UK

Emerton, L. (1999b) 'Balancing the opportunity costs of wildlife conservation for communities around lake Mburo national park, Uganda', Evaluating Eden Discussion Paper 5, September, International Institute for Environment and Development, London, UK

Emerton, L. (2000) *Economics and the Convention on Biological Diversity*, IUCN, Gland, Switzerland

Emerton, L. and Funda, I. M. (1999) 'Making wildlife economically viable for communities living around the Western Serengeti, Tanzania', Evaluating Eden Series, Working Paper No. 1, March, International Institute for Environment and Development, London, UK

Erickson, J. D. (2000) 'Endangering the economics of extinction', *Wildlife Society Bulletin*, (Special Coverage), vol 28, no 1, pp34–41

FAO (2005) *State of the World's Forests 2005*, Food and Agricultural Organization, Rome, Italy

Fisher, A. C., Krutilla, J. V. and Cicchetti, C. J. (1972) 'The economics of environmental preservation: A theoretical and empirical analysis', *American Economic Review*, vol 62, no 6, September, pp605–619

Fisher, M. (2004) 'Household welfare and forest dependence in southern Malawi', *Environment and Development Economics*, vol 9, pp135–154

Flint, M. (1992) 'Biological diversity and developing countries', in Markandya, A. and Richardson, J. (eds) *The Earthscan Reader in Enrivonmental Economics*, Earthscan, London

Fraser, I. and Chisholm, T. (2000) 'Conservation or cultural heritage? Cattle grazing in the Victoria Alpine National Park', *Ecological Economics*, vol 33, pp63–75

Gadgil, M. (1992) 'Conserving biodiversity as if people matter: A case study from India', *Ambio*, vol 21, no 3, May, pp266–270

Gadgil, M. and Rao, P. R. S. (1998) *Nurturing Biodiversity – An Indian Agenda*, Environment and Development Series, Centre for Environment Education, Ahmedabad

Godoy, R., Lubowski, R. and Markandya, A (1993) 'A method for the economic valuation of non-timber tropical forest products', *Economic Botany*, vol 47, no 3, pp220–233

Gowdy, J. M. (1997) 'The value of biodiversity: Markets, society, and ecosystems', *Land Economics*, vol 73, no 1, pp25–41

Gowdy, J. M. and McDaniel, C. N. (1995) 'One world, one experiment: Addressing the biodiversity–economic conflict', *Ecological Economics*, vol 15, pp181–192

Hadker, N., Sharma, S., David, A. and Muraleedharan, T. R. (1997) 'Willingness-to-pay for Borivli national park: Evidence from a contingent valuation', *Ecological Economics*, vol 21, pp105–122

Hanemann, W. M. (1999) 'Valuing the environment through contingent valuation', *Journal of Economic Perspectives*, vol 8, no 4, pp19–43

Hardin, G. (1968) 'The tragedy of the commons', *Science*, vol 162, pp1243–1248

Hoehn, J. and Loomis, J. (1993) 'Substitution effects in the valuation of multiple environmental programs', *Journal of Environmental Economics and Management*, vol 25, pp56–75

Howarth, R. B. and Norgaard, R. B. (1992) 'Environmental valuation under sustainable development', *The American Economic Review*, vol 82, pp473–477

Hyde, W. (1989) 'Marginal cost of managing endangered species: The case of the red-cockaded woodpecker', *The Journal of Agricultural Economics Research*, vol 41, no 2, pp12–19

India, Government of (1993) 'Project Elephant', December, Ministry of Environment and Forests, New Delhi

India, Government of (2001) 'Biodiversity' chapter 9 in *India-State of the Environment 2001*, Ministry of Environment and Forests, New Delhi

India, Government of (2002) *National Biodiversity Strategy and Action Plan (NBSAP) Project*, *Executive Summaries of Biodiversity Strategy and Action Plans*, December, Ministry of Environment and Forests, New Delhi

ITTO (1991) 'Status and potential of non-timber products in the sustainable development of tropical forests', Proceedings of an International Seminar held at Kamakura, Japan, 17 November, 1990, ITTO Technical Series No.11, International Tropical Timber Organisation, Yokohama, Japan

IUCN (2000) *2000 IUCN Red List of Threatened Species*, The IUCN Species Survival Commission, World Conservation Union, Gland, Switzerland

Jakobsson, K. M. and Dragun, A. K. (1996) *Contingent Valuation and Endangered Species: Methodological issues and applications*, Edward Elgar, Brookfield, VT

Jyothis, S. (2000) 'Willingness to participate in biodiversity conservation in Periyar tiger reserve: A contingent valuation', ISEC Working Paper No. 67, ISEC, Bangalore

Jyothis, S. (2002) 'Economics of biodiversity conservation – a case study of Western Ghat region, Kerala', ISEC, Bangalore, PhD Thesis, unpublished

Kahneman, D. and Knetsch, J (1991) 'Valuing public goods: The purchase of moral satisfaction', *Journal of Environmental Economics and Management*, vol 22, pp57–70

Kakujaha-Matundu, O. and Perrings, C. (2000) Biodiversity conservation and land use options in semi-arid lands: The case of Nyae-Nyae in Nambia, in Perrings, C. (ed) *The Economics of Biodiversity Conservation in Sub-Saharan Africa – Mending the Ark*, Edward Elgar, Cheltenham

Karanth, K. U. and Nichols, J. D. (2000) 'Ecological status and conservation of tigers in India – final technical report to the division of international conservation', US Fish and Wildlife Service, Washinton DC, Wildlife Conservation Society, New York, Centre for Wildlife Studies, Bangalore, India

Karanth, K. U., Bhargav, P. and Kumar, S. (2001) *Karnataka Tiger Conservation Project*, Final Report to Save the Tiger Fund, Wildlife Conservation Society, New York

Karnataka Forest Department (undated) 'Nagarhole National Park', Karnataka Forest Department, Bangalore

Karnataka Forest Department and Department for International Development (1999) 'Western Ghats forestry project – project experience and achievements', 1992–2000, December, Project Directorate, Western Ghats Forestry Project, Bangalore

Karnataka, Government of (1989) 'Statistical Brochure 1987', Karnataka Forest Department, Bangalore

Karnataka, Government of (1999), 'Statistical Brochure 1999', Karnataka Forest Department, Bangalore

Kotchen, M. J. and Reiling, S. D. (2000) 'Environmental attitudes, motivations, and contingent valuation of nonuse values: A case study involving endangered species', *Ecological Economics*, vol 32, pp93–107

Koziell, I (2000) *Diversity not Adversity – Sustaining Livelihoods with Biodiversity*, International Institute of Environment and Development, London, UK

Koziell, I. and Saunden, J. (eds) (2001) *Living off Biodiversity – Explaining Livelihoods and Biodiversity Issues in National Resources Management*, International Institute of Environment and Development, London, UK

Kramer, R. A. and Mercer, D. E. (1997) 'Valuing a global environment good: US residents' willingness to pay to protect tropical rain forests', *Land Economics*, vol 73, no 2, pp196–210

Kramer, R. A., Richter, D. D., Pattanayak, S. and Sharma, N. P. (1997) 'Ecological economic analysis of watershed protection in Eastern Madagascar', *Journal of Environmental Economics and Management*, vol 49, pp277–295

Kramer, R. A., Sharma, N. and Munasinghe, M. (1995), *Valuing Tropical Forests – Methodology and Case Study of Madagascar*, World Bank Environment Paper No. 13, World Bank, Washington

Kruess, A. and Tscharntke, T. (2002) 'Contrasting responses of plant and insect diversity to variation in grazing intensity', *Biological Conservation*, vol 106, pp293–302

Lal, J. B. (1992) 'Economic value of India's forest stock', in Agarwal, A. (ed) *The Price of Forests*, Proceedings of a Seminar on the Economics of the Sustainable Use of Forest Resources, Centre for Science and Environment, New Delhi

Lampietti, J. A. and Dixon, J. A. (1995) *To see the Forest for the Trees: A guide to non-timber forest benefits*, Environment Department Paper No. 013, July, The World Bank, Washington DC

Loomis, J. B. (1988) 'Contingent valuation using dichotomous choice models', *Journal of Leisure Research*, vol 20, no 1, pp46–56

Loomis, J. B. (2000) 'Can environmental economic valuation techniques aid ecological economics and wildlife conservation', *Wildlife Society Bulletin*, vol 28, no 1, pp52–60

Loomis, J. B. and White, D. S. (1996) 'Economic benefits of rare and endangered species: Summary and meta-analysis', *Ecological Economics*, vol 18, pp197–206

Manoharan, T. R., Muraleedharan, P. K. and Anitha, V. (1999) 'Economic valuation of nonmarket benefits of forests', paper presented at Training Programme in Environmental Economics, 5–9 July, ISEC, Bangalore

Melkani, V. K. (2001) 'Tiger conservation in India – past, present and future', *The Indian Forester*, vol 127, no 10, October, Wildlife Special, Dehra Dun, pp1081–1097

Mendelssohn, G. (1999) 'The relevance of economic valuation for species conserva-
tion policy: The case of the African elephant', in O'Connor, M. and Spash, C. (eds)
Valuation and the Environment – Theory, Method and Practice, Advances in Ecological
Economics, Edward Elgar, Cheltenham and Northampton

Metrick, A. and Weitzman, M. L. (1996) 'Patterns of behaviour in endangered species
prevention', *Land Economics*, vol 72, pp1–16

Miller, J. R. (1981) 'Irreversible land use and the preservation of endangered species',
Journal of Environmental Economics and Management, vol 8, pp19–26

Mishra, S. N. and Sharma, R. K. (1990) *Livestock Development In India: An Appraisal*,
Vikas, New Delhi

Montgomery, C., Brown, G. M. and Adams, D. M. (1994) 'The marginal cost of species preservation: The northern spotted owl', *Journal of Environmental Economics and
Management*, vol 26, pp111–128

Moran, D. (1994) 'Contingent valuation and biodiversity: Measuring the user surplus of
Kenyan protected areas', *Biodiversity and Conservation*, vol 3, pp663–684

Moran, D., Pearce, D. Wendelaar, A. (1997) 'Investing in biodiversity: An economic perspective on global priority setting', *Biodiversity and Conservation*, vol 6, pp1219–1243

Munasinghe, M. and McNeely, J. (eds) (1994) *Protected Area Economics and Policy – Linking
Conservation and Sustainable Development*, World Bank and World Conservation Union
(IUCN), World Bank, Washington

Murty, M. N. and Menkhaus, S. M. (1994) 'Economic aspects of wildlife protection
in the developing countries – A case study of Keoladeo National Park, Bharatpur',
Working Paper No. 163/94, Institute of Economic Growth, Delhi

Myers, N. (1988) 'Threatened biotas: 'Hotspots' in tropical forests', *The Environmentalist*,
vol 8, no 3, pp187–208

Myers, N. (1990) 'The biodiversity challenge: Expanded hotspots analysis', *The
Environmentalist*, vol 10, no 4, pp243–256

Myers, N. (1997) 'Rarity' book review, *Biodiversity and Conservation*, vol 6, pp1317–1320

Myers, N., Mittermeier, R. M., Mittermeier, C. G., Fonseca, G. A. B. and Kent, J. (2000)
'Biodiversity hotspots for conservation priorities', *Nature*, vol 403, 24 February, pp853–858

Nadkarni, M. V., Ninan, K. N. and Pasha, S. A. (1994) *The Economic and Financial
Viability of Social Forestry Projects – A Study of Selected Projects in Karnataka*, SPWD
and Ford Foundation, New Delhi

Nadkarni, M. V., Pasha, S. A. and Prabhakar, L. S. (1989) *Political Economy of Forest Use
and Management*, Sage, New Delhi

Navrud, S. and Mungatana, E. D. (1994) 'Environmental valuation in developing countries: The recreational value of wildlife viewing', *Ecological Economics*, vol 11, no 2,
pp135–151

Ninan, K. N. (1996) *Forest Use and Management in Japan and India – A Comparative
Study*, VRF Series, No. 286, Institute of Developing Economies, Tokyo, Japan

Ninan, K. N. and Sathyapalan, J. (2005) 'The economics of biodiversity conservation – A
study of a coffee growing region in the Western Ghats of India', *Ecological Economics*,
vol 55, no 1, pp61–72

Ninan, K. N., Jyothis, S., Babu, P. and Ramakrishnappa, V. (2001) *Economic Analysis of
Biodiversity Conservation: The Case of Tropical Forests in the Western Ghats*, India, ISEC,
Bangalore

Norton-Griffiths, M. and Southey, C. (1995) 'The opportunity costs of biodiversity conservation in Kenya', *Ecological Economics*, vol 12, pp125139

O'Neill, J. (1997) 'Managing without prices: The monetary valuation of biodiversity', *Ambio*, vol 26, no 8, December, pp546–550

Oksanen, M. (1997), 'The moral value of biodiversity', *Ambio*, vol 26, 8, December, pp541–545

Overseas Development Administration (1991) *Biological Diversity and Developing Countries – Issues and Options*, Natural Resources and Environment Department, London

Pearce, D. W. (1991) 'An economic approach to saving the tropical forests', in Helm, D. (ed) *Economic Policy Towards the Environment*, pp239–262, Blackwell Publishers, Oxford

Pearce, D. (1995) *Blueprint 4 – Capturing Global Environmental Value*, CSERGE, Earthscan, London

Pearce, D. and Moran, D. (1994) *The Economic Value of Biodiversity*, Earthscan, London

Perrings, C. (1995) 'The economic value of biodiversity' chapter 12 in Heywood, V. H. (ed) *Global Biodiversity Assessment*, United Nations Environment Programme, Cambridge University Press, Cambridge

Perrings, C. (2000), *The Economics of Biodiversity Conservation in Sub-Saharan Africa – Mending the Ark*, Edward Elgar, Cheltenham and Northampton

Perrings, C. and Lovett, J. C. (2000) 'Policies for biodiversity conservation in sub-Saharan Africa', in Perrings, C (ed.) *The Economics of Biodiversity Conservation in Sub-Saharan Africa – Mending the Ark*, Edward Elgar, Cheltenham and Northampton

Perrings, C., Folke, C, and Maler, K. G. (1992) 'The ecology and economics of biodiversity loss: The research agenda', *Ambio*, vol 21, no 3, May, pp201–211

Peters, C. M., Gentry, A. H. and Mendelsohn, R. O. (1989) 'Valuation of an Amazonian rainforest', *Nature*, vol 339, no 29, June, pp655–656

Polasky, S. and Solow, A. R. (1995) 'On the value of a collection of species', *Journal of Environmental Economics and Management*, vol 29, 2, pp298–303

Porter, R. C. (1982) 'The new approach to wilderness preservation through benefit–cost-analysis', *Journal of Environmental Economics and Management*, vol 9, pp59–80

Porter, S., Ferver, S., Aylward, B. (2003) 'The profitability of nature tourism in Zululand', in Aylward, B. and Lutz, E. (eds) *Nature Tourism, Conservation and Development in Kwazulu-Natal, South Africa*, World Bank, Washington DC

Portney, P. R (1994) 'The contingent valuation debate: Why economists should care', *Journal of Economic Perspectives*, vol 8, no 4, Fall, pp3–17

Putz, F. E., Redford, K. H., Robinson, J. G., Fimbel, R. and Blate, G. M. (2000) *Biodiversity Conservation in the Context of Tropical Forest Management*, Biodiversity Series, Impact Studies, Environment Department, Paper No.75, September, World Bank, Washington, DC

Ramesh, B. R., Menon, S. and Bawa, K. S. (1997) 'A vegetation based approach to biodiversity gap analysis in the Agastyamalai region, western Ghats, India', *Ambio*, vol 26, no 8, December, pp529–536

Randall, A. (1988) 'Human preferences, economics and the preservation of species', in Norton, B. G. (ed) *The Preservation of Species – The Value of Biological Diversity*, Princeton University Press, Princeton, NJ

Reddy, R. C. and Bishop, R. C. (1991) 'Endangered species and the safe minimum stand-ard', *American Journal of Agricultural Economics*, vol 73, no 2, pp309–312

Reddy, S. R. C. and Chakravarty, S. P. (1999) 'Forest dependence and income distribu-tion in a subsistence economy: Evidence from India', *World Development*, vol 27, no 7, pp141–149

Rook, A. J., Dumont, B, Isselstein, J., Osoro, K., WallisDeVries, M. F., Parente, G. and Mills, J. (2004) 'Matching type of livestock to desired biodiversity outcomes in pas-tures – a review', *Biological Conservation*, vol 119, pp137–150

Samples, K. C., Dixon, J. A. and Gowen, M. M. (1986) 'Information disclosure and en-dangered species valuation', *Land Economics*, vol 62, no 3, pp306–312

SCBD (2001a) *The Value of Forest Ecosystems*, CBD Technical Series No. 4, Secretariat of the Convention on Biological Diversity, Montreal, Canada

SCBD (2001b) *Sustainable Management of Non-Timber Forest Resources*, CBD Technical Series No. 6, November, Secretariat of the Convention on Biological Diversity, Montreal, Canada

Scriven, L. and Eloff, T. (2003) 'Markets derived from nature tourism in South Africa and Kwazulu-Natal: A survey of sale of live game', in Aylward, B. and Lutz, E. (eds) *Nature Tourism, Conservation and Development in Kwazulu-Natal, South Africa*, World Bank, Washington DC

Shanley, P., Pierce, A. R., Laird, S. A. and Guillen, A. (eds) (2002) *Tapping the Green Market – Certification and Management of Non-Timber Forest Products*, People and Plants Conservation Series, Earthscan, London

Shyamsundar, P. and Kramer, R. A. (1996) 'Tropical forest protection: An empirical analysis of the costs borne by local people', *Journal of Environmental Economics and Management*, vol 31, no 2, pp129–145

Shyamsundar, P. and Kramer, R. A. (1997) 'Biodiversity conservation – at what cost? A study of households in the vicinity of Madagascar's Mantadia National Park', *Ambio*, vol 26, no 3, May, pp180–184

Simpson, R. D. (1999) 'The price of biodiversity', *Issues in Science and Technology*, Online, Spring, www.issues.org/15.3/simpson.htm

Silori, C. S. and Mishra, B. K. (2001) 'Assessment of livestock grazing pressure in and around the elephant corridors in Mudumalai Wildlife Sanctuary, South India', *Biodiversity and Conservation*, vol 10, pp2181–2195

Solow, A., Polasky, S. and Broadus, J. (1993) 'On the measurement of biological diversity', *Journal of Environmental Economics and Management*, vol 24, pp60–68

Spash, C. I. and Hanley, N. (1995) 'Preferences, information, and biodiversity preserva-tion', *Ecological Economics*, vol 12, no 3, pp191–208

Stevens, T. H., Echeverria, J., Glass, R. J., Hager, T. and More, T. A. (1991) 'Measuring the existence value of wildlife: What do CVM estimates really show?' *Land Economics*, vol 67, pp390–400

Stevens, T. H., More, T. A. and Glass, R. J. (1994) 'Interpretation and temporal stabil-ity of CV bids for wildlife existence: A panel study', *Land Economics*, vol 70, no 3, pp335–363

Swanson, T. M. (1995) *The Economics and Ecology of Biodiversity Decline: The Forces Driving Global Change*, Cambridge University Press, Cambridge

Swanson, T. M. (1997) *Global Action For Biodiversity*, Earthscan, London

Tewari, D. N. (1993) 'Conservation of Biodiversity', Paper presented at the Indo-British Workshop on Biodiversity and Forest Ecosystems, organized by Karnataka Forest Department and DFID, 4–6 February, Bangalore

Thapar, V, (2005) 'The dying roar-tiger, tiger burning bright: Only in forests of Government files', *The Indian Express*, 26 February (www.indianexpress.com)

Tisdell, C. (1999) *Biodiversity, Conservation and Sustainable Development – Principles and practices with Asian examples*, Edward Elgar, Cheltenham

Tisdell, C. and Zhu, X. (1998) 'Protected area, agricultural pests and economic damage – conflicts with elephants and pests in Yunnan', *Environmentalist*, vol 18, no 2) pp109–118

UNEP (2001), *Global Biodiversity Outlook*, Secretariat of the Convention on Biological Diversity, November, Montreal, Canada

Wells, M, (1992) 'Biodiversity conservation, affluence and poverty: Mismatched costs and benefits and efforts to remedy them', *Ambio*, vol 21, no 3, May, pp266–270

Whittington, D. (1998) 'Administering contingent valuation surveys in developing countries', *World Development*, 28, no 1, pp21–30

World Bank (1993) *India – Policies and Issues in Forest Sector Development*, Report No. 10965-IN, Agricultural Operations Division, Country Department II, South Asia Regional Office

World Bank (1996) *India Eco-Development Project*, Project Document, Global Environment Facility, South Asia Dept. II, Agriculture and Water Division, Report No. 14914-IN

World Resources Institute (2005) *Ecosystems and Human Well-being-biodiversity Synthesis*, Millennium Ecosystem Assessment, Washington, DC

www.cifor.cgiar.org

www.fao.org

www.junglelodges.com

www.indiastat.com

www.worldenergy.org

Xue, D. and Tisdell, C. (2001) 'Valuing ecological functions of biodiversity in changbaishan mountain biosphere reserve in North East China', *Biodiversity and Conservation*, vol 10, pp467–481

Index

Page numbers in *italics* refer to figures, tables and boxes